ALSO BY JIM ROGERS

Investment Biker
Adventure Capitalist

HOT COMMODITIES

HOW ANYONE CAN INVEST PROFITABLY IN THE WORLD'S BEST MARKET

JIM ROGERS

RANDOM HOUSE TRADE PAPERBACKS

NEW YORK

For my Baby Girl,
who owns commodities but does not yet
own stocks or bonds

2007 Random House Trade Paperback Edition

Published in the United States by Random House Trade Paperbacks,
an imprint of The Random House Publishing Group,
a division of Random House, Inc., New York.

RANDOM HOUSE TRADE PAPERBACKS and colophon are trademarks
of Random House, Inc.

LIBRARY OF CONGRESS CATALOGING-IN-PUBLICATION DATA

Rogers, Jim
Hot commodities: how anyone can invest profitably in the world's best market /
Jim Rogers.
p.   cm.
Includes index.
ISBN 978-0-8129-7371-6
1. Commodity exchanges.   2. Futures market.   I. Title.
HG6046.R637 2004   332.63'28—dc22   2004058480

Printed in the United States of America

www.atrandom.com

9 8 7 6 5 4 3 2 1

Book design by Jo Anne Metsch

CONTENTS

INTRODUCTION

COMMODITIES get no respect.

Too many so-called smart investors consider themselves diversified if they have money in stocks, bonds, real estate, and maybe, for the sophisticates, some currencies, or timber. But commodities rarely, if ever, hit the radar screen.

It doesn't make sense to ignore a whole asset class—particularly one that has done quite well over time, contrary to all the myths about how risky, volatile, complex, and downright dangerous putting money in commodities is supposed to be. Successful investors look for opportunities to buy value cheap and hold it long-term, regardless of the market. So what if commodities are new to you. All it takes is a little homework, and there is no better motivator to be a fast study than the prospect of making some money. Let me tell you a story about one investor who started out knowing zero about commodities (and every other kind of investment) and ended up doing just fine.

In 1964, on a whim, I took a summer job in a firm on Wall Street. All I knew about Wall Street was that it was located somewhere in New York City and that something bad had happened there in 1929. Frankly, I didn't even know that there was a difference between a stock and a bond. But it was clear that there was money to be made on Wall Street, and being a poor kid from Demopolis, Alabama, who had already been lucky enough to go to Yale, I was eager to make some money to buy my freedom.

And while my ignorance about the financial world was profound, I had always been interested in current affairs and history, and it was a revelation to learn that someone on Wall Street would actually pay me for figuring out that a revolution in Chile would drive up the price of copper. My luck continued with a scholarship to Oxford, where I studied politics, philosophy, and economics; I also began using what I had learned in my summer job to invest my scholarship dollars before it was time to pay the bursar at Balliol College. After Oxford, I did a stint in the U.S. Army, where I distinguished myself mainly by investing the post commander's money in the stock market for a tidy return. Having served my country, I returned to New York in 1968 to begin my career in high finance. I had $600 in my pocket.

My arrival on Wall Street coincided, as it turned out, with the final run-up of a two-decade-long post–World War II bull market in stocks. At the time, who knew that '68 was the end for stocks? Not I, certainly. I was much too busy learning the ropes of the markets to focus much on the big picture. And I still had a lot to learn.

My inexperience turned out to be a huge advantage. Once I learned the primary lesson of investing—buy value on the cheap—I began searching the markets, any market, for undervalued assets. Unlike most of my colleagues on Wall Street who had trouble being disloyal to the stock market that had been so good to them for decades, I was eyeing every opportunity that sashayed by, and not many stocks deserved even a second look, objectively. As the bear market settled into the 1970s, I began to notice a lot of opportunities in commodities. I'm not quite sure precisely when I started studying commodities seriously, but a look at my bookshelves reveals that I bought my first *CRB Commodity Yearbook,* the annually published bible of commodities traders, in 1971 and have every one since.

I vaguely recall studying the CRB charts for various raw materials; when I saw a sharp rise, I analyzed why the prices of that commodity went up so quickly. I studied trends in supply and demand; I looked for evidence of aging plants and production or new exploration for metals and mines. I paid attention to weather reports: A cold winter meant higher prices for heating oil and natural gas; a warm winter in Florida meant that orange juice would be cheaper next year. And my abiding interest in history and politics reminded me that what was happening in the rest of the world affected prices on Wall Street. Knowing that the War Between the States in the 1860s cut off supplies of cotton to England, pushing prices so high that soon the English were planting cotton everywhere they could scrape up the soil, was extremely useful in understanding why worldwide commodity prices were rising again more than 100 years later.

That self-education in raw materials was years ago, and I do not remember all the nuances. What I do recall clearly, though, and with considerable nostalgia, is that I found myself in the middle of my first bull market, which happened to be in commodities, and I rode that bull for the next decade. Stocks, you see, are not the only asset classes that behave like bulls and bears.

In fact, that early education in commodity investing played a role in my success as the co-manager of an offshore hedge fund analyzing the worldwide flow of capital, raw materials, goods, and information. I was able to retire in 1980 at the age of 37. The stock market, however, was mainly a disaster: The Dow closed at 995.15 in 1966, and in 1982 it was back at 800—a full 20 percent decline after 16 years. (And I'm not even adjusting for inflation during a 16-year period of inflation that was the worst in U.S. history.) Americans were actually pulling their money out of mutual funds. In 1979, a now famous cover of *Business Week* proclaimed, "Equities Are Dead!"

I didn't think so. When I remarked in public in 1982 that the bear market in stocks was over, and it was probably time to invest in stocks again, people thought I was crazy. That was a good sign. By then I had realized that I had made most of my money investing where others didn't, and the conventional wisdom of the time was way too cautious about stocks. It was time to go the other way. When the Dow moved up to 1,200 in 1983, more than a 50 percent rise in just a year, the experts began warning, "You better sell. This is crazy. It's going too far too fast." And then, of course, came one of the great bull markets in history, with the Dow topping 11,000 in 1999. The Dow and the S&P indexes rose more than tenfold during the 1980s and 1990s. By 2000, the Nasdaq had soared 25 times its 1980 level.

But it wasn't going to keep going up. Markets never do. Eighteen years is a long time in market years—the average age, in fact, of bull markets in stocks and commodities in the twentieth century. In 1998, I began to notice that a lot of stocks were heading south. At the time, I was appearing weekly on a program on CNBC, and I started talking about investing in commodities and how the fast-growing Chinese economy would drive the demand for raw materials—and everyone looked at me as if I were crazy. Again. I contributed a few articles about commodities to the *Wall Street Journal* and *Barron's;* and when reporters called me to discuss the state of the economy or the markets, I kept turning the conversation to commodities.

No one listened. After all, the Dow and Nasdaq were at undreamed of heights. Ordinarily sensible, hardworking Americans had stock prices streaming across the bottom of their PC screens. Not so sensible Americans had quit their jobs to make their living day-trading. Three books were published in 1999 by alleged stock-market experts entitled *Dow 36,000, Dow 40,000, The Dow 100,000.* That same year, more than one-third of the covers of

Business Week—and five 100-page special supplements—were about "The Internet Revolution." No. 24 on *Fortune*'s "100 Best Companies to Work For" in 2000 was Enron, whose stock went to $90 that year. The *Wall Street Journal* and the *New York Times* were running learned articles denying that there was a classic stock-market speculative "bubble" in the works. "This time it's different," they said. It wasn't just a curious, new moment in the economy. It wasn't only a "new economy," it was "The New Economy!" Millions of Americans entered the stock market, and mutual-fund sales went through the roof. A Gallup poll at the time reported that 60 percent of all Americans were in the stock market in some way. When you walked into a bar or the nineteenth hole anywhere in America, everyone was watching CNBC!

And they said I was crazy. Whenever someone claims that investing has become different this time around, I grab my money and run. The only thing I could determine that was "new" about the New Economy was that it seemed to be a place where companies valued in zillions by Wall Street weren't required to make a profit. That surely defied common sense, never mind economics and history. Corporate earnings could never justify those share prices. There was certainly nothing new under the sun about losing money—or your mind—in the middle of widespread market hysteria. Whenever I see everyone rushing to bet their money on what's hot, I remind myself of Bernard Baruch, the Wall Street legend and adviser to U.S. presidents. During the stock-market craze of the late 1920s, Baruch stopped for a shoeshine one day and the guy working on his shoes began giving *him* stock tips. His shoes looking fine, Baruch headed back to the office—and sold everything.

I had my own Bernard Baruch moment in mid-1998 as most people were transfixed by the astonishing and continued rise of a group of glamour tech stocks. Cisco, Nortel, and JDS Uniphase, for instance, kept going up, and Microsoft never went down. I noticed that most other shares were actually declining. I de-emphasized the stock market and went back to my *CRB Commodity Yearbook*s and other sources to see what the deal was with the markets in agricultural products, energy, grains, metal, livestock, and life's other valuable things. They were incredibly undervalued, it turned out; in fact, once you factored in inflation, commodity prices were approaching lows not seen since the Depression! No sooner had I immersed myself in commodities than Merrill Lynch, Pierce, Fenner & Smith, the largest brokerage firm in the world, announced that it was getting out of the commodities business. In the 1970s, Merrill Lynch had made huge profits from trading commodities. This was now a tiny percentage of the firm's revenue.

I couldn't stop smiling. Surely, if *everyone,* including the wise men (and now women) at Merrill Lynch, thought that no American investor in his (or her) right mind would want to buy commodities it was definitely the time for this American to start buying commodities—and at bargain rates, no less. Further confirmation came when a few other commodity bulls who had read my articles or heard me on TV discussing commodities began calling me with offers to partner up to trade commodities. I wasn't interested. I had been retired from professional trading for nearly 20 years. Besides, I was about to embark on a three-year round-the-world trip that would coincide with the turn of the new millennium; keeping a sharp eye on zigs and zags of the various commodities markets as I drove around the continent of Africa or across Siberia and through China would have been a logistical impossibility.

Still, I didn't want to miss out on the first stage of a new bull market that only a few others had noticed. So I decided to start a commodities index fund. For years, studies have shown that the most efficient and profitable way to invest is through "index funds," so called because they are tied to such major indexes as the S&P 500 and the Russell 2,000 or 1,000. Instead of trying to beat the averages in the market, you join them by purchasing a fund that features a basket of stocks guaranteed to match the average, no matter what. You put up your money and the index fund buys shares in the 500 large companies that make up the S&P Index or the 2,000 "small cap" firms or 1,000 growth stocks in the Russell Indexes, and that's that. Your investment is on automatic pilot. No nonstop transaction fees for trading stocks, no big management commissions, and no decisions to make. Your success depends on the market averages rather than on the genius of a fund manager. The S&P goes up—or down—and so does your fund. The evidence is bountiful that such averages outperform most managed funds.

Confident that commodity prices were going to rise across the board, automatic pilot was exactly what I was looking for. I knew of four such indexes for commodities, and I began shopping for one that I might license. The best known at the time was the CRB Futures Index, operated by the same people who publish the commodities yearbook that had been my primer on commodities.* Investigating the CRB Index, I quickly discovered a major problem: Its 17 components were equally weighted. That means that crude oil constituted the same percentage in the fund as orange juice. I don't know about you, but in my life oil plays a much larger role than orange juice.

I headed off to see an old college friend who ran the *Wall Street Journal* about hooking me up with the Dow Jones Index. "I want to license your commodities index," I said, and he looked at me as if I were nuts: "We don't have a commodities index." When I informed him that such an animal was listed daily in the pages of his newspaper, he was astonished—and thus gave me more proof of investors' disregard for commodities, since even the editor at the nation's leading business paper didn't care about them. I soon discovered that the Dow Jones Commodities Index hadn't been revised since at least the 1960s. I went to see another old friend at Reuters, the international news agency, whose index had been around for years; he, too, had no idea that his company

*It is now officially the Reuters-CRB Futures Price Index.

had such an animal. I soon discovered that the Reuters commodities index hadn't been revised since the 1930s.*

My next stop was Goldman Sachs, which was promoting its own
commodities index established in 1992. Immediately, I saw a major
flaw in the Goldman Sachs Commodity Index (GSCI): Sixty-five
percent of the fund was weighted toward hydrocarbons. As important as oil and other energy-related commodities are to the world, I
did not think they deserved nearly two-thirds of any index. And if
it were true that hydrocarbons were that important, you'd be better off buying oil and natural-gas futures. The GSCI was assigning
weights according to increases in prices, which meant that the
index changed wildly every few years. Anyone investing in the
GSCI today would have no idea what he would own even three
years later; nor would Goldman Sachs. In my opinion, that's not a
proper index. I wanted consistency, stability, and transparency.

I sought out information about the *Journal of Commerce* index
for commodities, which also had been around for years—and
showed it: Included in the index's mix among the usual commodities
were hides and tallow. It's true that we all wear leather shoes and
blow out birthday candles once a year, but neither hides nor tallow
is traded on any exchange these days, so pricing such materials
would be problematic. But rice is traded on an exchange. Half the
world eats rice every day, yet not one of the existing indexes included
this commodity. All the indexes were, in fact, too Americancentric.

I concluded that the kind of well-balanced, consistent international commodities index I was looking for didn't exist. It was just
more proof that nobody gave a damn about commodities. Such
blatant disregard of an entire asset class that was about to take off
reminded me of the stocks-are-dead mind-set of the early 1980s—
just about the time the Dow began its meteoric rise from 800 to

---

*In 1999, Dow Jones partnered with AIG to create a revised index, the Dow
Jones-AIG Commodities Index, which I find has serious problems, too. Reuters
has now joined forces with the Commodity Research Bureau for the Reuters-
CRB Futures Price Index. Both of these indexes now also suffer from the flaw
that they change unpredictably year after year, therefore lacking consistency, stability, and transparency.

11,000. I realized that if I was going to invest in commodities I would have to create my own index and fund. So I did. The Rogers Raw Materials Index Fund opened for business August 1, 1998 based on the Rogers International Commodities Index (RICI). It features a basket of 36 commodities that help make the global economy go round and that would be an effective measure of the price action of raw materials not just in the United States but around the world. The selection and weighting of the items in the fund are reviewed annually, and weights for the next year are assigned every December. So far, the changes have been minimal. (For a list of the RICI components, see Appendix.)

On January 1, 1999, I began my trip around the world, driving through 116 countries and racking up 152,000 miles in three years—and along the way ringing in the new millennium by marrying my traveling companion, Paige Parker, on January 1, 2000. Many people asked me how I would manage my money while I was traveling in remote areas of Siberia, China, and Africa. When I told them that I had some of my money in a commodities index fund, they looked at me with wonder and some concern for my welfare and sanity. After all my talk about the rosy future of commodities futures, the markets were down. The RICI, in fact, had lost 11.14 percent of its value at the end of 1998. But I was content. I had done my research, which had convinced me that the bull market in stocks was over. Sixty percent of U.S. stocks were down in 1998, and the same pattern continued in 1999. The bull in commodities was under way. (It turned out that we were off by a few weeks of getting the absolute bottom.)

When Paige and I returned from our trip—to a post–September 11 America—the index was up 80 percent. (By September 2006, it was up 254 percent.) While we were away, the dot-com bubble went bang. People remarked on how "lucky" I was to have avoided all the pain. I tried to be kind. I was now old enough to know that anytime you move away from the herd, the herd will criticize you, indeed revile you; it will call you "crazy." But that's a good thing for an investor: Nearly every time I strayed from the herd, I've made a lot of money. Wandering away from the action is the way to find the new action. I had touted commodities and China, and everyone said I was crazy. But when you make some money going against the grain, you're no longer crazy; you're just "lucky."

Back in the olden days, in the early 1970s, when the days of cheap natural gas and oil were numbered, I remember sitting down with one of the few hedge-fund operators extant in those days, a graduate of Harvard College and the Harvard Business School. I explained to him that oil and gas supplies were being depleted, pipelines have few reserves of gas, prices were dirt cheap, and that he should buy shares in as many oil and natural-gas companies and anything associated with them that he could find. The man scorned my advice—even with prices already rising.

In 1973, war broke out in the Middle East; oil prices skyrocketed. The Arabs boycotted the U.S. for supporting Israel. Oil prices went up even more. I bumped into my friend the hedge-fund manager. "You sure were lucky," he said. I was astonished. Hadn't I explained long before war and boycotts broke out that oil prices were sure to rise because supplies were already down and nothing was in the pipeline? I reminded him that OPEC had been established in 1960 in an attempt to raise oil prices. For the next decade, the OPEC oil ministers would meet every year and solemnly raise the price of oil. But the market ignored them, and the price stayed low. By the 1970s, however, the supply-and-demand balance was back in oil's favor, and prices were bound to rise no matter what OPEC did. High prices had nothing to do with the Arab-Israel situation, and to prove it, within four months the Arabs called off the boycott. The Saudis weren't about to let politics keep them from making a whole lot of moola off those record-high oil prices—which continued for years after the war and the boycott ended (and, more astonishingly, even after supplies exceeded demand in 1978).

I have learned that when you've done your homework, once you recognize that supply and demand is totally out of whack, and you make your move, you are definitely going to get very lucky. This, my friends, is one of those times.

HOT COMMODITIES

THE NEXT NEW
THING IS—THINGS

A NEW bull market is under way, and it is in commodities—the "raw materials," "natural resources," "hard assets," and "real things" that are the essentials of not just your life but the lives of everyone in the world. Every time you walk into the supermarket or the mall, you're surrounded by commodities that are traded around the world. When you get into your car or truck, you are surrounded by other widely traded commodities. Without the commodities "futures markets" to set and regulate prices, the things we all need in life would be scarce and often too expensive. These essentials include oil, natural gas, wheat, corn, cotton, soybeans, aluminum, copper, silver, gold, cattle, hogs, pork bellies, sugar, coffee, cocoa, rice, wool, rubber, lumber, and the 80 or so other things listed in the traders' bible, the Commodity Research Bureau (CRB) Yearbook.

Commodities are so pervasive that, in my view, you really cannot be a successful investor in stocks, bonds, or currencies without understanding them. You must understand commodities even if you only invest in stocks and bonds. Commodities belong in every truly diversified portfolio. Investing in commodities can be a hedge against a bear market in stocks, rampant inflation, even a major downturn in the economy. Commodities are not the "risky business" they have been made out to be. In fact, I believe that investing in commodities will represent an enormous opportunity for the next decade or so.

For most investors, commodities trading is a land of mystery full of legendary dragons. Intelligent, well-informed people who can recite P/E ratios of large caps and small caps, who study the balance sheets of high techs and biotechs, semiconductors, and small banks in the South, self-proclaimed "savvy investors" who follow bond prices and yields more closely than the baseball box scores and who might even have an eye on the dollar versus the euro, the yen, and the Swiss franc, know nothing about commodities. And if they do know something, it's typically second- or third-hand information, usually mistaken, and, more often than not, involves a cautionary tale about "a brother-in-law who lost his shirt in soybeans." Like Americans who never travel to foreign countries for fear of being humiliated or cheated because they don't know the local language and customs, investors who shy away from commodities are missing out on an incredible opportunity.

You cannot ignore an entire sector of the marketplace—not if you really want to be considered an "intelligent investor." If a friend of yours who was heavily invested in the stock market went through the 1990s without even considering buying a technology stock, and ignored what was happening in the world of Microsoft, Cisco, Amazon, eBay, and even IBM, surely you would find such behavior strange. Yet that is precisely what most investors have done with respect to commodities.

One reason that companies and stocks did so well in the 1980s and 1990s was that raw materials were in a bear market: Cheap commodity prices removed the cost and margin pressures from companies that depend on natural resources to do business. Investors who figured out that the commodity *bear* market was ending in the late 1990s realized that the stock bull market would be ending, too. The CNBC anchors were still giggling with glee, still advising to buy more dot-com shares, while the smart investors were exiting the market and moving to commodities. They could see that the costs of doing business would soon start eating away at profits—and that stock prices would soon follow.

It is hardly the bush leagues. In fact, natural resources are the largest nonfinancial market on the planet. The annual production of just 35 of the most active commodities traded every day in New York, Chicago, Kansas City, London, Paris, and Tokyo is worth $2.2 *trillion*. The volume of dollars traded on the commodities exchanges is several times that of the common stocks traded on all U.S. stock exchanges. (Commodities dealings for many times more than that amount take place outside the commodities exchanges.) And wherever there is a market, there are opportunities to make money. I know—the business pages of your newspaper, the financial magazines, and CNBC devote most of their time and space to stocks. According to the media and other stock-market "experts," the equities bull is forever hiding just around that next corner on Wall Street. But millions of investors who listened to the experts back in 1998–2001 about "the New Economy" got hammered in the stock market and are still trying to get back to even. The smart investor looks for opportunities to acquire value on the cheap, with one eye out for a dynamic change in the offing that might make that investment even more valuable.

Today, commodities fill both bills. The commodity bear market ended in 1998, when prices were approaching 20-year lows (equal to Depression levels, when adjusted for inflation). That year Merrill Lynch, the largest brokerage firm in the U.S., decided to leave the commodities business, and I began a commodities index fund to capitalize on the end of the bear market.

I am convinced that value and strength in the commodities markets will continue for years to come—that we are, in fact, in the

midst of a long-term secular commodities bull market. The twentieth century saw three long commodities bulls (1906–1923,
1933–1953, 1968–1982), each lasting an average of a little more
than 17 years. The new millennium has begun with another boom
in real things. In my opinion it began in early 1999. The aim of this
book is to explain *why,* showing, along the way, *how* to profit
from it. Better still, by understanding natural resources, you will
become a better investor in every other asset class.

There is no mystery to it. What could be more straightforward
in this world than its very basic materials? Corn is corn, lead is
lead, and even gold is just another thing whose price depends on
how much of the stuff is around and how eager people are to own
it. And there is certainly no magic to figuring out the direction in
which prices will go in the long term. These alternating, long bear
and bull markets in metals, hydrocarbons, livestock, grains, and
other agricultural products do not fall from the sky. They are
prime players in history, the offspring of the basic economic principles of supply and demand. When supplies and inventories are
plentiful, prices will be low; but once supplies are allowed to become depleted and demand increases, prices will rise, just as inevitably. It has not taken any genius on my part to understand this
dynamic; it's just the way the world works. But the investor who
sees this supply-and-demand balance going out of whack and is
willing to put some money on the table will be rewarded many-
fold.

We are now in one of those periods when a new bull market is
under way—and it is in commodities. And when that happens it's
time to get a lot more money into *things.* Do you see another alternative for your money that I'm missing?

· **Stocks.** Most equities are overpriced on a historic basis; P/E
(price-earnings) ratios for the Nasdaq are in the stratosphere. In
fact, at every level of consideration—price-earnings ratios, price-
to-book ratios, dividend-yield ratios—corporate equities are all

extremely expensive compared with past markets. Do you really think stocks will be able to soar from such exalted levels?

· **Bonds.** With interest rates lower than they've been in decades, the bond market is not about to make you rich—especially as rates go up. The yields on long-term government bonds are pathetic, while better-paying corporate bonds are expensive. And if your financial consultant advises you to buy bonds issued by the "government-sponsored" mortgage agency Fannie Mae or Freddie Mac, hang up the phone. The White House, Congress, HUD, and federal regulators are all gunning for both agencies. Sitting on top of $7.3 trillion in home mortgages, Fannie and Freddie are scandals in the making. (N.B.: "Government-sponsored" does not mean "government-backed"; if either Freddie or Fannie goes down, Uncle Sam is not obliged to give you your money back.)

· **Real Estate.** Housing is already too expensive to be much of an investment, at least in those places where you'd be willing to live. (You've even missed the real-estate booms in the U.K., Spain, Australia, New Zealand, and other countries where prices have accelerated beyond their historical average rates of increase.) U.S. housing prices rose faster than the rate of inflation for more than eight years; home-equity values may be inflated by as much as 20 to 30 percent. In New York and Southern California, housing prices have doubled in the past five years. A massive speculative bubble in the U.S. housing market seems to be floating from coast to coast, and as it bursts (as bubbles always do) some serious pain is in store for the millions of Americans who have been borrowing against their home equity at record rates—$750 billion in 2003. The resulting loss in wealth could be between $2 trillion and $3 trillion, sparking an economic downturn reminiscent of the one that resulted when the dot-com stock bubble went kaboom. Even if the air stays in the real-estate market, prices are way too high for investors to make a lot of money.

· *Currencies.* The U.S. is already the world's largest debtor nation—with more than $9 *trillion* in outstanding international
IOUs, and increasing by $1 trillion every 15 months. For the past
20 years, we have been borrowing heavily in the world's financial
markets to finance large trade deficits—now about $700 billion a
year (or 6 percent of GDP, the highest ever). Our interest payments to service those debts in 2005 alone totaled $350 billion.
That's roughly a billion dollars a day just to keep the dollar
afloat. We are now living off other people's money. With the
White House in a race with the Federal Reserve to spend money
faster than the Fed can print it, the dollar is shakier than ever.
Foreign investors eyeing our balance sheets are beginning to see a
banana republic emerging on our shores, and many have already
bailed. (In the 12-month period between June 2003 and June
2004, net foreign investment in the U.S. was a negative $155 bil-
lion.) During past trade deficits, it was foreign investment that financed our standard of living; now it's being paid for by foreign
buyers of U.S. bonds—mainly Asian banks, including the Chinese—looking to keep their own currencies under control.
Should those lenders decide that they would rather not finance
our profligate ways, the dollar will decline even more, interest
rates will rise, and so will inflation. Foreigners have already
begun to sell U.S. dollars. But to where do you run? The Swiss
franc and the Japanese yen are stronger than the dollar, but those
governments are also playing monetary monopoly, fiddling with
the money supply and the interest rates to make their products
more competitive. If you had changed your dollars for euros at
the end of 2001 when the euro was worth 89 cents, in September
2006, your euros would have gone up to $1.27, a very nice 42 per-
cent gain. But the euro, too, is a flawed currency long-term. If
anyone has a fix on a great currency, let me know.

Commodities, in fact, have been outperforming stocks, bonds, and
real estate for years now. The Rogers International Commodities

Index, which I founded, was up 254 percent eight years after its start on August 1, 1998, while the Lehman Long Treasury Bond Index was up only 67 percent and the S&P 500 Index of major stocks was up 32 percent. After a seven-year period ending in 2006, of the two stock mutual funds with the most assets under management—the Vanguard 500 Index and Fidelity Magellan—Fidelity's was in negative numbers and Vanguard was up only 35 percent after seven years.

How do your stocks stack up against these gains in commodities? Of course, you might be a much more talented stock picker than most. But even if you're an absolute wizard you ought to be putting some of your winnings into commodities—or companies and countries that produce them—if only in the interest of being genuinely diversified.

I suspect that the prospect of immersing yourself in the ups and downs of soybeans, sugar, cotton, crude oil, or even gold might not strike you as "fun." Admittedly, I have often relished buying a great company cheap and holding it long-term; to be sure, finding the next GE, Microsoft, or Amgen can be an intellectual as well as a profitable adventure. But let me assure you that when the price of sugar futures went from 1.4 cents to 66 cents between 1966 and 1974, those holding cheap sugar had a whole lot of fun watching sugar rise *more than 45 times*. Back in the 1970s, when oil went from $3 a barrel to $34 in just six years, man, that was where you wanted to be! Those who invested in commodities in 1998 made nearly 254 percent eight years later.

I don't know about you, but for me that's fun.

OPEN YOUR MIND—TO COMMODITIES

A friend of mine recently called his broker at a major New York investment firm to discuss moving a modest chunk of his portfolio into commodities. "You're aware of how risky commodities are, right?" she said. He said he was aware of the risks involved in investing in anything. The broker took that as a "No," and proceeded to tell a story about her colleague who had "one of the big corner offices" on the same floor. "He was heavily into commodities," she said. Then, after a pause pregnant with the offer of some wise, free advice, she whispered, "He's no longer with the company." When my friend insisted that he still wanted to explore commodities, she confessed that she couldn't help him; she had never bothered to get her license to deal in commodities, mainly because there had never been a good reason to do so. After a bull market in stocks that has lasted longer than the careers of many of today's financial managers and consultants, not to mention the journalists who feed off them, it is understandable that most investors and their advisers have trouble wrapping their minds around the prospect of investing in commodities. The last time serious money was being made in commodities, these people were in college or maybe even junior high school. Some may even have been in diapers.

Most investors could use some mental deprogramming. At certain points in history, stocks (and bonds) are not the best investments to make. If I had advised you, for example, in 1982 to put all your money into an S&P 500 Index fund, you would have thought I was insane. Stocks had been going sideways for more than a decade. But commodities were on a roll: Sugar went up 1,290 percent between 1969 and 1974; corn went up 295 percent. Oil went up 15 times in the 1970s, to $40 a barrel; gold and silver rose more than 20 times in a decade; and the price of many other commodities spiked. By 1979, that famous *Business Week* cover had already proclaimed, "Equities Are Dead!" In 1982, the Dow Jones Industrial Average was under 800—*down nearly 20 percent from its first almost 1,000 close of 995.15 in 1966.* (The Dow didn't officially hit 1,000 until November 1972.) Everyone knew that as an asset class corporate equities were *finito*. What they didn't know was that they were already in the early stages of a bull market for stocks that would last nearly 20 years.

Today the cycle has turned back to commodities. How can I be so certain that commodity prices will continue to rise over the next 12 to 15 years? I'm not certain about anything. "Certainty" is an incomprehensible word to any rational and responsible investor. Only political ideologues, religious fanatics, and other madmen believe they have all the answers. Happily, you need neither omniscience nor certainty to get rich. All you have to do is pay attention to where the opportunities are in the markets, keep an eye out for major changes that might affect them, and then act rationally and responsibly. That also means seriously considering markets other than real estate, stocks, and bonds, none of which are likely to appreciate significantly in the next decade. At this particular moment in history, it means taking commodities seriously.

Of course, it would be nice if I could claim that I've come to this conclusion as a result of my own uncommon genius. But the advent of every commodities bull market is due to the most basic principle of economics: supply and demand.

WHY COMMODITIES—NOW?

Quite simply, the current supply-and-demand balance for commodities worldwide is way out of whack—a classic sign of a long bull market on the way.

When I was a child in the 1950s, my family would drive from Alabama, where we lived, to Oklahoma to visit my grandparents. I can still remember being amazed to see fires in the fields along the road. No one seemed to care. It was only decades later, as a young man on Wall Street looking around for some investment opportunities, that I learned the reason for those fires along the Oklahoma roads of my childhood. There were oil fields out there, and in 1956 the Supreme Court had ruled that the government had the right to regulate the price of natural gas. Washington kept natural gas so cheap that it was more economical for those Oklahoma producers to "flare" it—burn it off—than to produce it while pumping oil.

And there was certainly no financial incentive for anyone to look for new sources of gas or oil, for that matter, which was plentiful (and thus inexpensive) in the 1950s and 1960s. Drilling companies went out of business, and exploration dropped off.

The same was true for most other commodities—lots of supply, low prices. By the early 1970s, those prices had begun to rise. Why? Time turns even excess inventories into empty warehouses. No matter how much of a given commodity there is, if supplies are not maintained on a regular basis they will become depleted, leading to price increases. More and more Americans were driving bigger cars; cold winters still required heating oil; and air-conditioning made it possible for more people to thrive in areas of the nation where the heat and the humidity had once discouraged enterprise. And then all those stockpiles of natural gas and oil began to disappear—with nothing to replace them, because no one had been able to make a buck in the hydrocarbon business for years. Soon investors were falling over one another in an effort to capitalize on escalating prices.

Between 1966 and 1982, the stock market went nowhere and with double-digit interest rates the bond market collapsed. Meanwhile, commodities boomed. But high prices soon did their normal work of encouraging new supply while cutting demand. Companies began drilling for oil, opening up new mines, and planting corn and soybeans. Gold plunged from $850 in 1980 to $300 in 1982, sugar went all the way back down to 2.5 cents in 1985 from the 66 cent price reached in 1974, while oil collapsed to less than $10 a barrel in 1986.

And then the cycle began to repeat itself. With supplies of commodities high and prices low, investors looking for value opportunities eventually returned to the stock market in the mid-1980s. That, too, was predictable: Investors never chase bears. By the 1990s, U.S. investors, mesmerized by the Internet bubble, were funneling every cent they had into company shares of "growth stocks" selling for more than 50 times earnings. In 1999 alone,

venture capitalists invested $42 billion—more than the three pre-
vious years *combined*; IPOs raised $68 billion, *40 percent more
than any year on record*. Not one IPO was for a new sugar plantation, lead mine, or offshore drilling rig, I can assure you. In the
meantime, metals mines and oil and gas fields were becoming depleted.

To me, it was déjà vu. The oversupply of two decades had created low prices that eventually spawned a bull market in commodities—just what happened in the late sixties. Once again,
commodities had been plentiful and cheap. The Asian and Russian
crises of 1997 and 1998 led to the final liquidation of those regions' commodity inventories at fire-sale prices—and worldwide
prices hit bottom. During these decades of depleting supply, demand for commodities continued to grow. Asia boomed; the
economies of the West and the rest of the world also grew. And,
once again, Americans began consuming commodities at an ex-
pansive and carefree rate. Years of cheap oil had given drivers a
taste for gas-guzzlers again. Everyone seemed to be driving SUVs
that only movie stars used to own, driving fuel-economy averages
to the lowest levels in 20 years. Those new McMansions rising
around the nation, thanks to record-low mortgage rates, required
lots of heating and cooling. Big cars and houses also eat up huge
supplies of lumber, steel, aluminum, platinum, palladium, and lead
for vehicle batteries. Europeans, too, were experiencing a housing
boom and driving more and bigger cars than ever, including SUVs.
Natural gas, cleaner and more efficient than oil or coal, had become the fuel of choice for North American power plants. Demand
in the energy and industrial metals sectors increased further with
the widespread economic recovery in Asia. South Korea has become one of the world's leading importers of commodities. Short
of scrap, Japan is racking up record imports of refined copper.

And then there was China, gobbling up commodities like the
giant economic dragon it was destined to be. I was in China in
1999, and was astonished at the changes that had taken place

since my previous visit at the beginning of the decade. In my last book, *Adventure Capitalist,* I included a photograph we took in Shanghai that summed up China's economic growth perfectly: A young Chinese girl, fashionably dressed, carefully made up and with color in her hair, sits on her motor scooter talking on a cell phone. I don't think that's what Mao Zedong had in mind when he launched millions of Red Guards throughout the country in the 1960s to root out "Western influences."

Communist China is now home to some of the best capitalists on the planet. Driving through the countryside, we saw men and women working from dawn until dusk, and when the sun went down we saw them improving the roads—already the best roads in the world, in my opinion—under floodlights. Shanghai is quickly emerging as one of the world's most exciting, economically robust cities. Giorgio Armani has opened up a new flagship shop in Shanghai; Prada and Louis Vuitton already have at least nine stores each in China, while Ermenegildo Zegna, one of Armani's prime competitors, has opened 29 shops since his early arrival in China in 1991.

China has had the fastest growing economy in the world for years, expanding more than 9 percent on average each year since 1980. Chinese factories and builders are cranking out everything from television sets, computers, and cars to shopping malls and urban town houses. China is now the biggest user of cell phones on the planet, and it's quickly heading to No. 1 in Internet use. It has passed Japan to become the No. 2 consumer of oil in the world, next to the U.S.—and the No. 1 consumer of copper and steel. Based on reports from China's National Bureau of Statistics, the nation consumed one-third of the global supply of steel in 2003, more than the U.S. and Japan combined. A major *exporter* of commodities not long ago, China currently imports half of its copper, three-fifths of its iron ore, and one-third of its oil. The People's Republic is also draining European recycling plants of every bit of scrap they can produce.

With more than 1.3 billion people to feed, China faces a mind-boggling demand for foodstuffs. The Chinese are now eating more meat than ever before, though their meat consumption is still lower than the per capita levels in other Asian countries, Europe, and the U.S. All those cattle, sheep, and chickens to feed a population more than four times the size of the U.S. will also require more *corn* feed. In addition, China is now importing soy from as far away as Brazil and Australia. A growing sweet tooth among its more affluent people—candies and other confectionaries have become a fashionable gift for hosts—has also boosted Chinese sugar imports.

All this demand has come at a time when China is short of virtually every raw material it needs. Nor are its neighbors in any position to chip in. With few homegrown commodities of their own, South Korea and Japan are now competing with China for raw materials. In fact, most of Asia has grown dramatically over the past 25 years, pushing up demand further. India's economy, too, has been growing at its most rapid rate in 15 years, supposedly expanding more than 8 percent in the past few years—which would make it the second-fastest-growing economy in the world after China—and thus increasing its demand for goods. And while Russia may have vast deposits of oil and minerals, the country is falling apart economically as privateers and mafia capitalists strip their nation's assets, undercutting world supply in the long run and further hiking prices.

Ironically, U.S. investors were too distracted by their own booming economy and stock market in the 1990s to invest any money in increasing productive capacity of raw materials, agricultural products, and other hard assets. And thus the seeds of the current commodities bull market were sown throughout the world: exploding demand for commodities at the very time that supplies were becoming depleted and investment in the natural resources infrastructure was virtually nonexistent. With that kind of supply-and-demand imbalance, prices can go in only one direction, and that's up.

RUNNING ON EMPTY (AGAIN)

"We're stuck with a commodity that we have to have," said Dave Wilson, president of an Idaho construction company that builds luxury homes, lamenting the high price of lumber in April 2004. "We have to pay whatever they charge."

Welcome to the commodities bull market, Dave. Users of virtually any commodity around the world could have said the same thing. They need stuff, and they want it *yesterday at low prices*, but there's nothing in the pipeline. Let's take a quick look at current capacity in several prime areas:

Oil. No major oil field has been discovered in the world for more than 35 years. Some of the largest discoveries of oil—the multibillion-barrel reservoirs known as "giants" or "elephants"—are 50 to 70 years old. U.S. production peaked in the early 1970s and then began declining—and that also includes Alaska's giant North Slope reservoir. North Sea production peaked in 1999, and some geologists and petroleum analysts have concluded that the oil fields of the current world champion producer, Saudi Arabia, are just years away from declining or may already have reached their peak. Whatever oil is left is likely to be a lot more expensive to find and get to market. The U.S. has not built a new oil refinery since 1976—and the number of domestic refineries has actually decreased by more than half since 1982 (from 321 to 149). There were 4,530 rigs in the U.S. at the end of 1981 actively exploring for oil and natural gas. In 2004, according to industry figures, the total was 1,201.

In fact, no one seems absolutely certain how much oil most nations have, since countries never allow independent audits. The Organization of Petroleum Exporting Countries (OPEC) determines quotas based on each member nation's oil reserves, thus providing an incentive to inflate their numbers. Take a quick look at the OPEC member list—Algeria, Indonesia, Iran, Iraq, Kuwait,

Libya, Nigeria, Qatar, Saudi Arabia, United Arab Emirates, Venezuela—and tell me which nation you would trust not to inflate its reserve numbers.

U.S. officials and oil-company executives have looked to oil-rich Russia for salvation. But Russian oil technology is backward. And while the Russians are pumping plenty of oil, they do not have the pipeline capacity to get more than half of it to market. In the meantime, ingenious privateers have been stripping the nation's oil assets as fast as they can send the money to Swiss bank accounts, and the Russian government has once again begun meddling in the oil business. Russian oil is not likely to push prices down. I would also be concerned about the political stability of Venezuela, the world's fifth-largest exporter of oil; and Nigeria, with large offshore oil deposits, will struggle to survive as a viable political entity. Unless someone discovers some more "giant"—and accessible—oil fields soon, the world faces declining production.

Natural Gas. Production in North America has not kept pace with demand, and the prospect of supplies catching up is remote for the next decade or so. Federal officials and industry executives have been expressing their alarm in public over the prospect of prolonged natural-gas shortages. Like oil fields around the world, the known gas deposits are getting on in years; producers have already picked off most of the low-hanging fruit. New deposits have been identified, but, like new oil, the gas is deeper and more expensive to extract; and the capital investment dollars haven't been there for years to find new supplies. Gas fields in Canada and the northern slope of Alaska are still without the pipeline infrastructure necessary to speed the gas to market. Environmental regulations also make it tougher to dig new wells, and even with permission, local restrictions sometimes limit drilling to only three and a half months of the year.

As demand and prices increased in 2003, the necessary steps for increased natural-gas production were under way. In 2003, drilling rigs actually increased by a third—though in 2004 those rigs had yet to increase gas production. The U.S. government has encouraged the building of new natural-gas terminals on the East and West Coasts and the Gulf of Mexico that could handle large amounts of imported natural gas in liquefied form. Energy companies moved ahead with plans for 25 or so terminals, but they ran into formidable opposition on environmental and safety grounds. (Liquefied natural gas can leak from transport tankers or storage terminals—and explode.) Seven projects have been canceled. If any of the others make it to completion, that will be years away, as natural-gas supplies continue to diminish. One sure sign of low supplies: Ted Turner, who took a major hit on his AOL stock, has allowed drilling rigs on his prize 588,000-acre ranch in New Mexico—to exploit natural-gas reserves.

Metals. Virtually no new mine shafts have been opened in 20 years worldwide. As the demand for copper, silver, iron ore, aluminum, palladium, and lead increases, where are the new mines, not to mention the new deposits? Small mining and metals exploration firms have reported that venture capitalists have ignored them for years. In 2004, I met with a group of Canadian mining CEOs who, in spite of the current boom in their own markets, conceded that they had virtually no new mines opening in the near future. In fact, they had invited me to explain why I thought a bull market was under way as part of their efforts to determine whether to increase spending. Others have begun to get the message.

But even if more metals mines were on the horizon, where are the new smelters to make them usable? In 2004, aluminum smelting capacity alone was growing at about half its annual rate since 1961. According to a report in the *Wall Street Journal* in May 2004, 8 of 10 smelters in the Pacific Northwest had been idled or closed down in the past few years as a result of high energy costs. Alcoa, the world's largest aluminum company, announced plans for a $1 billion smelter on the island of Trinidad and was breaking ground for another in Iceland—the first to be built in 20 years. In the meantime, however, supplies are expected to dwindle for the next few years. The last lead smelter was built in the U.S. in 1969. Of the actual mining exploration reportedly taking place in the past few years, more than half of it was for gold.

Sugar. Have you heard of anyone opening a sugar plantation lately? Supplies are diminishing, and by some accounts the world sugar market is expected to exceed world sugar demand by 2.3 million tons between 2005 and 2006—as worldwide demand has begun to exceed supply. Sugar has also become an energy commodity, having been turned into ethanol, a clear alcohol that can be used in its pure form to power vehicles with special engines or blended with gasoline to produce "gasohol." More than 60 percent of the world's ethanol is produced from sugar. Brazil, the world's largest producer and exporter, has been using half its sugar crop to power the nation's cars. By 2005, 60 percent of Brazil's new cars produced by Volkswagen, General Motors, and Fiat were "flex-fuel" and able to run on gasohol—a number that will only increase with the price of oil and gasoline. Japan is also committed to using more of the cleaner ethanol fuel, as new emissions standards are introduced to meet the Kyoto Protocol deadline of 2012. The Brazilian industry has already promoted ethanol sales in China. (Ethanol use is increasing in the U.S., though most of it is made from corn.) More sugar in the gas tank means less for export—and higher prices.

Low supplies, increasing demand, nothing in the pipeline. All the pieces are in place for happy days for commodity investors. Bottlenecks in the supply chain have goosed prices even further. There are not enough ships worldwide to ferry existing commodities to their destinations, and those in operation will be using up more, expensive fuel.

While predicting exact prices is not my expertise (or my investment strategy, for that matter), I do know that in mid-1999 commodity prices, when adjusted for inflation, were lower than at any time since the Depression. So even at today's highs, when you factor in inflation there is still plenty of room for most commodities to go even higher. (Crude oil's record high in the 1970s would be over $90 a barrel in today's dollars.) History tells us that in every bull market nearly everything reaches an all-time high. I haven't even factored in war and terrorism—and that's because the commodity bull market would thrive without that terrible duo. Historically, however, war and political chaos have never been good for anything but pushing commodity prices higher, unfortunately.

That prices are likely to rise for years to come is reason enough to invest in commodities. But there is another factor that makes such a prospect even more comforting.

WHEN STOCKS GO DOWN—COMMODITIES GO UP

Historically, there has been a negative correlation between the price movement of stocks and commodities. On any chart of bull markets in stocks and commodities, they are parallel lines going in separate directions. Commodities were hot in the period between 1906 and 1923, when stocks went nowhere—and the reverse was the case during the Roaring Twenties. Many of us still remember the hot commodities—and cold stocks—of the 1970s. Quite the opposite was the case during the 1980s and 1990s. Now the cycle is turning in favor of commodities. Studies have confirmed this negative correlation between stocks and stuff. Two recent studies, for example, headed by Barry Bannister, a capital-goods analyst for Stifel Nicolaus and Co., the financial services company, show that for the past 130 years "stocks and commodities have alternated leadership in regular cycles averaging 18 years." Bannister

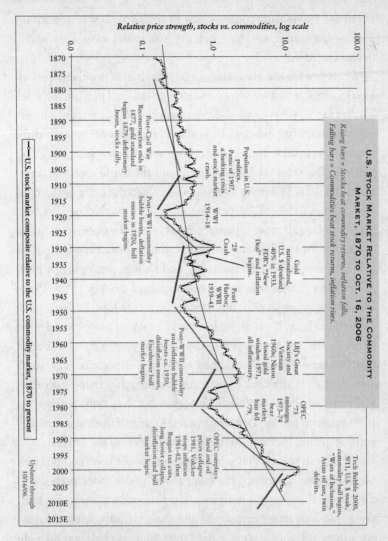

U.S. STOCK MARKET RELATIVE TO THE COMMODITY MARKET, 1870 TO OCT. 16, 2006

Relative price strength, stocks vs. commodities, log scale

Rising bars = Stocks beat commodity returns, inflation falls.
Falling bars = Commodities beat stock returns, inflation rises.

— U.S. stock market composite relative to the U.S. commodity market, 1870 to present

Updated through 10/16/06.

Post-Civil War Reconstruction ends in 1877, gold standard begins 1879, deflationary boom, stocks rally.

Populism in U.S. politics, Panic of 1907, a banking crisis and stock market crash.

Post-WWI commodity bubble bursts, deflation ensues in 1920, bull market begins.

WWI 1914-18

'29 Crash

Gold nationalized, U.S. $ devalued 40% in 1933, FDR's "New Deal" and reflation begins.

Pearl Harbor, WWII 1939-45

Post-WWII commodity and inflation bubble bursts ca. 1950, disinflation ensues, Eisenhower bull market begins.

LBJ's Great Society and Vietnam 1960s, Nixon closed gold window 1971, all inflationary.

OPEC '73 embargo, 1973-74 bear market; Iran fell '79.

OPEC overplays hand and oil prices collapse 1981, Volcker stops inflation 1981-82, then Reagan tax cuts, long Soviet collapse, disinflation and bull market begin.

Tech Bubble 2000, 9/11, U.S. $ weak, commodity bull begins, "Wars of Inclusion," Asian oil use, twin deficits.

Source: Barry Bannister, Strategist for Stifel Nicolaus & Co. Stock market prices are from the Cowles Commission study ordered by Standard & Poors, combined with the S&P 500 post-1960. For Commodities, 1870 to 1890 are the Warren & Pearson U.S. commodity price average. 1891 to 1913 is the WPI from the BLS and other agencies. 1914 to 1956 is the PPI for All Commodities modern series, about two-thirds of which we feel are classic commodities, and 1957 to present is the KR-CRB Commodity Futures Index.

heard me talking up commodities in the early 2000s and kindly sent me his own research on bull markets in stocks and commodities since 1880.*

When you look at these trends on a graph, it is positively eerie. It looks as if God himself were a trader who enjoyed playing the stock market for 18 years or so and then switched to futures, until he got bored again, after another 18 years or so, and went back into the stock market. Why the negative correlation? I'm not sure, but I have a theory. Consider the Kellogg Company, the world's leading cereal producer, with $8 billion in total sales. When the price of the massive supplies of wheat, corn, sugar, and paper that Kellogg needs to make and box all those different cereals is low, the company is likely to make a lot more money. At worst, the cost of doing business is under control; at best, it's declining, and Kellogg makes bigger profits at bigger margins. In the commodity bear market of the 1980s and 1990s, when commodity prices were very low, Kellogg stock did extremely well—moving from a $2 stock to more than $40 in 1999. By the end of that year—and the first year of the commodity bull market—Kellogg stock had sunk by 50 percent. The stock inched up over the next eight years—Kellogg has made major acquisitions outside the cereal business—but has only reached its 1999 range in the last couple of years. Kellogg's stock did virtually nothing during the last commodity bull market in the 1970s.

It stands to reason that when the prices of the commodities Kellogg needs are going up, the company is under more pressure to control costs and profit margins. And so a rising commodity market would hurt many companies and their margins, while decreasing prices for those same goods over long periods would help them. In theory. And that is my theory for this apparent reverse

*Barry Bannister and Paul Forward, "The Inflation Cycle of 2002 to 2015," Equity Research Industrial Portfolio Strategy, Legg Mason (April 19, 2002). Bannister, "War, Legacy Debt, and Social Costs As Catalysts for a U.S. Inflation Cycle," Legg Mason (May 16, 2003). In both studies, the authors point to a new bull market in commodities that is under way. I agree.

correlation between stock and commodity prices. It would also explain why commodity-producing companies (oil and mining companies, for example) and those that support and serve them (oil-rig manufacturers, tanker and container owners, trucking firms that haul metals and scrap, and so on) tend to do well during commodity bull markets.

I have not sat down and done a study of this phenomenon. In fact, I always used to recommend it as a dissertation topic for ambitious graduate students, but the hard data has been coming in. Bannister and an associate actually began their analysis of the commodities and equities markets by asking their clients, "Do commodity-serving companies deserve your capital?" They concluded that, while stocks for most companies went down during a commodity bull market, companies connected to the commodities business—their focus was manufacturers of heavy machinery used in agriculture, such as John Deere and Caterpillar—were likely to do quite well. That, too, would be explained by my theory. When oil prices were making record highs in 2006, the stock pickers on CNBC were shaking their heads about how awful the market was—except for oil and other energy-related companies, which, of course, was exactly what happened during the last bear market for stocks (and commodities bull) in the 1970s. While the stock market was going nowhere generally, there were some great success stories among oil and oil service companies.

This trend is no fluke, evidently—at least according to an even more recent, and extremely important, study from the Yale International Center for Finance entitled "Facts and Fantasies About Commodity Futures," which was published while I was writing this book.* To study simple properties of commodities futures as an asset class, the authors created their own commodities index of returns on future contracts between July 1959 and March 2004.

* "Facts and Fantasies About Commodity Futures," by Gary Gorton and K. Geert Rouwenhorst, Yale ICF Working Paper No. 04-20, June 14, 2004.

They, too, found that returns from investments in commodities were "negatively correlated" with equity returns (and bonds, too). This result, they explained, was "due, in significant part, to different behavior [between stocks and commodities] over the business cycle." When the stock market is in decline or just going sideways, investors are always looking for a hedge. Ignoring commodities in a bear stock market, as so many tend to do, turns out to be quite irrational—and fiscally irresponsible.

THE NATION'S ECONOMIC HEALTH IS NOT A DECIDING FACTOR

The twentieth century's longest bull market in commodities began during the Great Depression in 1933 and grew even stronger during that period, a period that serves as the very standard for "hard times" in America. Economies all around the world suffered, yet commodity prices kept rising. And thirty-odd years later, during the famous worldwide recession of the 1970s, commodity prices skyrocketed again.

In both cases, supplies had dwindled during previous years, while demand rose or at least remained flat. Supply and demand, that's what it's about. When the stock market is on fire, as it was during the twenties and the sixties, investors ignore companies that specialize in raw materials and other goods. And then, no matter how badly the economy is doing, the necessities of life (food, heat, shelter) and the basic means for jump-starting the economy (construction, mining, agriculture) sustain demand for commodities.

And even when demand dwindles, prices can still climb. How? If the supply falls faster than current demand, the supply-and-demand imbalances only increase—and so will prices. You can't just turn on the spigot at a copper mine. Ramping up production of an existing mine takes years. And once the product is depleted there will be a supply vacuum. Finding new mines, exploiting them, and bringing the metals to market, as I have pointed out, can take decades.

The Yale study also concludes that "commodity futures are positively correlated with inflation, unexpected inflation, and changes in expected inflation." That was pretty obvious to those of us who participated in the commodity bull market during the 1970s, when double-digit inflation was rampant. Investors worry about inflation, particularly the unexpected variety, because it cuts the purchasing power of their returns and other income. Looking for a hedge, some head for stocks, others head for short-term government bonds and treasuries. Back in the 1970s, as a young investor searching for ways to make money I actually drifted into commodities for the first time because I saw so little value anywhere else. I certainly had no idea that was the way the world worked during a long-term bull market for commodities. (At the time, I didn't even know that I was in the middle of a big commodities boom.) According to the authors of "Facts and Fantasies About Commodity Futures," commodities have been a better hedge against inflation than stocks *and* bonds for the past 45 years.

Today, as a much more experienced investor, I would have been dumbfounded if Professors Gorton and Rouwenhorst had discovered otherwise. But many people are confused about inflation. I am constantly asked about inflation (and "deflation") during speaking engagements. People refer to it as if it were some kind of magical entity that existed on its own, independently of market mechanisms. But what is inflation but higher prices? And higher prices do not happen without a reason or cause. And if I'm right that current supply-and-demand imbalances will be pushing up most commodity prices for years to come, that's the root of inflation. Most people just don't notice it until those higher commodity prices are passed along to them—when more expensive oil and metals, for example, raise the price of their cars and gasoline. If inflation were a marching band, higher commodity prices would be the majorettes leading the musicians down the street. And by investing in commodities you can beat the band.

WARNING! THERE WILL BE SETBACKS

I cannot promise a stairway to heaven. No bull market in any asset has ever gone straight up; periodic corrections will always occur. In this bull, too, there will be corrections; things will go down. And when they do the smart investor will buy more. In the last commodities bull, which ran from 1968 to 1982, commodities went up and down slightly for the first three years and then spiked more than 200 percent on the CRB Index, went down a bit, then up a bit—and then plunged 53 percent over the next year. Commodities gained 22 percent on the CRB by 1977, only to lose 15 percent of that gain the following year. After five years of ups and downs in the same range, one might have thought that commodities had stalled. But one would have been very wrong—and would have missed another 104 percent spike in prices before that bull market ended in 1982.

The stories of particular commodities were also filled with corrections. In the late 1960s, gold, for instance, was at $35 an ounce. In 1975, it skyrocketed to $200 in anticipation of the effects of the recent decision by the U.S. government to allow Americans to own gold again. Within the year, gold lost 50 percent of its value, plunging back to $100. A lot of people sold their gold. Too bad for them, because gold proceeded to go up eight and a half more times—to $870 an ounce in January 1980! When oil made its historic rise to $40 a barrel in the 1970s, there were periodic dips along the way. A look at the performance chart for the Rogers International Commodities Index launched on August 1, 1998, about four months before the bull really began, shows plenty of ups and downs, particularly in 2001, when commodity prices for the 35

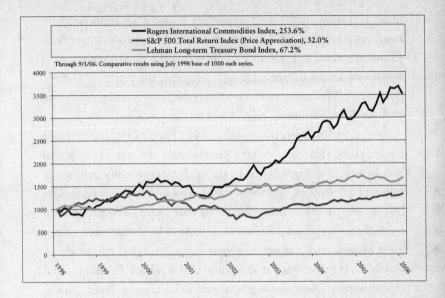

goods included in the index were down 18.51 percent for the year because of 9/11. Experienced traders expect setbacks, and when they see prices going down they simply buy more.

WARNING NO. 2! CHINA HAS CAUSED SOME OF THE GAIN—AND WILL CAUSE SOME PAIN

In the near future, you may see headlines reporting "China in Turmoil!" With an economy that's been growing at a phenomenal rate for a decade (more than 9 percent in 2006, which was at least three times faster than the U.S. economy), there are bound to be some problems. Mix a massive amount of new market capitalism into a centrally controlled Communist system, and you generate enough confusion and inexperience for a hard landing or two.

When the political and economic shock comes, it will send waves throughout the world. Japan's current growth is dependent

upon China, which is also importing massive amounts of commodities from the rest of the world. When the prime minister of
China suggested in the spring of 2004 that the economy needed to
be slowed down in order to stall inflation, the prices of copper,
gold, and oil fell on the news—and so did shares on the Asian and
U.S. stock exchanges.

I will take up China in more detail in Chapter Five, but up front
I want to be clear that when China sneezes the rest of the world
will be reaching for aspirin. In particular, commodity prices will
fall, and a lot of investors will panic. You and I, however, will be
buying more commodities. We know that history and simple economics are on our side: Supply and demand have conspired to create a historic bull market in commodities, and that means prices
should continue to rise at least until 2015. Those 1.3 billion and
still counting Chinese are not about to disappear. Buying more
commodities cheap during those setbacks for the market is where
you will make some real money.

WHAT IS THE DIFFERENCE BETWEEN
A CONSOLIDATION AND THE END
OF A BULL MARKET?

A consolidation is caused by a glitch in the supply-and-demand
relationship. When the Chinese government actually forced
large banks to tighten up loans to manufacturers in an effort to
slow the economy, that put a further crimp in metal prices. But
as long as worldwide supplies are still low, and demand is still
high, once China starts importing commodities again prices are
likely to rise. A consolidation is simply a *temporary* decrease in
prices.

The signal that a bull market is over is a series of fundamental
changes in the way we live. In 1972, for example, the Club of
Rome predicted that the world would soon run out of natural re-

sources. Oil went from $3 a barrel to $34, and the prognosticators were publishing charts with oil prices heading for $100 by the
mid-80s. President Jimmy Carter soon had Americans wearing
sweaters, turning down their thermostats, buying smaller cars,
and cursing OPEC. European nations began using nuclear power
plants instead of oil to generate electricity, further decreasing oil
demand. And then oil from new deposits discovered in the North
Sea and Alaska began to come on line, increasing supply. By 1978,
oil production had exceeded demand for the first time in years—a
major fundamental shift, which should have signaled the end of
the bull market. (Prices, however, continued to rise for two more
years, proving that human beings can make markets move in
strange ways. The last leg of a bull market always ends in hysteria; the last leg of a bear market always ends in panic.) If scientists
discover that orange juice causes cancer, the news will not result in
a simple correction in the orange juice market; it will be the death
of it.

When you see headlines about the discovery of new oil reserves
or wind farms popping up outside major cities, when you see new
mines coming on line, when you discover that stockpiles of all
kinds of commodities are rising, those are fundamental shifts—
then it's time to get your money out of commodities. The bull market will be over.

Those days, in my opinion, are a decade away, at least.

REVIEW BOX:
THE BRIEF FOR COMMODITIES

- The 1980s and 1990s saw a bear market in commodities. Rarely have commodities been as inexpensive as they have been in recent years—when compared with the Consumer Price Index or the price of other financial assets, such as stocks and bonds.

- This long bear market in commodities has created a sharp reduction in capacity—and thus large supply-and-demand imbalances. Quite simply, demand is increasing and supply is extremely low and declining, and it will take years for this imbalance to improve.

- As economies in Asia continue to grow, there will be a strong worldwide demand for all commodities. China, in particular, has quickly moved from a major exporter to an importer of commodities, consuming iron ore, copper, oil, soybeans, and other raw materials voraciously.

- Historically, the prices of commodities show a negative correlation to the price moves of stocks, bonds, and other financial instruments. When stocks are down, commodities are up, and vice versa. That means if you are not investing in commodities, you are not genuinely diversified.

- Commodities are tangible assets that offer different characteristics—and no credit risk. They are also liquid. Commodities are traded on open markets throughout the world, and their prices are listed in the press and other media.

- Commodity prices can rise even when the economy is stuck in reverse.

- Commodity returns outpace inflation.

- Stock prices can go to zero. Commodities cannot. Unlike shares in a company, commodities are real things that are always likely to be worth something to somebody.

- The U.S. Federal Reserve and other central banks in the world have been pursuing a policy of debasing their paper currencies. Hard, tangible assets will, once again, be the place where value and growth can be found—the real money.

- The U.S. Federal Reserve's policy of monetary stimulus and rapid credit expansion will continue to push up the prices of hard assets such as precious metals and other commodities—as more and more money chases a diminishing supply of assets. And while central banks have the power to create money as quickly as they can warm up the printing presses, they cannot create new raw materials or foodstuffs out of thin air or speed up the customary procedures for bringing what is available to market.

- History shows that war and political chaos only push commodity prices higher, unfortunately.

2

"BUT . . ."

RECENTLY, at a party in New York, I mentioned that I had been talking to various groups in the U.S. and Europe about investment opportunities in commodities. Before I could get out one more word, a woman interrupted me. "Commodities!" she exclaimed, with the kind of incredulity in her voice that Manhattanites reserve for people moving to Los Angeles. "But my brother invested in pork bellies and lost his shirt. And he's an economist!" Everyone seems to have a relative who took a beating in the commodities market, and this fact (or fiction) is considered sufficient reason that no sane person would ever risk playing around with such dangerous things. That this particular victim was also a professional economist makes the warning seem even more ominous. I, however, couldn't help laughing.

Billions of dollars are invested in commodities every day. Without the commodity futures markets, many of the things that you depend on in life, from that first cup of coffee in the morning to the aluminum in your storm door to the wool in your new suit, would be either scarce or nonexistent, and certainly more expensive. To be sure, investing in anything has its risks. A lot of Ph.D.s in economics lost money in the dot-com debacle, too. (On New Year's Day in 2002, the *Wall Street Journal* published its annual survey of economists for the upcoming year. Although the economy had been sagging for almost a year, not one of the 55 economists thought that it was in for a serious decline. One hundred percent were wrong—and proof that Ph.D. economists are as prone to mob psychology as the rest of us.)

There are several other bromides out there for why "ordinary people" should not invest in commodities, and I want to lay these myths to rest, once and for all, so that we can get on with the more interesting business of how you can begin to make some money investing in the next-generation asset class.

ABOUT THAT RELATIVE OF YOURS
WHO GOT WIPED OUT—

He was inexperienced. You can learn. Most likely, he was buying on thin margin—the minimum deposit a broker requires to take a position in a particular commodity—and when the market went against him he lost big-time.

Here's how it happens: Like stocks, commodities can be bought on margin. Unlike stocks, however, where by law you have to put up at least 50 percent of the price of the shares, the margins on commodities can be even lower than 5 percent: You can buy $100 worth of soybeans for $5. If soybeans go up to $105, you've doubled your money. Beautiful. But if soybeans go down $5, you're wiped out. Not so beautiful.

Experienced, smart speculators can make tons of money buying on margin. They also know that they can lose tons, too. But they can usually afford it. Your relative was in over his head. If he had bought $100 worth of soybeans in the same way that he can buy

IBM—for $100 (or maybe even $50)—he would be happy when it goes up $5 and a lot less sad should it go down $5.

"BUT WHAT ABOUT TECHNOLOGY?"

Whenever I mention commodities in public, someone always points out that we now live in a high-tech world where natural resources will never be as valuable as they were when we had a smokestack economy. But if you read your history you'll discover that technological advances are as old as history itself: The introduction of the sleek and beautiful Yankee clipper ship dazzled the world in the mid-nineteenth century, loaded with cargo, sailing down the trade winds at 20 knots and more, averaging more than 400 miles in 24 hours and able to make it from U.S. ports around Cape Horn to Hong Kong in 80 days; within a decade, the clippers had been replaced by the steamship, no faster but not dependent on wind power; and before long the next big thing in transport had taken over, the railroad, which, of course, was the original Internet—and prices in commodities still went up. In the twentieth century came electricity, the telephone, and radio (three more Internets) and then television (a fourth Internet). There was also the automobile, the airplane, the semiconductor—and in the midst of all of these truly revolutionary technological breakthroughs came periodic, multiyear commodity bull markets.

Even a revolutionary technological breakthrough in a particular commodity-related industry will not necessarily lower prices. For decades, drilling below 5,000 feet or offshore was virtually impossible. Then in the 1960s the Hughes diamond drill bit was invented and an explosion of technological advances in oil drilling and exploration followed. Drilling efficiency—and oil deposits—were available that had been unthinkable before this technological breakthrough. Soon there were wells 25,000 feet deep and offshore oil rigs multiplied around the world.

Yet oil prices went up more than 1,000 percent in the 15-year period between 1965 and 1980. When the supply and demand in raw materials is seriously out of whack, the emergence of new technology will not necessarily restore the balance quickly. To be sure, changes in technology, for example, have made the economy less dependent on oil. But we still use plenty of it, and whenever there isn't enough prices will rise. Computers or robots may do amazing things, but they cannot find oil or copper where there is none or make sugar, cotton, coffee, or livestock grow faster than nature allows. We can put in orders all day long on our computers for lead, but all that Internet technology will be in vain if there are no new lead mines. Technology can neither feed us nor keep us warm, and the demand for commodities will never disappear.

"BUT ISN'T IT ONLY SPECULATION AND THE LOWER DOLLAR THAT ARE INFLATING PRICES?"

Certainly, speculators who jump in and out of commodities can push up prices. And the dollar has been a pale remnant of itself—down against the euro almost 40 percent from the beginning of 2002 until the start of 2004 and at a three-year low against the Japanese yen. Since commodities are traded in dollars, a weak dollar will make prices appear higher. Crude oil rose 64 percent in dollars over that two-year period, but only 16 percent in euros.

But the dollar strengthened in the spring of 2004, and a funny thing happened: Commodity prices kept going up. The global recovery, particularly in Asia, was for real. We are now watching a fundamental structural shift in commodities markets, and it is called "supply"—and "China," a nation that will be consuming extraordinary supplies of all kinds of commodities for years to come. I will explain why in more detail in a later chapter. For now, however, here's the story: dwindling supplies and increasing demand. And the dollar has nothing to do with either. Let me also remind you of the 1970s, when inflation in the U.S. was about 10 percent a year, the dollar wasn't buying anywhere near what it used to, and the economy was in a major recession—and commodity prices kept rising. We're talking another long-term bull market in commodities, and neither speculators nor a weak dollar can make that happen. Speculators can have a short-term effect only. For example, if they drive up the price of oil artificially, oil producers with excess supplies will gleefully dump their oil on the market driving the price back down. Both the dollar and speculation can have a marginal effect, but the market itself is bigger than they are.

"BUT MY STOCK BROKER TELLS ME THAT INVESTING IN COMMODITIES IS RISKY."

Tell me again about all those Cisco shares you owned back in 2000. Or JDS Uniphase, or Global Crossing? So many risky stocks made the turning of the new millennium a not so happy time for many, who watched their portfolios evaporate.

If you do your homework and remain rational and responsible, you can invest in commodities with perhaps *less* risk than playing the stock market. You don't need me to emphasize that investing in anything is a risky business. But let me point out something that you might not have realized: There has been more volatility in the Nasdaq in recent years than in any commodities index. Cisco, Yahoo!, and even Microsoft have been much more volatile than soybeans, sugar, or metals. Compared with the risk record of most tech stocks, commodities look safe enough to be part of any organization's "widows and orphans fund."

According to "Facts and Fantasies About Commodity Futures," the Yale study cited in the first chapter, the "high risk" of investing in commodities does not square with the facts. Comparing returns for stocks, commodities, and bonds between 1959 and 2004, the authors found that the average annual return on their commodities index "has been comparable to the return on the SP500." The returns from commodities and the S&P 500 beat those from corporate bonds during that same period. They found that the volatility of the commodities futures under analysis was slightly below that of the stock in the S&P 500. They also found evidence that "equities have more downside risk relative to commodities."[*]

How about buying shares in commodity-producing companies instead of buying commodities themselves? That's about as far as some financial advisers will go in the direction of commodities. But investing in commodity-producing companies can turn out to be an even riskier bet than sticking with buying the things outright. Supply and demand will move the price of copper, for instance, while the share prices of Phelps Dodge, America's largest publicly traded copper company, can depend on such less predictable factors as the overall condition of the stock market, the company's balance sheet, its executive team, labor problems, environmental issues, and so on. Oil skyrocketed in the 1970s, but some oil stocks did not do that well. The Yale study found that investing in commodities companies is not necessarily a substitute for commodities futures. The authors found that from 1962 to 2003, "the cumulative performance of futures has been *triple* the cumulative performance of 'matching' equities"[†] (italics mine).

And let me remind you of one more important difference between commodities and stocks: Commodities cannot go to zero, while shares in Enron can (and did).

"But with Prices Already up for Several Years, Haven't I Missed Out?"

In the twentieth century, commodities markets, both bulls and bears, lasted for cycles averaging 17–18 years. And here's why.

---

[*]Gorton and Rouwenhorst, "Facts and Fantasies About Commodity Futures," pp. 9–13.
[†]"Facts and Fantasies About Commodity Futures," p. 30.

Let's say you and I are looking for an opportunity to make money. We do our homework, and we notice that lead is extremely cheap. On the face of it, lead might seem to be an asset whose time has passed. If you walked into a room in any major urban area in the U.S. and found a politician, a used-car salesman, and the owner of a lead mine, nobody would speak to the mine owner. He's in one of the most politically incorrect and least fashionable businesses in the world. Lead paint in old buildings continues to poison children; toxic lead residue in the air from leaded gasoline had been poisoning us all. And now that lead is no longer in either gasoline or paint, demand for it has dropped precipitously, and as a result maybe one lead mine has opened in the past 25 years.

But our investigations into the lead business have convinced us that there is still plenty of demand. These days, most of the available lead is used for "lead-acid batteries," the kind of battery you have in your car or truck. And with increasing economic growth in the world's two most populous nations, tens of millions of Chinese and Indians are beginning to trade their bicycles in for motor scooters, cars, and trucks that require these batteries, demanding more and more lead.

The existing lead mines are bound to be running out. Mines do not last forever. And neither do existing inventories, if they are not increased. With supply down, and demand likely to rise—only 4 percent of those 1.3 billion Chinese own cars—lead looks like a good bet.

Better still, lead is cheap. Therefore we're going into the lead business.

It will, however, take some doing. First, we have to find a new lead deposit—no easy task. But we luck out and find a major new source of lead. Now we must go to Wall Street to raise the money to build our lead mine. Investors are cool to our proposal: They will give us zillions for an information technology start-up, but no one is interested in anything as "old economy" as a lead mine. But we're persistent, and we finally raise enough money to go into the lead mining business with the help of a smart venture capitalist who also sees the prospects in lead. In fact, by now lead prices may be creeping up. Of course, we have to get government permission, and then there are the environmentalists to cope with. Brilliantly, we move through the bureaucracy and satisfy the environmental concerns—but we're still a long way from producing lead. The deposits we found were in the middle of nowhere, and we will have to build roads through the wilderness; we will, in fact, have to create a sizable infrastructure to support this mining venture, from the world headquarters of our mining firm to the trucks, construction workers, miners, and the cabins where they will live. That infrastructure takes time. But we make it happen, and eventually, years later, our mine is on stream, and we're mining lead, finally.

You cannot, however, take lead from the ground and put it directly into an automobile battery. You need a smelter. But nobody has built a smelter since years before the last lead mine was dug. And if the environmentalists were opposed to the opening of your lead mine, they'll be ready to do battle at the mention of smelters. Smelters are miserable places that spew toxic smoke into the air, and nobody wants one within miles of them. But we find an area nearby that is desperate enough for jobs to put up with our smelter. Now we have to find the money to build it!

And so it goes. In the meantime, as we're racking up the years and the millions to get into the position to make money meeting that increasing shortage of lead we spotted years ago, prices have risen exponentially. The demand is on us—and everyone has noticed that lead is a smart market in which to be. Suddenly, others are trying to find lead and build mines. They, too, will have to go through the long, drawn-out process of making it happen. And lead prices will keep going up, no matter what. The world's vehicles still need their lead-acid batteries.

That is what makes bull markets in commodities last for so long. Conversely, once all the new lead mines come on stream, their owners will be mining as much lead as they can to take advantage of the high prices and demand. The new mines have to pay back their financiers. Eventually, however, warehouses will be filled with lead, more than is needed, and the prices will move downward. It will take years to use up all that capacity, the price of lead will go nowhere—which means that a bear market is under way. That bear market, in turn, will last for years, until the existing mines become depleted.

Luckily, we are now at that stage where, after a long bear market in metals, capacities are down, while demand worldwide has grown. Companies are beginning to realize that it's time to get back into the mining business. Meanwhile, we investors have a decade or more to ride the rise in prices before the new mines come on stream and capacities get high enough to push prices back down again.

Every single commodity traded takes time to be found, grown, produced, and shipped. Exploration and production for energy products and minerals take decades. Oil was discovered in the North Sea in 1969; North Sea oil went to market in 1977. Alaska's North Slope oil was discovered in 1968, and took nine years to get to market. Even a 1,200-pound steer takes more than two years from conception before it is "finished" and ready for slaughter; one coffee tree takes three to five years to grow to fruition. That is why bull markets in commodities last so long: When supplies of things are allowed to become depleted without increasing new capacity, it takes time even to recognize the change, much less to get production up to the point where it can meet demand.

So give commodities some respect—and take advantage of them as a potential investment. That they are riskier than stocks or bonds is bunk—pure myth that has finally been demolished. Investments in commodities have not just done better than bets on commodities-producing companies over the past 43 years; they have scored

triple the returns. Please tell that to the next financial adviser who
warns you off commodities. Better still, you have time to put your
toe in and learn as much as you can. The bull market under way
will last for years. There's still plenty of time left—and money to
be earned.

3

STEPPING UP TO COMMODITIES

IF you're still with me, you're probably eager to find out how to invest in this new bull market in commodities, but before you reach for your checkbook, however, I would recommend some serious research—into the commodities business, yes, but also into your own soul.

Anyone with any experience in the stock market already knows how important psychology is to successful investing. Emotion can drive the markets up or down, and the mind-set of individual investors fires those emotions. We all panic. Everyone. In 1980, I bet that oil would be going down—right before Iraq invaded Iran. War in the Middle East was not the best time to short oil. With everyone worried about a drop in oil production instead of the surplus I was betting on, prices ran up. I covered my short positions (i.e., bought them back at higher prices instead of the lower ones I had expected, and took the losses)—another dumb move. The poor fundamentals on oil that had existed before the war had not changed. But I panicked, as every investor does from time to time.

Your personality makes a difference. You have to look into the mirror and be absolutely candid about your own attitude toward risk, your ability to admit to having made a mistake, and your willingness to stray from the herd. If you have trouble admitting you're wrong, commodities will be as hard a school as any other investment area. Experienced commodities traders know that they will be wrong lots of times. If you are inclined to follow the conventional wisdom, that, too, is likely to be an obstacle to success. Almost every time I've made serious money, it's been by heading in the opposite direction of the crowd.

So before you put any money on the table, please, "Know thyself," and decide the best way—for you—to take advantage of the opportunities in front of you. All investors have their preferences. Some are eager and aggressive and want to control every move; others are timid and prefer to do as little as possible. Some see themselves as great traders with an eye for the next big move in prices. Others have no knack for it and would prefer to leave the wheeling and dealing to someone else.

I, for example, am the world's worst trader. The best traders are maestros of timing. Knowing when to get in and get out, they enter and exit markets fearlessly. Over decades as an investor, I have learned that the best way for me to make money is to find something cheap that I like, take a position, and hold it for the long term. I'm a lousy trader, and I avoid "short-term" investments.

Almost as important as self-knowledge, you'll need to pick the commodities you want to invest in and then learn everything you can about them. That may prove much more difficult than probing your psyche. The annual *CRB Commodity Yearbook* lists more than 100 specific commodities—from alcohol and aluminum to wheat and zinc. How to choose? In fact, the list of the most frequently traded commodities is a lot shorter. Reuters-CRB Futures Price Index, which has been around since 1956 under a number of owners and is listed in the business section of most newspapers, includes 19 heavily traded materials to give investors a sense of the movement in commodities markets. The Dow Jones-AIG Commodity Index, also in the financial pages, has 19 components. The Goldman Sachs Commodity Index currently includes 24 components. The Rogers International Commodity Index has 36. As I noted in the Introduction, each index allots different weightings to specific commodities: The Reuters-CRB alloted the same weightings to each of the 17 items on its list until its tenth revision in 2005. I wonder if they still do not have it right. For example, it now gives aluminum a 600 percent greater weight than wheat. Aluminum is a wonderful commodity, but most people in the world have never used it while nearly everyone in the world uses wheat every day. The Dow Jones-AIG figures the weightings according to the relative trading activity of an individual commodity averaged with the dollar adjusted for worldwide production data over five years. Or that is the party line. For example, I note the weighting of natural gas is up about 250 percent in the last few years. Natural gas production is declining if anything. It certainly is not up 250 percent. Cocoa has disappeared from the index now. Has the world stopped producing cocoa? The GSCI also claims to be weighted on world production and uses this as an explanation for its extremely high energy weighting. A look at the facts might raise questions about their claim of a "world production basis." For example, livestock was 26 percent of the GSCI in 1993 and was 4 percent in 2005. Are we really to believe livestock production has declined 80–90 percent over those dozen years? The facts are that Dow Jones, Goldman Sachs, and now Reuters-CRB increase their weightings as prices rise—not a sound way to invest, in my view, and certainly not the way the real world works. The RICI attempts to balance commodities according to their importance in international commerce. The components of these different indexes, however, are from the same five sectors: Energy, Metals, Grains, Food/Fiber, and Livestock (see Appendix).

These are commodity sectors that the potential commodities investor should be examining. I would recommend beginning modestly, searching for opportunities in one or two sectors, and then focusing on a specific commodity or two that intrigue you, for whatever reason. Say copper catches your eye (to stick with an example I've already used). The overriding question is:

WILL THE PRICE GO HIGHER?

Getting a fix on where copper prices might be headed will require some serious homework. The *CRB Commodity Yearbook* is an indispensable guide to all commodities, reporting "The Commodity Price Trend" for every year, including a brief summary of inventories and demand in recent years. But to get a more accurate fix on what the future might bring for any given commodity, you must look deeper into the Commodity Research Bureau's accumulated research and other government, industry, and media sources.

What to look for? The guidelines are simple: *supply and demand*.

SUPPLY

Information about past trends, current inventories, and future supplies of copper is publicly available. You just have to round it up. The *CRB Commodity Yearbook* reports different government and industry sources for supplies for previous years and offers estimates for the upcoming months, including detailed historical charts, along with special features analyzing various commodities and price trends.* Up-to-date supply figures can be found on U.S. government, state, and industry Web sites, and other countries have equivalent sources. The U.S. Geological Survey, for example, offers information about minerals, including charts of monthly and an-

---

*The *CRB Commodity Yearbook* is published by John Wiley & Sons and can be purchased through bookstores or the publisher at www.wiley.com. The price is $199, which includes a CD-ROM with the Commodity Research Bureau's analyses of commodities and appropriate charts going back, in some cases, to the 1950s. I do not use it for its analyses—only for its facts.

nual prices, along with supply, demand, and inventory figures as well as information about mine closings and openings. Industry associations and services (e.g., American Bureau of Metal Statistics, American Metal Market) are also a good source of data and analyses of trends.

Copper is sold on COMEX, the metals division of the New York Mercantile Exchange, and the London Metal Exchange (LME), which also offer plenty of free information. (As you begin studying a particular commodity or sector, you will quickly discover the most popular sources of information. Web sites are standard fare, too, these days.)

The primary variables to check are:

- How much production is there worldwide?
    How many tons of reserves are there?
    Is the production in areas that might experience turmoil?
    Are the reserves rich with copper or only marginally productive?
    What are the existing inventories?
    How many mines exist worldwide?
    How productive are these mines?
    What is the potential supply over the next 10 years?
- Are there new sources of supply?
    Old mines expanding?
    When?
    How much will this cost?
    How much copper will this expansion produce?
    How long will it take before additional supplies get to market?
- Are there new *potential* supplies?
    How much?
    How expensive to develop and then produce?
    How long before these new sources will be available?
    When will the new supplies get to market?

This kind of research will give you a good sense of how much copper (or any other commodity) there is *likely* to be over the next 10 years—barring unpredictable events, such as strikes, fires or other natural disasters, political problems in that country, and so on. In 2003, for instance, copper production was set back—and prices given a boost—following a series of accidents at an American-owned mine in Indonesia.*

DEMAND

Figuring how much copper will be needed over the next 10 years will require you to investigate the ins and outs of the copper business.

- What is this commodity most used for?
- Which of the current uses will continue? (The wireless revolution knocked out demand for telephone wires, which use copper.)
- What alternatives are available to replace it if the prices go too high? (Plastic pipes instead of copper ones, for instance.)
- What new technological advances might require this commodity that did not exist before? (Computers, for example, created a new need for copper parts used in the system's innards; cable systems picked up the slack in copper demand for telephone wires.)

Try to be as objective as possible about this research. We all have a tendency to see what we want to see in facts and figures, to make an investment seem hot even if the facts suggest otherwise. So if your research indicates that supply is high and demand is not likely to improve, learn to sell short or move on—but not before you consider the alternatives. If plastic pipes wipe out the demand for copper ones, the smart investor will recognize that in that blow to copper lies an opportunity: Plastic is an oil product, and more plastic piping might increase the demand for oil.

*Similar questions, of course, can be asked about all commodities. I analyze five commodities in greater detail in Chapters Six through Ten.

And remember, if copper declines enough in price and oil rises enough, the reverse might happen, too.

THE ALTERNATIVES

There are a number of ways to take advantage of the growing demand for commodities:

*1. Buy shares in companies that produce commodities
or service those companies.*

When professional stock pickers see commodity prices going up, they immediately look at the companies that specialize in those things—Phelps Dodge, for example, the Phoenix-based copper company that's one of the world's largest producers and trades on the New York Stock Exchange. When copper prices went from 60 cents in 1998 to $1 in the winter of 2004, the chairman of Phelps Dodge, J. Stephen Whistler, stated the obvious with considerable glee to a group of Wall Street executives: "We not only can make money at these kinds of prices, but we make a lot of money."

There are even some mutual funds that invest in commodity-related companies. But too often stock prices have little to do with how good a company really is or the value of its products. Other things can get in the way:

- *Status—and psychology—of the pertinent stock market.* In the 1970s, the price of oil kept rising, and some oil stocks went nowhere. That is not to say there wasn't any value in energy companies. Some oil and oil service companies did very well. But there was a bear market in stocks, and investors were looking for opportunities elsewhere. A company's fundamentals can be perfect, and the price of the commodity it produces can be going higher, yet shares in that company may stagnate along with the market. The stock market too often runs on emotion; hope, greed, fear, and panic are not inclined to pay close attention to growing imbalances between supply and demand. In 2002 and

2003, Wall Street was forecasting low earnings for oil companies; even when oil was heading to $40 a barrel and above in 2004 (and profits from S&P energy companies had increased by 63 percent in 2003), the energy analysts still couldn't believe it was for real. Why? They were analyzing oil as if it were a stock—making the mistaken assumption that any big price move would soon revert to the historical mean. In the meantime, they ignored the fact that demand in the U.S. and Asia was rising faster than supplies, not to mention unrest in Venezuela, a war in Iraq, and fears that terrorism in Saudi Arabia would disrupt supplies. In other words, the stock guys were ignoring everything about what makes oil prices go up or down. Oil was at a historic high, and oil stocks were mired in a sluggish stock market.

· *Government policies.* At the end of the first quarter of 2004, while most companies were reporting increased earnings, jobs were picking up, and economists were giving a thumbs-up to the strength of the U.S. economy, investors continued to sell. The Dow, the S&P 500, and the Nasdaq Composite Index were all down for the quarter. No one seemed able to take their eyes off the sword of Damocles hanging over the entire market—the threat of an interest-rate rise that would undercut earnings and make debt more expensive. Even though money had been almost free for years, the stock market couldn't wrap its head around higher rates. The news from the war front in Iraq was even worse than usual. And thus, in the midst of a bull market in commodities, the stocks of companies that produced them shifted into neutral. Governments also control and change other policies such as environmental, labor, pension, and import-export laws and regulations. These are often negatives for some companies, but are almost always positive for the commodities themselves. For example: The U.S. has decided not to drill for more oil in Alaska—bad for companies doing business there but good for the price of oil.

• *Management.* In recent years, the average investor has learned a lot about how CEOs, CFOs, and boards filled with hand-picked cronies can undermine a company. The top brass at Enron may really have believed they had—as the title of a recent book about the scandal put it—"the smartest guys in the room," but we now know that the company was managed by people whose ingenuity ran in the direction of creating fiction. When oil went to $40 a barrel in the spring of 2004, oil stocks were outperforming what could only be generously called a sluggish market. Royal Dutch Shell, however, lagged behind its competitors, largely because of a scandal that it had overreported its oil reserves by 22 percent— with the full knowledge of some top executives.

• *Balance sheets and accounting practices.* Enron, WorldCom, Tyco, Adelphia, Cendant. Need I say more? The most vigilant investor cannot control financial finagling and puffed-up earnings reports. How many companies these days are fudging their expectations just to be able to beat them? Companies with debt or pension problems may lag even as commodity prices rise.

• *Unpredictable Events.* Sudden corporate or political scandals, strikes, environmental problems, war, and terrorism can move the stock markets lower. Investors, no matter how tireless, cannot cover every contingency. In spite of higher prices for steel and increased demand, in 2004 U.S. Steel's first-quarter profits were substantially higher than those for the previous year. The company's stock, however, lagged behind that of its competitors. One reason was U.S. Steel's operations in Serbia and Slovakia, where income had reportedly dropped 38 percent. Slovakia's historical entry into the European Union meant that it had to renege on tax benefits it had promised the U.S. company, undercutting the company's expansion plans. Steel shot up, and it seemed like a no-brainer to most people to buy U.S. Steel. But how many investors had their eye on the situation in

Slovakia? In the first half of the first decade of the new millennium, after the attacks of September 11, 2001, the magnitude of the power of "unpredictable events" on the stock market was clear; in fact, one of the most predictable variables in the market was that as soon as the stock indexes began to climb, war and terror, whether real or threatened, scared investors away from the market.

There are scores of copper stocks around the world, so analyzing them all, with their different managements, balance sheets, unions, pension plans, governments, local stock markets, notes to each financial statement, different accounting systems, environmentalists, and so on, can be a never-ending process. The smart investor looking into a copper company first has to examine the supply-demand dynamics of copper. Why not just stop after that analysis and buy or sell the copper itself? It saves a lot of effort and reduces mistakes.

And, over time, investing in copper is likely to bring a higher return. The Yale study "Facts and Fantasies About Commodity Futures" reported that the returns from commodities were *three times* those of companies producing those commodities. I have just given the reasons why.

2. Invest in countries that produce commodities.

Canada and Australia are two examples of major commodity-producing countries. Both are rich in natural resources and are home to some of the largest mines in the world. And, predictably, as commodity prices have risen in recent years the economies of both countries have grown, too. Retailers, restaurant and hotel chains, indeed businesses of every type, will do better in commodity-rich nations than in countries that are short of natural resources. Currencies will also perform better in nations exporting rather than importing commodities. The Canadian dollar was worth U.S. $1.06 during the commodity bull market in the 1970s.

It declined to about U.S. $.60 in the subsequent commodity bear market. Bonds in these countries will often perform in tandem with the economies of such nations. Likewise, their stock markets are also likely to prosper.

I have invested in Canada and Australia and have certainly done better than I would had I limited myself to investing in the U.S. alone. I also have put money into New Zealand, a small country rich in resources that has prospered in recent years. Other commodity-rich nations have also enjoyed economic growth. In 2003–04, Brazil, also a major exporter of commodities and the world's biggest producer and exporter of sugar, was recovering from an economic crisis and was flush with cash as a result of huge foreign-exchange reserves. Chile is the world's leading exporter of copper. Bolivia is sitting on huge deposits of natural gas, something that the U.S. desperately needs. Bolivia's fortunes are likely to improve and will be worth investing in eventually.

But it's not as simple as finding a country rich in resources and parking some of your money there. Emerging economies are always susceptible to external threats. Any pullback in China, which passed the U.S. as the world's No. 1 consumer of copper in 2002, is bound to hurt Chile. Brazil exports iron ore, pulp, and steel to China, and a slowdown on the Chinese end will cause pain in Brazil. Rising U.S. interest rates also have a ripple effect around the world.

Commodity-rich countries will also face internal threats, which are often less predictable by outside investors, who are not likely to be experts in the political situations of other countries. Venezuela is the world's fifth-largest exporter of oil—and has a left-wing strongman in charge who values his relationship with Fidel Castro more than his dealings with the state-controlled oil industry. Malaysia, whose economy is also based on natural resources, was ruled by an economic incompetent from 1981 to 2003; new leadership *might* bring some new opportunities. Brazil remains one of my favorite places in the world to visit, but as the Brazilians say, "Brazil is the

next great country in the world, always has been, always will be."
(They will also tell you that "Brazil is God's gift to mankind—and
then He sent the Brazilians to screw it up.")

Russia and the former Soviet republics around the Caspian Sea
are also extremely rich in natural resources, but, in my opinion,
the entire region is already a disaster on the way to a catastrophe.
I wouldn't invest a nickel there. Likewise, Nigeria is rich in oil but
extremely poor in political leadership. South Africa is another
commodities-rich nation with huge and growing internal political
tensions and crime rates. Its fine infrastructure is under-
maintained and running down; the movement of people from the
country to the cities has created vast shantytowns that can be
nothing but depositories of hostility and unrest. The only thing
holding the place together is Nelson Mandela, a powerful symbol
of hope, who is pushing 90.

The inevitable problems in Russia and South Africa, which will
make it increasingly difficult for these countries to exploit their
natural resources and get them to market, are two of the reasons I
am bullish on commodities.

3. Invest in real estate in areas and countries rich in commodities.

I would not advise anyone to buy a house in New York or
Boston—or London, for that matter. Not only have those cities
been subject to overpriced real estate for years but their economies
are much too dependent on financial services, a market sector that
has not done well in previous commodity bull markets. If you
want to speculate in real estate, buy a house at the lake in a farm
state (Iowa, for example, or Nebraska) or in an oil and natural-gas
area (Oklahoma), or a mining state (Montana or Colorado),
where communities will benefit from the rising prices in metals,
energy, and agricultural products. If you had bought property several years ago in such commodities-rich countries as Canada, New
Zealand, Australia, and Chile, you would have increased your equity severalfold.

4. Buy commodities.

In my opinion, buying commodities in some form is the best way to take advantage of rising prices. You don't have to move to Australia or even Colorado to buy copper. Copper does not view itself as "the smartest guy in the room." Copper, in fact, is pretty dumb and simple: If there's too much copper, the price will go down; if there's too little, it's going up. Even if you buy copper stocks, you first have to determine the supply/demand outlook for copper. Why go to all the extra trouble and risk of buying stocks or investing in countries? And, maybe best of all, copper doesn't care what Alan Greenspan and the Federal Reserve think, or do. And, unlike the stock price of a troubled company, copper will never go to zero.

You probably know someone who has some gold bars or a bag of gold or silver coins stashed in a bank vault. But where would you stash $50,000 worth of copper, corn, sugar, or pork bellies? Fortunately, there are several other ways to buy commodities that range from complex to simple, from very risky to less so.

Many commodities investors prefer to manage their own trades—just as many stock market investors prefer to manage their own portfolio. Savvy stock pickers don't buy just any stock; they analyze the company, investigate the business it's in, check out the competition. Some commodities traders prefer to do their own analysis of the market, check out trends in supply and demand, investigate the political and labor situation in the country the commodity comes from, and so on. But no matter how hands-on you want to be as a trader, you will still need a person or a firm to broker the trades on your behalf, and generally that person must be registered with the Commodities Futures Trading Commission (CFTC), the federal agency that oversees the commodities business in the U.S. Virtually all the major brokerage firms have departments that handle futures trading, though services and research information can differ. Some traders prefer to rely on the advice of their brokerage firm or the executive assigned to their account. Some even pay for independent trading advice.

If you think you're a trader—and many people, unlike myself, really do have a knack for trading—you can open up your own account:

- *Individual Account.* Trades are executed for you, and no one else. You can open an individual account directly with a registered *futures commission merchant* (FCM), who will receive your funds, manage them, confirm your trades, and make sure the required minimums are in the account. Or you can go through an *introducing broker,* a firm that's in the business of soliciting or accepting futures orders, which are then handled by an FCM. Introducing brokers do not handle your money or trades, but they do offer trading services. No one can make any transaction for your account without your approval. (This is also known as a Non-Discretionary Individual Account.) This kind of account is for self-confident investors who are prepared to spend whatever time it takes tracking futures markets in a chosen commodity. For the less confident trader, there is, however, another alternative: a managed account.

- *Managed Account.* This is an individual account that you allow someone else to manage, buying or selling for your account at the manager's discretion, with your authority through a written power of attorney. (This arrangement is also known as a Discretionary Individual Account.) You, of course, will be responsible for any losses your account manager runs into, so make sure that you know as much as possible about a given manager's experience and credentials. Keep in mind that these managers are usually involved in other accounts, too. But they must keep all their accounts separate, and they cannot share profits or losses between accounts. You should also make sure that your trading philosophy squares with the manager's. It is up to you, of course, to make your objectives clear. In addition, you should be absolutely clear about the minimums required for your account, as well as all the management and transaction fees.

On the basis that two heads for commodities are better than one, some traders like to hire a *commodity trading adviser* (CTA), an individual or firm that does just as the title suggests—advises on trading, including what kind of positions to take in the market (i.e., betting that prices will rise or fall), and when to get out or liquidate those positions. All for a fee, of course. The CTA becomes your private expert, paid to be at the other end of the phone to answer questions about the trades you are making for your individual account. CTAs also will manage your money for you and send periodic statements of your status. CTA's must meet certain training, experience, and financial requirements set by the federal government.

• *Trading Futures Options.* Taking a cue from the stock market, commodity exchanges made options available for some commodities in the 1980s. Just as in trading commodities outright, you can trade options on futures contracts with the aim of speculating on the price rising ("call options") or declining ("put options"). A put or a call gives you the right—but not the obligation—to buy a particular futures contract at a specific price (the "strike price"). The appeal of options is that you can profit from the upside potential of the price going your way without the downside risk in trading futures contracts. The only money the futures options trader can lose is the price paid for the option, known as the "premium." Personally, I am not a big fan of purchasing options, most of which end up as losses. If prices do not move in any direction, you cannot exercise your option. The Chicago Mercantile Exchange actually examined expiring and exercised options over the three-year period from 1997 through 1999 and found that an average of more than 75 percent of all options held to their expiration day ended up worthless. The odds thus are with the *sellers* of commodity options, who get to keep all of those expired premiums. It is definitely another way to profit from commodities, and I often sell options. But the risks of selling (or "writing") options are comparable to trading the actual futures contract, and beginners should be aware of that. Entire books have been written about trading options on commodities futures, and this is not one of them. But anyone exploring the possibilities of profiting from the bull market in commodities should know about the option of futures options.

For those who are no more eager to trade commodities on their own than they are to be a stock day-trader, there are the commodity equivalents of mutual and index funds.

• *Commodity Pool.* A venture, generally a limited partnership, in which the funds of numerous investors are combined with the goal of trading commodity futures. Also known as a "commodity fund" or "futures fund," this pool of money is traded as an individual account. Your cut of the profits (or losses) is figured in proportion to the amount you have in the fund. Like a stock mutual fund, a pool is bound to be more diversified than an individual account. More important, since most pools are limited partnerships, your downside risk is typically limited to the money you put into the fund. (Should the market move swiftly against the speculator trading his own account, the losses could be considerable.) Nevertheless, like any investment in any market where there can be volatility, prices can go against you, and the diversification of a commodity pool is hardly fail-safe. And, like mutual funds, not all commodity pools are created equal. A lot rides on who is administering the pool, the **commodity pool operator** (CPO), who structures the fund, hiring and supervising the traders making the day's transactions on the floor of the exchange with the fund's money. Check out a variety of funds and see how well their CPOs have done over time. And there's no need to be shy: A commodity pool, by law, cannot even accept your money without disclosing the record of the CPO, who the principals in the fund are, what commodity trading advisers they depend on, and who actually makes the trades.

• *Mutual Funds.* They are still rare for commodities. In fact, as I write, I know of only two, and neither is totally committed to commodities. With $5 billion in assets, the largest is the PIMCO CommodityRealReturn Strategy Fund (PCRAX), which takes a position in commodities through derivative instruments linked to the performance of the Dow Jones-AIG Commodity Index, "backed up," according to PIMCO, "by a portfolio of inflation-indexed bonds and other fixed-income securities." The other closest thing to a commodities mutual fund is the Oppenheimer Real Asset Fund (QRAAX) with $885 million in assets. According to the company, "the fund invests primarily in hybrid instruments, futures and forward contracts, options, swaps, investment-grade bonds, money markets, and the U.S. Government debt." The Oppenheimer fund uses the Goldman Sachs Commodity Index. As the bull market in commodities continues (and other asset classes languish), watch for the introduction of more commodity mutual funds.

• *Index Investing.* Studies have shown that the cheapest and most sensible way for most people to invest is in index funds, which have historically outperformed more than two-thirds of managed funds. You write your check, and your money is on automatic pilot, rising and falling according to the prices of the basket of commodities you have purchased. One of the ways that I invest in commodities is through an index fund. Unhappy with the existing commodities indexes, as I noted earlier, I created the Rogers International Commodity Index and my own index fund, the Rogers International Commodity Index Fund, which is open to individual investors as well as institutions. Several investment companies offer products based on the index. I think it's the best. But please don't take my word for it. Independent evaluations are made regularly of all the existing indexes in every asset class, such as those done by Seamans Capital. The other indexes do not offer funds for investors. But two of them are traded in New York and Chicago in the form of financial futures such as those for stocks tied to the S&P 500 Index, the Nasdaq 100, the Russell 1000, and many other indexes. In conjunction with the Reuters-CRB Futures Price Index, the New York Board of Trade (NYBOT) markets a futures contract based on that index, while the Chicago Mercantile Exchange (CME) offers a futures contract tied to the Goldman Sachs Commodity Index.

How do you find a broker, if you decide to trade commodities? Carefully. References from a friend, relative, or business associate with experience in trading commodities is a common first step. But keep in mind that this will be an important relationship, as anyone with experience with stock brokers or financial consultants knows. The right commodities broker for your friend might not be the broker for you. You must feel comfortable with any person in a position to help you make (or lose) money. Trust is crucial. Therefore, it is important to interview a prospective broker and probably wise to talk to more than one.

If you're already following the equity, bond, and other markets and working with one of the big "full-service" brokerage firms, you can ask your financial consultant whether the company trades commodities. Not all of them do. But it's worth asking, particularly if you've been very happy with the firm's service in other areas. But keep in mind that during the commodities bear market of the 1980s and 1990s, only a fraction of the big firms' earnings came from commodities, and most have neglected that side of their business. Nevertheless, a trusted financial consultant is likely to aim you in the right direction.

I've noticed that the commodities exchanges also offer listings of brokerages, such as the Chicago Mercantile Exchange's "Find a Broker" program. Check out the exchange Web sites for leads (see Appendix). Brokerage firms are also likely to have their own Web sites, so you can do some homework before you make your call. Make sure you are clear about your goals in the market, and make sure the broker is equally clear about them. It is also a good idea to have a sense of what commodities you might be interested in trading. I advise you to start with one or two. Make sure the broker has experience in those commodities with a good grasp of the supply and demand fundamentals. If you expect a lot of advice and hand-holding, you must find a broker up to that task. Try to get as much information about a broker's or the firm's track record. If anyone tells you that they will never lose any of your money, run for your life. It is virtually impossible to win all the time in any market. Buyer beware!

And be very clear about the financial requirements—the commission and transaction fees, the minimum size of the account that they're willing to accept, the minimum deposits that must be in those accounts, and all the margin requirements. Reputable, licensed firms have all of this on paper, and will send it to you before your first meeting with a prospective broker. Read all of that carefully. In fact, before you make a move to find a broker, read the next chapter, and I promise you that by the end of it, you'll be a much more educated shopper for a commodities broker.

No matter how you decide to invest in commodities—whether you limit yourself to an index fund or a commodity pool or are eager to get involved in trading futures, either on your own or with some version of a managed account, you ought to familiarize yourself with how the commodities futures markets work. I believe, in fact, that no matter what you prefer to invest in, you will be more successful if you understand the commodities markets. In the next chapter, I offer a primer on what every novice must know before he or she puts some real money on the table.

4

STEPPING INTO THE
COMMODITIES MARKETS

STEPPING into a commodities market is a lot like visiting a foreign country without speaking the language. Before you put any money on the table (and even if you are leaving the trading up to someone else), you should familiarize yourself with the lingo. I would even recommend a tour of a commodities exchange, a true wonder of the financial world and an unusual opportunity to observe the free market in action. Take your children to see a bit of the olden days before it's soon displaced by more efficient, cheaper electronic trading.

The U.S., in fact, is one of the few places in which these anachronisms still exist. The controlled chaos and energy of hundreds of men in colored jackets waving pieces of paper in the air, making hand signals, and screaming at one another is a sight to behold. The sheer physicality of the place is in itself amazing (and a good reason that many women are not inclined to seek careers in the *commodity pits*). These traders speak their own language, which bears some resemblance to English: "going long," "locals," "ticks," "liquidate." There's lots of talk about "margins" ("margin account," "margin call," "initial margin," "maintenance margin"). Metaphors abound: "jumping in," "jumping out," "expiring," "crashing," "dumping," "liquidating." And some terms seem descended from another language altogether: "contango," the opposite of which is—English teachers and copy editors, please shield your eyes—"backwardation." Like the stock market (or any specialty, from baseball to marketing, from plumbing to art history), the commodities game has its own jargon and codes. To master commodityspeak is to begin to understand how trading commodities actually works. This chapter will move through the history of the mechanisms of the commodities markets, and in doing so, terminology (indicated in bold) necessary for understanding commodities will be defined and explained in the context of a real working exchange.

Before we turn to the lingo, however, it's important to begin with the two most fundamental concepts of commodities trading: supply and demand. These two forces prop up the market and drive future prices. Simple enough. What is not as simple is predicting what those prices might be down the road. For a commodities producer or user, big swings in prices are the difference between making money and losing it—or even staying in business. Commodities producers—farmers growing wheat or cotton, mining companies bringing metals to market, or companies or countries sitting on lots of oil—work hard to hone business plans and strategies for selling products at a price higher than it costs to produce and market them. But unpredictable events can get in the way, from bad weather and changes in government policies to labor strikes and, these days, acts of terror, causing production and supply problems and thus raising prices.

Users of commodities—cereal companies, for instance, gasoline and heating-oil operations, or car and appliance manufacturers that need huge amounts of aluminum and copper—must also develop prices for their products that have a shot at beating the prices of their competitors. They, too, are at the mercy of events and trends they cannot control, principally fluctuations in supply and demand. If, for example, supplies of copper or aluminum are tight, car manufacturers will have to pay more for what they need, pushing up the costs of their cars and slimming their profit margins.

In unregulated markets like commodities, strange things are always happening, and volatility is quite normal. Such fluctuations in price create considerable financial risks for those businesses that depend on buying and selling commodities. And that's if they can find the right buyer and seller and settle on the right price. *And* their profits also depend on whether the stuff gets delivered at the right time to the right place. *And* on whether the buyer can actually pay on delivery. If I agree to buy my home-heating oil from you, and you never show up, I'm stuck without any oil to heat my house. As angry as I might be, what can I do? I can't call the cops. Sure, I can try to take you to court, but in the meantime I'll freeze.

Commodities producers and consumers do not need that kind of risk in their lives. Fortunately, it is a risk they need not bear. Instead of throwing themselves at the mercy of the volatile physical market, they can lock in a price and lay off their risks by buying contracts in the **futures market.** This futures market, like any other market, brings together buyers and sellers; it provides the physical space where supply meets demand.

THE BASICS OF FUTURES

To start at the beginning:

> *"Trading commodities" and "trading futures"*
> *are the same thing.*

It wasn't always so. Once upon a time, American farmers transported recently harvested crops by horse and wagon or rail to the big cities every fall, and the bigger and better their harvests were, and the more corn, wheat, and hay piled up, the lower prices fell. Often there was more stuff than there was space for storage. Corn and wheat rotted in the streets—the same stuff that people wished they had the following spring, when low supplies turned basic foodstuffs into extravagances beyond the means of ordinary people. Farmers produced goods that companies needed, but it was every man for himself trying to buy and sell at reasonable prices, at the mercy of the weather, poor transportation, and wheeling and dealing. Railroads charged exorbitant shipping rates, "middlemen" took unreasonable profits, and banks were stingy with credit. For America's first 80 years, this is how agricultural commodities were traded in the U.S. It was hardly evidence of American ingenuity.

You will remember from Economics 101 the principle that "markets are usually a good way to organize economic activity." Nowhere is this as obvious as in the commodities business, where the emergence of an official market—an **exchange**—makes business for commodities sellers and buyers a whole lot more efficient and less risky than was the case in those old but not so good days. In 1848, to meet the need for a central marketplace, 82 Chicago merchants founded the Chicago Board of Trade (CBOT) in a local flour store, the first **commodities exchange** in the U.S. Within a year, according to the exchange's official history, the CBOT was using "to arrive" contracts for the future delivery of flour, timothy seed, and hay. According to the CBOT, the earliest **forward contract** was recorded in 1851—for 3,000 bushels of corn that was not for **spot delivery** (handed over "on the spot"). By 1860, there were 2 million farmers in the U.S., responsible for 82 percent of the nation's exports. Agricultural commodities fueled the young nation's economic growth, but farmers too often saw others getting rich off their hard work. Soon they began to organize into "cooperatives" and "granges" to protect themselves from sharp operators and to put pressure on politicians to enact legislation designed to protect farmers. They also began to work with local merchants to figure out more efficient and profitable ways to market their goods. In 1865, at the end of the War Between the States, the CBOT formalized grain trading with the development of standardized agreements to buy and sell fixed amounts of a certain commodity at a specified location at a future time for a predetermined price called **futures contracts**.

It was a brilliant innovation—though one more example of reinventing the wheel. The Japanese were selling rice futures in the seventeenth century. But the new Chicago exchange helped balance the supply and demand for agricultural products and addressed the problems of fixing prices, delivery, credit, and many other unpredictable variables of an unregulated trade in physical commodities taking place on a vast continent. As useful as forward contracts were, they were still only privately negotiated deals between a buyer and a seller for exactly what was available when the seller wanted to sell it and where. Both sides had to find each other and depend on each other. Both the wheat sellers and the buyers were looking for a way to standardize their deals, decrease the inevitable risks of dealing in agricultural products, increase their opportunities, and give themselves a way out of deals they had already made. Anyone who has seen a cowboy movie can sympathize with the difficulties of moving thousands of head of longhorns from Texas to Chicago. No one has to lead a herd of cattle into the Chicago Mercantile Exchange (CME), which was founded in 1898 and is now the largest futures exchange in the U.S.; or lug barrels of oil onto the floor of the New York Mercantile Exchange (NYMEX), which was established in 1872 to trade butter and cheese and is now the world's largest exchange dealing only in commodities. At the turn of the twentieth century, there were roughly 1,000 commodities exchanges in the U.S. There are now seven exchanges specializing in commodities (see Appendix).

Although the *New York Times* and the *Wall Street Journal* act as if commodities did not trade any place other than the U.S. (except for their Brent crude oil futures listing from the U.K. trading at London's International Petroleum Exchange), there is plenty of action elsewhere in exchanges around the world. In addition to trading on the COMEX division of the New York Mercantile Exchange (NYMEX), high-grade copper futures, for example, are also traded on the London Metal Exchange (LME) and the Shanghai Futures Exchange. The world's biggest exporter of sugar is Brazil, so it is not surprising that sugar futures are traded at that nation's Bolsa de Mercadorias & Futuros (BM&F), which is also Latin America's main commodity exchange. But sugar also trades on exchanges in Japan and England, as well as on the Coffee, Sugar & Cocoa Exchange (CSCE) division of the New York Board of Trade (NYBOT). (See Appendix.)

The brilliance of commodities futures is that they turn all of those physical goods, those valuable assets that you can touch and even smell, into paper that can be traded with ease. The information from those futures contracts is what ends up on the floor of the U.S. exchanges written on the **pit cards** that those traders in the colored jackets are waving, noting everything you need to know about a given contract. And thus Africans can sell cocoa and oil to Americans, who can buy Brazilian sugar and copper from Chile— without ever boarding an airplane. U.S. consumers and producers of commodities can enter the futures market to make sure they get a good price for what they are selling or need without worrying (too much) about becoming a victim of market forces that they cannot control. Every futures deal includes four main standards:

1. Quantity—how much of a given commodity will be bought or sold. One contract always equals 5,000 bushels of corn, for example, 1,000 barrels of oil, 25,000 pounds of copper, or 100 troy ounces of gold. (See Appendix for complete list.)

2. Description—heating oil, for example, to distinguish it from crude oil or natural gas; a corn contract and another for soybeans (and a separate one for soybean oil, etc.).

3. Delivery date and location—where the seller delivers the commodity and the buyer picks it up: Heating oil arrives in New York Harbor every month of the year, and wheat might be delivered—in March, July, September, or December, the standard months for wheat delivery—to a grain elevator in Omaha, Chicago, St. Louis, or Kansas City, for example. Every commodity has predetermined months of the year and locations for delivery. (See Appendix.)

4. Payment terms—not within 60 days like most bills, or the three days you have to pay for a stock. In futures, payment is strictly cash. At the close of trading every day, profits and losses for every contract are totaled.

This information is what those floor traders are screaming— "What month do you want it for, how many contracts, how much?" They are part of the tradition of the **open outcry**—traders and brokers in brightly colored jackets literally shouting out bids and offers in a large arena, or **trading pit**. The open outcry remains the primary method of trading commodities in the U.S. That's the way the price gets set.* (Futures contracts also contain other specific information, including the hours that the exchange is open, the months that the commodity is listed, and minimum price fluctuations, which differ from one commodity to another. For this information for the most popularly traded commodities, see Appendix.)

Notice how different buying and selling commodities is from dealing in other assets. Unlike corporate stocks, paintings, automobiles, stamps, or even baseball cards, commodities are **fungible**— absolutely interchangeable. One gallon of heating oil or diesel is

---

*Almost all futures trading outside the U.S. is done on electronic trading platforms, where bids and offers are posted on a computerized trading system. Doubtless, the days of those colored jackets and the shouting guys who we~ them are numbered.

like any other gallon of that oil. Five thousand bushels of wheat right here is no different from the 5,000 bushels of the stuff over there. Even 100 troy ounces of gold is, well, 100 troy ounces of gold. Apart from their usefulness and value, there is nothing unique about these materials. That trait makes it easy to substitute one batch for another for purposes of shipment or storage at different times. Their fungibility also makes commodity futures portable and easily transferred—one contract for oil or cotton is the same as any other. All that trading activity also makes commodity futures highly **liquid**—that is, they can be bought and sold with relative ease, and quickly, without affecting the price. This fungibility and liquidity are among the reasons I find commodities so much simpler than stocks. Copper is copper all over the world. If there is too much, the price will go down. If there is too little, it will rise.

Exchanges also introduce stability and regulations not found in the physical commodities market. Producers and users don't have to go searching for one another. If you have a commodity to sell or want to buy one, the exchange stands in for the other side. And while you or I could fail to show up to make or accept a delivery of a physical commodity, an exchange cannot play fast and loose. Every exchange has rules of governance and a board of directors, not to mention all its members watching for any sign of a misstep, thus making an exchange a self-regulating market. In 1936, Congress passed the Commodity Exchange Act, the statute regulating U.S. futures markets. The Department of Agriculture enforced the CEA until 1974, when Congress supported the creation of the Commodity Futures Trading Commission (CFTC), an independent federal agency established to oversee existing futures contracts and the creation of new ones. (NYMEX has announced plans to create steel futures, and U.S. ethanol producers have developed contracts for their product, as is now the case in Brazil.)

Such efficiency, organization, and rules make life a lot easier for commodities buyers and sellers—and has turned trading futures contracts into a popular pastime involving *trillions* of dollars every year. During the course of my own investment career, the evolution in futures has been remarkable. When I started trading commodities in the late 1960s, the futures markets had not strayed far from its agricultural beginnings in post–Civil War Chicago. Wheat, corn, soybeans, cotton, and sugar were where the action was. Livestock futures were initiated only in the 1960s. And while today crude oil dominates the commodities indexes (and the news), crude oil and gasoline futures didn't come on the market until the late 1970s. Financial futures (for U.S. Treasury bills and bonds and international currencies) were introduced in the 1970s, and stock index futures (Dow Jones Industrial Average, S&P 500, NYSE Composite, etc.) were added to the shopping list during the following decade. And while the popular imagination still thinks of great fortunes won and lost in soybeans, cattle, and oil, the fact is that most of the money in futures is now in the financial arena, where certain contracts for euros or Treasury bills can be valued at one million dollars each. (A standard grain contract for corn, wheat, or soybeans is limited to 5,000 bushels. At $3.00 a bushel, one wheat contract would be worth $15,000. Real money, to be sure, but nowhere near the kind of stakes in financial futures.)

Risk in the commodities business, however, never goes away. Indeed, it is risk that fuels commodities exchanges. On the floor of every exchange, they are *trading risk*.

LAYING OFF RISK

Futures fix a price. But the price of futures themselves is never fixed. The process is never-ending, fluctuating up and down, according to the supply-and-demand estimates of buyers and sellers about what a particular commodity will be worth at a given time in the future. (The longest contract is generally for two years; the shortest will be whatever you can find available for the nearest month's maturity date when delivery is required, usually a matter of weeks or even days. As we'll see, "spot" prices is now; futures is later, but because you have to get rid of the contract before you take delivery, cutting it too close is stupid.)

Prices change based on new information (an insect infestation threatens the wheat crop, for example, or political conflict threatens a commodity-producing country), or new developments occur (Brazil will use more of its sugar for ethanol, thus decreasing worldwide exports; the popularity of low-carbohydrate diets has put people off carbohydrate-rich orange juice). Often traders reassess forecasts of future supply and demand, and the price of a particular futures contract is bid up or down accordingly. In June, the price of a December heating-oil futures contract represents what buyers and sellers then *think* about the value of heating oil next winter. But within a few months people might learn that heating oil is in tighter supply than anyone realized, pushing the price upward. By November, meteorologists might be predicting the warmest winter in history, pushing the price back down.

Such supply-and-demand factors have influenced prices ever since markets were created in antiquity, but setting prices was a willy-nilly affair. The advent of futures markets created an ongoing gauge of supply and demand, finally putting a price tag on the future value of a given commodity—a great benefit to buyers, sellers, and the economy as a whole.

But the price could be wrong. The only certainty in futures trading is that prices change. Imagine that I own a chocolate company. Business is fine, but I toss and turn at night, worried about the price of the cocoa that I need to make my chocolate. In fact, it's been an anxious few decades for us chocolate moguls. The world's largest producer of cocoa happens to be the Ivory Coast, which also happens to be the site of what seems to be eternal civil war and religious strife. A bad day in that West African nation could send the price of cocoa to the sky—and my profits spiraling in the opposite direction. And, lest you think being in the candy business is kid stuff, about 3 billion pounds of chocolate get eaten every year in the U.S. alone, making chocolate a $13 billion industry.

It's June, and the price I paid for my current cocoa stock assures me of a profit; the current market price—$1,280 per ton—is also decent. But I know that I'll need more cocoa six months from now and I can't be sure what the price will be. To protect myself now against those unpredictable events in far-off Africa, I can buy cocoa in the futures market, where the price for December cocoa is currently $1,300. I decide to buy 10 contracts and call my broker to make the purchase. Since the standardized amount in a single cocoa contract is 10 tons, each contract will be worth $13,000, making my total purchase price 10 times that, or $130,000.

It's a pretty good price, $20 more than the current going rate and way below the historic December high for cocoa, which was more than $2,000 a ton. My company can now go about its business (and I can sleep at night), knowing that if the Ivory Coast blows up six months from now, sending the price of cocoa through the roof and my manufacturing costs with it, those costs will be offset by the rise in value of my futures contracts, which I can sell.

Protecting against a spike in the prices in this way is called a **hedge**. Anyone who has invested in the stock market—indeed, anyone who reads the business pages of the newspapers—has at least heard about "hedging" and "hedge funds," once a rare entity and now much too common for comfort. Hedge funds are in the business of protecting their own and other people's money from dangerous price movements. They market themselves as better than the average investor or stock picker, with more sophisticated strategies, but I used to be a hedge-fund manager, and I know it's not rocket science. Basically, successful hedgers have the knack of protecting one investment by making another. Commodities consumers can also hedge their purchases, just as my cocoa company did.

And what if things quiet down in the Ivory Coast, as they periodically do, sending the price down $20 a ton in six months? I will be holding cocoa futures that have suddenly become very expensive. Maybe I wasn't so smart, after all, to stake out a **long** position in cocoa futures. But therein lies another lesson:

Hedging is a defensive move.

I can buy my cocoa in the cash market at the lower rate, offsetting my futures position. To be sure, I didn't make money when the price went down or when it went up. But hedging is not about making money; it's protection against *losing too much*. After all, having insurance doesn't prevent bad things from happening.

Producers of commodities also hedge in the futures market. Say you're a big oil company, pumping your share of "sweet light crude," the best-quality oil used for gasoline. You've got oil to sell—1,000 barrels, you estimate. But it's in the ground, and even though the price of oil is $60 a barrel right now—which is historically quite high—no one can be absolutely sure the price will be so good when your oil is actually pumped and ready to go to market in six months' time. The oil producer can sell his oil in the futures market at the New York Mercantile Exchange—for 1,000 times $60—and then go about business without worrying that the price will go down before those 1,000 barrels of sweet crude can be pumped. The company has set a price for the oil it has in the ground, protecting, or **hedging,** against a fall in prices.

And thus the futures market becomes a haven for risk-averse commodities producers and buyers. But commercial futures markets could not exist, without adding to buyers and sellers of commodities a third player: the **speculator**.

PROFITING FROM RISK

Speculator is a dirty word in most circles. But in the world of commodities the speculator is crucial, the grease in the system that keeps the markets moving *and* keeps it liquid. It is the speculator who puts the exchange in the commodities: When those producers and consumers of commodities hedge their risks in the futures market, on the other side of their trade stands the speculator—major Wall Street banks, hedge funds, and private individuals who buy and sell futures contracts for no other reason than to make money. Also known by the less emotionally charged (and thus preferred) label **trader,** a speculator never has to touch (or smell) a commodity. Speculators do not even have to visit the floor of the exchange, operating through brokers who watch their accounts and represent them in the buying and selling of futures contracts from other brokers and **locals,** exchange members or **floor traders,** who trade futures for themselves through the open outcry system.

It is the speculators who set the price, according to the risks they "speculate" in the market. Every day the exchange is like a big auction where the traders find out how much they think a given commodity is worth. Some see the price going up; others see it going down. Their willingness to bid on contracts accordingly is what gives these volatile markets their stability and their liquidity. Like commodities buyers and producers, the speculator takes a position in the market. Unlike hedgers, who use futures to protect themselves from the dangers of the market, speculators jump into the fray eager to benefit from its ups and downs.

Speculators can trade futures in any commodity, though most of them tend to specialize. Unlike the big consumers and producers of commodities, they get in and out of the market—and with no risk associated with the actual physical goods. Most traders aren't interested in taking possession of a single kernel of corn, gallon of oil, or big, fat hog. Studies have shown that less than 3 percent of futures contracts result in delivery or use of the underlying commodity. Pickup or delivery isn't required until the exact delivery date in the contract. To make sure they do not end up the owners of 5,000 bushels of corn or $20,000 worth of beef, speculators **close out** or **unwind** their future positions before the expiration dates—i.e., sell or buy them on the exchange, thus **liquidating** their contracts.

As a general rule, speculators never trade contracts during the delivery month and therefore avoid even the possibility of having to take delivery. Most traders holding a December futures contract will get out in November. (If someone mistakenly doesn't get out on time, the corn, beef, or coffee will not end up in his driveway; the trader will, however, get a warehouse or grain-elevator receipt along with the additional financial responsibilities of paying for storage. Add that to the full price of the contract, and the financial penalty for inattention is considerable.)

The task of speculation is simple:

Pick a direction in the market and hope it goes that way.

Skilled futures traders have scores of strategies and variations thereof to try to squeeze a profit from the market. The two most basic ways of making money are when prices go up and when they go down.

GOING LONG—OR SHORT

You can buy a futures contract and hold it **long,** betting that it will appreciate (buy low, sell high). The trader who has analyzed the supply-and-demand situation for cocoa, including a close look at the political situation in the Ivory Coast, has concluded that things have been much too peaceful there and the lid is likely to blow before the year, pushing prices up. He decides to buy one futures contract and **go long** cocoa. Here's how this scenario might play out:

- Remember my cocoa company that hedged its December cocoa, buying it at $1,300 a ton in June? Traders might have bought cocoa futures at $1,300, but it's now September, and the open-market price of December cocoa is already up to $1,310.

- The current owner of one contract isn't ignorant of the Ivory Coast situation, but he doesn't think prices will rise more than another $10. He's willing to sell.

- The speculator's broker bids $1,315 and finally gets it on the open outcry system for $1,320. That's a tidy profit for the seller of $20 per ton—or $200 for one contract ($20 times 10 metric tons in the standard cocoa contract).

- The following day, violence breaks out in the Ivory Coast, and the price of December cocoa shoots up another $40. The trader can sell and take his profit or wait for it to go higher before the December delivery date.

And what if he waits and is wrong—peace suddenly breaks out in the Ivory Coast, sending cocoa prices straight back to $1,300? He would be forced to take his medicine and sell his position at a loss and hope that tomorrow is a better trading day.

But a speculator can also sell futures **short,** betting that the price will fall (sell high, buy low). **Short selling** is one of the most confusing moves for first-time investors. For pros, however, it's one of the handiest tools for turning someone else's misfortune into a profit. I can still remember that moment, as a college student working for the first time at a Wall Street firm one summer, when I learned that you could make money betting that a company's stock was going to *go down.* And imagine my delight when I found out that you could actually (and legally) sell stocks that you didn't even own.

I know it sounds strange, but we do sell things that we don't own or have all the time. The car dealer sells you a particular model or color that he doesn't have on the lot. When gasoline prices skyrocketed in the 1970s and again today, there were waiting lists for fuel-efficient and hybrid cars that had yet to come off the assembly line. Magazine companies sell us subscriptions for magazines they do not have but hope to deliver. Concertgoers routinely buy tickets for future events. If Placido Domingo gets a cold or Britney Spears hurts her knee, and the concert is canceled, the impresario (short seller) will have to give ticket buyers their money back (**cover his position**).

The way shorting works in stocks is that you find a company that you think is grossly overvalued whose share prices you believe will soon be heading southward. Back in the final days of the dot-com bubble, you could've thrown a dart at the Nasdaq listings and come up with a candidate to sell short. Cisco reached its historic high of $82 in 2000; JDS Uniphase was more than $140 at about the same time. The smart short sellers back then—"the shorts"—were calling their brokers and asking them to sell piles of CSCO and JDSU shares.

Here's how it works. When most people make an investment, they try to buy something cheap and sell it for more. They buy 100 shares of XYZ stock at $10 a share, for example, and sell them when the price hits $15 a share—for a $500 profit. Selling short is exactly the same process—but reversed: You *sell* something at $15 and you buy it at $10. You make the same transaction, and in this case you make exactly the same amount of money, but in reverse order. You have sold it and then bought it. Betting that the price will go down, you sell high and buy low, profiting from the difference. You can do this with stocks, bonds, currencies, and commodities.

How can you sell assets that you don't own? Simple: You *borrow* them—from your banker, your broker, your friend, whoever actually has some or has access to them. They lend you, for example, 100 shares of XYZ company, you sell it at $15 a share price for a total of $1,500. Then when the price falls to $10 a share, you buy 100 shares for $1,000. You then return the 100 shares to the lender, $500 better off. Of course, if you had bet wrong—and XYZ's share had kept rising—you would have to dig into your pocket and pay the difference.

The commodities speculator can also benefit from falling prices. Unlike the stock market, where it is conceivable that a given stock might be so fairly priced that there are no short positions at all, in the futures market there is a short position for every long one. When someone wins, someone else loses, and vice versa. (When you bet on the Green Bay Packers to win, you are expecting their opponent to lose. You are *shorting* the opposition.) Also unlike the stock, bond, and currency markets, the commodities speculator who decides to sell short doesn't have the problem of finding someone who has the actual asset so that he can borrow it and then sell it. What he's selling is not the actual physical commodity but a *contract* for its future delivery. All the speculator has to do is ask his broker to sell a particular contract at a particular price (or the closest to it) and wait for the price to go down. Instead of borrowing anything, he puts up some collateral, but not much—just 5 or 10 percent of the contract's worth. Here's how a short seller might play the cocoa situation:

- After that stint of violence in the Ivory Coast, another trader might reason that $1,360 is much too high a price for December cocoa, reflecting fear more than the fundamentals of cocoa supply and demand. There is no shortage of cocoa.

- Betting prices will go down, he requests that his broker **sell short** one December futures contract at the $1,360 price, hoping to close the transaction before the December delivery by buying an identical contract before then at a much lower (and offsetting) price. (Total value of one contract of 10 metric tons: $13,600.) The broker executes the trade.

- The speculator isn't about to give anyone any cocoa. As we've seen, most traders in the futures markets close out their transactions before delivery. But the futures market was invented to protect consumers and producers from risk, so *some* traders are thinking about delivery. The cocoa farmer who believes the price is likely to go down can sell the December contract at that $1,360 price for a metric ton, hoping that when it's time to deliver that cocoa the price will be lower and he'll make a profit—while his neighbors are delivering their cocoa and getting that lower price for their stuff.

• Within a month the United Nations announces that it will be sending a peacekeeping force to the region, and the price of cocoa begins to fall. The speculator made the right call to sell cocoa. The price has gone down to $1,340 a metric ton. He has his broker purchase another, identical cocoa contract at the market price. The broker manages to get the contract for $1,330—for a profit of $30 per metric ton, or $300 for the short seller.

Sometimes traders sell short without a good reason. They simply feel a big decline in their bones. In 1987, I went short soybeans after the price had flown up over $9.00 per bushel. All the traders I knew were buying like mad and offered very bullish arguments for further price increases. By then, however, I had learned many lessons about the hysteria of markets. Hardly anyone notices the beginning of a bull market. But as prices keep rising, savvy investors get the picture, and soon others turn just as bullish eventually as prices continue to rise in spite of the periodic consolidation that occurs in markets. Everyone in the market is making money, which does not go unnoticed by everyone outside the market, and many more people get sucked in. Soon formerly rational people are quitting their jobs to become day traders. Wild hysteria rules— and I am shorting. By shorting soybeans in 1987, I was shorting another round of hysteria. The price of soybeans fell, and I made some money. While shorting hysteria is usually correct, I recommend also trying to have good fundamental reasons for believing that the price is likely to decline.

The speculator's profit lies in the difference between his original price and a cheaper one. If he's wrong, and prices rise, he will have to cover his short position by buying futures at the higher price, thus losing money.

And every speculator will get it wrong at one time or another. I vividly remember shorting oil in 1980. Prices had been rising for years, even though increased production and conservation were building up supplies. In 1978, supplies actually *surpassed* demand—but prices kept going up, irrationally. By 1980, I figured the market would soon notice that the fundamentals of oil were completely out of whack and decided to bet against oil. What I didn't anticipate was that our friend (and he was an ally back then) Saddam Hussein would invade the Islamic Republic of Iran, then run by the Ayatollah Khomeini. Two members of OPEC in a major shooting war against each other is not a good time to bet that oil prices will go down. In the run-up to the war, I managed to cover my shorts as prices began to skyrocket. (In hindsight I should have hung in there, because oil was genuinely overpriced and eventually the prices sank back down. I had been right about the fundamentals of oil, but I panicked, just like everyone else.)

Here's my general rule of thumb for shorting:

> *I don't like to sell something short unless it's* unbelievably *expensive.*

And I mean *unbelievably.* I've shorted lots of things in my life that were expensive, only to see them get more expensive. In my early days on Wall Street, I learned one of my greatest lessons about market hysteria when I shorted University Computing in 1970, selling it at $48 and waiting for it to descend. I ended up covering my shorts when the price reached $72. University Computing proceeded to go up to about $96—and then plummeted to $2. I was right to short the stock, but I still got wiped out, because, at the time, I didn't have the guts or the money to stick with my convictions that the stock was way overpriced. I was a lot smarter during the dot-com bubble, but I suspect a whole new generation of young wizards learned a similar lesson shorting tech stocks that kept rising into the stratosphere for no good reason at all. A fledgling tech company that was clearly overpriced and a classic candidate for shorting, JDS Uniphase went from $20 to $129 in a year. The trouble was that the market wasn't paying attention to real value. Newcomers to the market who thought it was a never-ending gravy train piled on for the ride. Incredibly, JDSU had more than another $20 to go before it plummeted to $80, climbed toward its high again—and then headed south to almost zero, where it stayed for the next three years.

When gold was moving from $100 straight upward in the 1970s, a rational investor might have considered shorting it at every 100-point rise. Was there anyone at $150 betting it would go straight to $860? (I didn't short gold back then, but I did sell it at $675, way too early, of course, but the top came in about four more days.) And when sugar went from 4 cents to 40 cents, also in the seventies, I suspect that many thought that commodity was *unbelievably* expensive. Unfortunately for those who shorted sugar at 40 cents, the price went over 66 cents before it fell back to reality.

STOP!

As you may have noticed, futures trading is a humbling vocation. Every trader must come to terms with losing, because all traders lose. In fact, *most* traders lose most of the time. It's the bottom line that counts—winning more than you lose. But since losses are unavoidable one other primary principle of trading is to *limit your losses*.

The futures trader has one handy tool to protect him from getting wiped out if the market suddenly moves against him: the **stop order.** You've bought a silver contract at $5.90 a troy ounce. You are long and expecting the price to rise, but you want to limit your loss to 10 cents an ounce. You can place a stop order—also called a **stop loss**—for your broker to sell an offsetting contract if the price of silver drops to $5.80. Should the price hit $5.80, the broker will *try* to make the trade. If you're shorting the price, betting the price will go down, the stop loss number will be higher. That order is automatic: You make it and forget about it. It's your broker's job to execute the trade when the market hits the stipulated price.

But there is no ironclad guarantee that a trade can be executed at the price you want. In a highly volatile market, the price of a given commodity can move so rapidly in one direction or the other that it may be impossible to jump out of your position at the desired stop sign. In that case, the broker is obligated only to execute your stop order at the best available price.

Generally, brokers will at least come close to the price you ordered. *Generally.* But the stop order is hardly the ultimate fail-safe. In an unusually volatile market, prices can reach their **daily trading limit.** This daily limit that exchanges set on all commodities is another difference between trading commodities futures and stocks or bonds (see Appendix). For example, currently corn can go up or down no more than 20 cents per contract per day. If corn closes Monday at $3.00 and on Tuesday it rises to $3.20, all trading will stop—except for those who want to trade at $3.20 or below. When prices hit that limit, the exchange can declare a **locked limit market.** That leaves the broker in a position where he may not be able to execute your order at any price if, for example, there are no sellers at $3.20. In this case, if there is serious hysteria, corn may go on Wednesday to $3.40 with no trades at all because there are no sellers. If you've sold corn at $3.00, you're in a serious bind. Your broker will not be able to get you out until corn goes high enough to bring sellers back into the market. There have been cases when commodities have been **limit up** or **limit down** for a week or two at a time, making it impossible for traders to liquidate losing positions that are racking up serious losses. Woe to the investor who is overleveraged at times like this.

The stop order can also be used to protect profits. If silver you bought at $5.80 goes to $6.10, it might also move down fairly rapidly. The speculator can set a stop at $6.00, assuring you of your 20 cent profit (or as close to that as your broker can get)—without limiting your position if the price continues to rise.

Whether traders go long or short, with a stop order or not, they will eventually have to settle up their accounts. For while they may be working for themselves or for a client, they are still part of an institution that keeps a close—and daily—watch on the bottom line.

THE BUSINESS OF COMMODITIES TRADING

The commodities market is "zero-based." That means that at the end of each day all positions are balanced: The winners—those who bet correctly on which direction the market went, up or down—collect from the losers. (Anyone who cannot ante up for the day's losses will have his position closed out immediately.) Their **margin accounts**—the equity that the traders have deposited with the firms that make the actual trades—thus **adjusted,** they are ready for more trading. This daily reckoning is a major difference between the commodities market and the stock market, where you have three business days in which to pay for a stock purchase.

Another important difference between trading stocks and trading commodities is the amount of money you need to put up as collateral to make a trade. While currently an investor must, by regulation, put up at least 50 percent of the price of a stock in order to purchase it, commodities trading allows more leverage. The minimum deposit for a trade required by brokerage firms— **initial margin**—can be as low as 2 percent of the cost of the current value of the futures contract the client wants to buy; typically, it is more like 5 to 10 percent. Brokerage firms often require a margin amount higher than the exchange minimums. Exchanges also pay close attention to the market, adjusting margin limits up or down according to the amount of risk in the market. In a highly volatile market, for instance, the exchange will be inclined to raise the initial margins—to protect the integrity of the futures markets as well as to protect overeager speculators from themselves. (The Chicago Board of Trade's initial margin for wheat in 2006, for example, was $700, or roughly 3 percent of the current value of one wheat contract, which, with wheat in the range of $4.50 a bushel, was about $22,500. In other words, you can buy $22,500 worth of wheat by putting up only $700. The CBOT's initial margin for corn during the same period was $450, or about 4 percent of the total futures contract for corn, which was worth about $11,250. The initial margin for oil at the New York Mercantile Exchange for a new customer was $4,725 in 2006, when oil had ascended. That meant you could trade one standard 1,000-barrel oil contract worth more than $60,000 with a minimum deposit of roughly 8 percent.)

Here's how that leverage works:

- On a particular day in February, you could buy (or sell) one August futures contract for soybeans (that come in minimums of 5,000 bushels each) priced at $5 a bushel (total value = $25,000) for an initial margin of 5 percent—or $1,250.

- If you're a buyer who is speculating that the price of soybeans will eventually rise, and come May it does—by 10 percent, or 50 cents a bushel—then your futures contract is now worth $27,500 (5,000 bushels multiplied by $5.50). You can sell that August contract for a $2,500 profit, tripling your money even though the price of beans rose only 10 percent. A very nice payday (minus commissions and transaction costs, of course).*

---

*In all the examples in this section, I have left out brokers' commissions and transactions costs—for the sake of argument and to keep the numbers as round as possible. Just like the equity and bond markets (and everything else in life), trading futures has its costs, and starting out, you should be very clear on what they are, from exchange to exchange, brokerage to brokerage.

- But if the August price of soybeans goes *down* by 50 cents a bushel in May, and you decide to sell, the loss amounts to $2,500. That not only wipes out your initial margin but puts you in the hole for another $1,250. Beans declined 10 percent, but you lost 200 percent.

> *Reminder: This is why that brother-in-law lost his shirt in soybeans.*

Just do the math. Speculators buying several contracts on margin stand to make huge profits on tiny stakes, if prices rise. If they go down, the more highly leveraged you are, the more you can lose.

> *And this is why, along with your brother-in-law, most commodities traders end up losing their trading capital.*

The loser in the above example can expect a phone call daily from his broker—a **margin call**—requesting him to cover his loss and immediately ante up his **maintenance margin,** the minimum deposit required by the exchange.

Serious Warning: Exchanges revise their margin requirements periodically, and brokerage firms will follow suit. Before you begin trading futures, you *must* familiarize yourself with the brokerage firm's **margin agreement**—the minimum amount of money you must deposit for a particular futures contract. Those low margins are extremely tempting. For professional speculators with a lot of nerve and a big chunk of money that they can afford to lose (**risk capital**) to back it up, leverage presents opportunities to make tons of money. But only a handful of even experienced commodities speculators are so fortunate. The rest of us have to be much more cautious—and far less leveraged, if at all. Anyone considering trading futures contracts must think long and hard about **leverage**. And once you actually begin trading, you must be absolutely clear about how much you stand to lose from a given contract should it go in the opposite direction that you desire. Keep in mind that you can buy oil or cotton or any commodity just like IBM—full price, cash on the barrelhead. And always keep in mind that risk capital should be money that you can really, really afford to lose. Money that you need for the mortgage, health care, your children's education, your retirement, and other such expenses does not belong in a margin account.

Once you set up a margin account with a brokerage firm, your broker will deposit sufficient funds with the appropriate exchange to cover your trading. Every futures exchange has its own **clearinghouse,** which pays out the profits to the day's winners and deducts the losers' losses. The clearinghouse is literally in the middle of every trade. Unlike trading physical commodities, futures buyers and sellers do not have to find each other; nor do they have any obligation to each other. And without ever meeting, each party can **liquidate** contracts—sell one that they have bought or buy one that they have sold. The clearinghouse is always on the other end of the trade as a guarantor. If I short December corn in July, my buyer will, in effect, be the clearinghouse at the Chicago Board of Trade, the U.S. exchange that handles corn. If my bet is right and the price of corn is down in September, I can buy that contract back and take my profits. The other side of that trade—the seller of the contract—will be the clearinghouse, which, by the way, is also regulated by the Commodities Futures Trading Commission.

DECODING THE COMMODITIES NEWS

If you haven't already done so, it's time to take a look at the commodities section of your local newspaper or the *Wall Street Journal* or *Barron's* to check out the prices of various commodities. What you see there may not make any sense at all. You may also have tuned in to CNBC and seen the commodities quotations streaming across your TV screen during the day. You'll have seen strings of meaningless letters and figures, such as

GH 355.5 . . . WU 369 . . . SN 725 . . . HOX 101 . . . CLN 39 . . .

Let's say you're interested in copper. To see how copper is doing these days, all you have to do is pick up a copy of the *Wall Street Journal* or the *New York Times* or the *Financial Times* of London, which now has a U.S. edition, and turn to the commodities section. While your local paper is likely to list only the previous day's closing prices for the most popular commodities futures (oil, corn, wheat, soybeans, cattle, pork bellies, sugar, and coffee, along with weekly spot prices for gold, silver, and copper), the *Journal* has an entire "Futures" page, reporting price movements according to category—Grain and Oilseed, Livestock, Food and Fiber, Metals, and Petroleum.

Under "Metals Futures," you will always find this heading in that day's *Journal:*

COPPER-HIGH (CMX) 25,000 lbs; cents per lb.

Translation: High-grade copper, traded on COMEX, the metals division of the New York Mercantile Exchange (NYMEX). The standard copper futures contract is for 25,000 pounds, and the unit in which copper futures are quoted is cents per pound. And as long as copper in the U.S. continues to trade on COMEX, this headline will never change.

Under it, you will find something like this:

	OPEN	HIGH	LOW	SETTLE	CHGE	LIFETIME HIGH	LOW	OPEN INT
June	124.30	124.40	123.50	124.05	–2.80	139.30	73.50	1,892

Under that you will find similar figures for July, September, November, December, the following May, July, and December, the other trading months for copper. But let's stick to June. The first four figures are the copper's opening price, the highest it fluctuated and the lowest, and the fixed price ended at the previous day's close—down

2.80 cents per pound, the Change. (*Barron's,* which publishes once a week, provides the week's high and low.) The next two numbers are the Lifetime High and Low, which give the reader a sense of the range of copper prices during the life of this futures contract or how close it might be to its lifetime price levels. "Open Interest" is just that—the interest traders have in the market—and the figure is for the number of outstanding, unliquidated contracts from the previous market close for that month's copper futures. When you buy and sell copper, you become a part of that number. When you liquidate your position, you may cause that number to decrease.

If you're interested in buying a December contract, you'll find different prices:

Dec   110.00   110.00   108.40   109.25   −260   119.00   99.00   856

Notice that the market is anticipating lower prices in December, which, according to historical levels, is the tendency, as you can see from the record high of 119. That day's total contracts for December copper is also less than for June, which is typical for futures several months out. But it also indicates that the December market is not as liquid as June's.

If you're a CNBC watcher, the network includes commodities prices in the top line of its continuous stream of quotations on the hour and every 10 minutes after that, during the day—after the headline "Commodities." This ticker can be positively maddening for the newcomer to commodities, a seemingly indecipherable string of letters and numbers. They are futures quotations—beginning with financials then stock indexes, followed by commodities: precious metals first, then grains, livestock, energy products, and other individual active movers.

A code that you will not be able to understand without a decoder, for most beginners, the commodities code is maddeningly illogical. But every language has things that, even within the context of the rules of that language, make no sense. People who are trying to learn English are frequently flummoxed by *though* and *tough,* and other languages have similar quirks that torture first-time speakers and readers. The same is true of commodities listings. Like stocks, commodities have their own abbreviations. Once they're decoded, however, they're pretty easy to remember. The delivery months are also abbreviated—for this year and next. Not so easy.

The CNBC stream offers the commodity, the most active delivery month, and the latest price. Here's the sort of thing you'll see:

GH 355.5 . . . WU 369 . . . SN 725 . . . HOX 101 . . . CLN 39 . . .

Translation: March gold was the most actively traded at $355.50 a troy ounce; September wheat was at $3.69 a bushel; and July soybeans are priced at $7.25 per bushel; November home-heating oil is currently trading at 101 cents per gallon; July light crude oil is going for $39 a barrel.

The abbreviations for commodities futures actually are, for the most part, what you would expect—C for corn, O for oats, NG for natural gas, and so on. (I have listed 35 commodities traded around the world in the Appendix, according to the sectors posted in the *Wall Street Journal*, along with the exchange they're traded on as well as the standard contract size and unit of sale.)

The abbreviations for the months are not as intuitive:

F   (January)
G   (February)
H   (March)
J   (April)
K   (May)
M   (June)
N   (July)
Q   (August)
U   (September)
V   (October)
X   (November)
Z   (December)

There is a logic to it—avoiding the letters used to abbreviate commodities (*S* for soybeans, for example) and *I* and *L,* which might be mistaken for numbers. But the best way to master the list is to memorize it and practice decoding the TV quotations. The stream runs quite quickly. I would recommend videotaping it so that you can rerun it or pause it in order to get a good look at the quotes.

THE NUMBERS

One more slight complication: Price quotations differ from one commodity to the next. As we have seen, some commodities are quoted in dollars per unit, others in cents. At first, the decimal points can be confusing—and misleading. If your experience is checking only the stock-market quotations, and you see July wheat in the newspaper priced at 299.75, you would be wrong to assume the price of wheat is $299.75 per bushel. And if you thought about it for a minute, you'd realize that you wouldn't be able to afford those Wheaties if the price was anywhere near that high. Wheat is cited in *cents* per bushel. The number "299.75" means $2.99 and three-quarters cents.

More confusing still for the commodities greenhorn are the TV quotes that might even shorten the number: GH 55.5, for example. That means March gold. But the price is not $55.50. Everyone following gold would know that the price was in the 400s and that 55.5 actually means $455.50.

The TV quotes—or a commentator or broker—might mention that a given commodity was "up two ticks." In commodityspeak, a *tick* is the minimum price movement for that particular commodity—up or down. Different commodities have different minimums—a fraction of a cent, a cent, 10 cents, a dollar, or points, which (to make things even more confusing) are used to represent the dollar value of the minimum price fluctuation. (This is generally derived by multiplying the contract size of the commodity being traded by the minimum price fluctuation. A sugar contract's standard size is 112,000 pounds, and the minimum price fluctuation is ¹⁄₁₀₀ of a cent per pound, making the dollar value of sugar's minimum price fluctuation $11.20—or one point.)

A tick from one commodity is thus not the same as a tick for another. Grains, for example, have ticks of ¼ of one cent. Since one CBOT grain contract is standardized at 5,000 bushels, a minimum price movement will be $0.0025 times 5,000—or $12.50. "Wheat was up two ticks today" means that the single contract price rose $25. The heating-oil minimum is one point (listed as 1 pt.)—or $4.20 (0.0001 times 42,000 gallons in the standard contract).

Once again, to make sense of broadcast or broker reports on price movements, you will have to know the value of the minimum for the commodity you're interested in. (See Appendix for a list of minimums.) Annoying, but what I can say? That's the way they do it, and you'll have to learn it and practice it. But most people will not be trading futures in every commodity. If you begin with one or a few, memorizing the price differentials and tick minimums will not seem like such a big deal.

Warning: Spending too much time staring at the commodities tape can be dangerous to your health—emotional as well as financial.

It's one thing to learn the codes of commodities trading in order to stay on top of the news and to be able to understand and talk to your broker. But don't get carried away. You can invest in commodities and never understand the tape at all, just as you can invest in the stocks of companies without ever knowing the symbols on the exchange. Watching the tape all day on TV, your computer, or at your broker's office is a good sign that you're hooked on trading and may be overleveraged. Leveraged traders *need* to watch every trade; their money is depending on the prices going their way. You do not want to be that person.

READY TO CONTANGO?

These commodity numbers reveal more than just price information. They also provide news and market clues, and it is important
for the novice not to take them at face value. If you look at the
Wall Street Journal "Futures" page again, you'll notice that the
current month's grain prices tend to be cheaper than later months.
That does not necessarily mean that if you are holding a December
wheat futures contract in February that is 50 cents a bushel higher,
you're ahead 50 cents. Even when nothing is happening, when the
supply-and-demand chain is working flawlessly, there will be dif-
ferences in prices owing to ordinary *carrying charges*—the total
cost of storing a commodity, including storage charges, insurance
fees, bank interest fees, and spoilage.

The cost of carrying charges is one reason so many commodities
sell for a premium in the future. Even if I own my own warehouse,
if I buy 1,000 pounds of sugar and store it in my warehouse, that
supply of sugar will cost me money every day to store and maintain. I've got to pay interest on the money I borrowed to buy the
sugar, transportation costs to move it, insurance premiums to protect it, overhead on my warehouse and employees. If it is now February, December wheat will have significantly higher storage costs
than March wheat. And while gold also requires storage, its insurance costs might be less than that for wheat, which is vulnerable to
spoilage and fire, while precious metals are not.

That's why futures often sell at a higher price farther away in
time, rising from the near month to the back months. Sugar sells
more for delivery in the future than for today because of the rational expectations of cost. Or, as commodities traders say, those
sugar contracts sell at *contango*—when such things as storage and
insurance costs of the underlying commodity cause the price of futures to exceed that of current, spot prices. (I wish I could tell you
where this colorful word comes from, but no one seems to know
its origin.) Suppose a drought this season drives sugar prices up to

10 cents a pound. Everyone knows that there's a limited supply of sugar for this crop year, but everyone needs it. You and I need sugar, Hershey's needs sugar for its chocolate; Nestlé's needs sugar for its candy, and so on. And they all need it during this crop year. And prices will be higher the further out in the year you go. And they will pay whatever they have to for it—a contango market.

But if you check the sugar futures contracts for delivery a year from now, sugar might be selling for *six* cents. Why? Because everyone assumes that with the price now so high producers will be trying to generate as much sugar as possible; also, the drought is likely to be over, and a normal crop will come in next year. With traders expecting plenty of sugar to be around a year from now, sugar for delivery then is selling at six cents—a *backwardation,* which is the opposite of *contango.*

THE NEXT STEP

I would now advise a break before proceeding to the next chapter. There is a lot of new information here and plenty of it is worth reviewing. And as complicated or confusing as some of it might be, just think how much progress you've made. Many readers may have begun this section not knowing a "margin" from a "margin call," or even that "trading commodities" and "trading futures" are the same thing. Now you have at least a basic vocabulary of the futures market, as well as an understanding of how to trade long or short and how to follow the commodities markets in the media. Along the way, you may also have been explaining all of this to friends and family. And if you haven't, I'd recommend trying to explain these concepts to someone else as a perfect test of what has sunk in and what you might need to review.

By now I hope you are looking at the entire world differently. Suddenly, such matter-of-fact things in your life as sugar and cotton, or other things that you never gave a moment's thought to, such as platinum or live hogs, are popping off the newspaper pages. Learning about commodities does that to people, opening them up to not just a whole new world but a whole new world of opportunities for making money.

But you really must *learn* about the commodities you invest in. Just checking the prices on the commodities page of the *Wall Street Journal* or on CNBC is not enough. Curiosity about one commodity or another is only a start. You must commit to serious, widespread homework and analysis. To understand why and when prices move for a given commodity, you must study historical as well as current trends in supply and demand. You must familiarize yourself with past bull and bear markets. You must keep an eye out for evidence for aging capacity, mines, and production as well as for openings of new operations and new exploration for mines and energy reserves. You must understand how weather affects agricultural commodities or heating oil supplies. Above all, you must keep in mind that commodities is a *world* market affected by political events and personalities in the countries that produce (and buy) them.

There are some who speculate mainly on the basis of commodities charts and technical analysis. They swear by various mathematical models and theories. Good luck to them. Frankly, in my experience, I've known few people who have gotten rich off technical analysis. (I do know people who've made a lot of money *selling* technical analysis or books about it.)

If you are intrigued by such techniques and theories, then by all means explore them. But that is not how I approach investing in commodities, or any other markets, as you may have gathered. I analyze the fundamentals, and the purpose of this book is to show how commodities work in the real world of supply and demand. In commodities trading, knowledge is the gateway to making money. I am not offering "hot tips." My goal is to show you how to think about commodities before you put any money on the table.

In the next chapters, I will analyze several commodities, showing current and past trends, why prices have moved up and down, and what may happen in the future. What I offer is hardly the final word on any of them. Please consider these discussions—like everything else in this book—as just the beginning of your education in how to think about commodities. Any serious speculator will have to do even more work, investigating these commodities and whatever others catch your fancy.

Above all, the new investor in commodities must begin to understand the most dominant force in the world commodities markets—China.

5

Notes from the
Wild, Wild East

I HAVE been to China about a dozen times since 1984, most recently in 2006. And I have seen extraordinary things there. I have even seen the future—and it presents some unprecedented opportunities for commodities investors. Here's how important I think China will be: My daughter, who was born in 2003, is learning Chinese. Her Chinese nanny speaks only Mandarin to her, and her Chinese is as fluent as her English. In her lifetime, Chinese will be the most important language in the world, next to English. If you are young and ambitious, learn Chinese. If you have ambitions for your children, persuade them to learn Chinese.

China will be the world's next great nation. Spain was the greatest economic power in the world in the sixteenth century; the rich and the powerful of the eighteenth-century world spoke French; the nineteenth century belonged to Britain; and the twentieth was the American century. The twenty-first will belong to China.

History has not been kind to empires. One powerful nation or another gets its turn to dominate the world politically, economically, and culturally, then it declines, and, eventually, falls—rarely to return. China will break that cycle.

A great empire for 200 years at the turn of the first millennium, during the Song dynasty, China engaged in international commerce with sailing ships that held more than 1,000 men. A genuine market economy linked coastal areas to the interior, and cities were developed specifically for industry, trade, and maritime commerce. China was using paper money in the eleventh century, long before the West. Stores in the capital of Kaifeng, then the world's second-largest city, were open 24 hours a day.

Soon the Chinese will get another turn in the sun. Within 20 years or so, their nation will have the world's biggest economy. The rest of us will have to figure out how best to benefit. We are witnessing one of the great economic successes in all of history. In the past two decades (a flash in China's long life), the country emerged from an impoverished peasant society, where famine had killed perhaps 40 million people as recently as 1959–61, to the world's sixth-largest economy and rising fast. In urban areas, the traditional greeting "Have you eaten today?" has been replaced by "Have you surfed the Net?" The first time I traveled across China in 1988 by motorcycle, there were no roads; I had to drive across the desert. When I returned in 1999 to make the trip again, this time by car, I found a cross-country motorway and, in my opinion, the best highway system in the world.

On that 1988 trip, I bought my first share in the future of China, a bank security, one of the few then publicly traded on the Shanghai Exchange, a ramshackle storefront down an unpaved street; it is framed on a wall in my house. When I went back to Shanghai in 1999, the signs of economic growth were everywhere: more cars, stylish young people, cell phones, booming Internet use, and building cranes filling the skyline. The stock exchange was in a shiny new office building, with a trading floor filled with 300 people working at computer terminals. I opened up a real account. I still have those shares, and I hope to leave them to my heirs.

When I returned to China in 2006, the economy was still grow-ing at a blistering rate. Its factories were churning out goods as fast as possible, and its infrastructure was developing rapidly, partly in anticipation of the 2008 Olympics and the Shanghai World's Fair in 2010. Consumer affluence and spending have increased expo-nentially. The Chinese are even building—Mao Zedong is surely not resting in peace over this news—golf courses. Companies from all over the world have been rushing to China to cash in on those 1.3 billion–plus consumers, 300 million of whom are younger than 20 years of age. (Think of it: There are more hopeful young people in China than the total population of the U.S.) Volkswagen already sells more cars in China than it does in Germany. General Motors is selling more than a quarter of a million Chevys and Buicks a year to the Chinese and has announced adding Cadillacs to the mix, hoping to sell 1.0 million cars per year by 2007.

Foreigners have also begun to invest in Chinese companies. In 2002, China replaced the U.S. as the largest recipient of foreign in-vestment. In 2003, Warren Buffett—who had rarely invested abroad before—bought into PetroChina, a large Chinese petro-chemical company that was listed on the New York Stock Ex-change in 2000. Buffett has since increased his ownership to 18.1 percent of the company, more than doubling his investment.

It will not, however, be all rivers of honey and gumdrop trees. China will undergo setbacks, just as Britain and the U.S. did in their rise to world dominance. But dominate China will. The na-tion's economic stats are astonishing:

- The Chinese economy has been growing faster than any other economy in the world—at an official rate in 2005 of more than 9 percent, though independent analysts at the time were saying that GDP was more like 12 or 13 percent. (By comparison, U.S. leaders were hoping that the Amer-ican economy would end the year with a growth rate of 4 percent.)

- The Chinese report that industrial production in 2004 was up 19.1 percent over the previous year. (While Chinese statistics may be no more reliable than those of other countries, it is safe to say that the economy is booming.)

- The Chinese have foreign reserves on hand of almost one trillion (a statistic that's hard to fake).

- China's more than $1.2 trillion economy is technically the world's sixth largest. But, according to the *CIA World Factbook*, when you compare the Chinese economy with the rest of the world according to "purchasing-power parity," it's second only to the U.S. economy. China's gross domestic product output is way ahead of both Japan's and Germany's.

China's standard of living, of course, lags far behind that of the U.S. and the rest of the advanced nations of the world. The country is pure potential—and part of that potential includes rising economic demand for natural resources and commodities of all kinds.

THE RISE OF "RED CAPITALISM"

In 1999, when I was in China, the then prime minister, Zhu Rongji, spoke at the Harvard Business School. During the question-and-answer period, a smart aleck asked, "Are you going to devalue the Chinese currency?" Since 1994, the Chinese currency, the renminbi, has been pegged to the U.S. dollar, and there had been a lot of speculation in the press that the Chinese would be making their currency convertible—the sine qua non for China to become a truly great economy. Rumors persisted that before the government made the currency convertible, it would devalue it. The premier assured the questioner that devaluation would not occur, and then invited the skeptics in the room to buy "puts" on the renminbi. Buying puts—the right to sell or go short—is a sophisticated way to profit from the collapse of a stock or currency. It was an extraordinary remark from the mouth of any politician, never mind a leader of the Chinese Communist Party. Zhu put the Harvard wise guy in his place while proving to a sophisticated audience of businesspeople that the premier of China knew a thing or two about playing the currency market.

That kind of financial sophistication permeates the Chinese bureaucracy as well as the business community. Some of the best capitalists in the world live and work in Communist China. Not so long ago, the government denounced entrepreneurs as "exploiters" and banned them from the Chinese Communist Party. But in 2001, then president Jiang Zemin praised business leaders for pushing ahead with modernization; now, a political party created to represent the interests of peasants and workers includes millionaire entrepreneurs. And therein lies the problem: How does a market economy champing at the bit function under a Leninist regime?

The central government has been learning how to benefit from the markets by trial and error. But Chinese bureaucrats are fast learners, supported by talented young economists, bankers, and financiers faced with the challenge of dealing with an unprecedented rate of growth in an increasingly globalized marketplace. For decades, the best and the brightest in China have aspired to careers in the Party and the government rather than in the private sector. These people now run China, so it should be no surprise that China has some of the most capable politicians in the world. Frankly, we should all wish these people well, regardless of their political beliefs or ours. Worldwide economic growth—indeed the stability of the world—depends on how well the leadership in Beijing manages its economy.

Despite the challenges, it seems to be doing fine. For no matter how long China's leaders persist in calling themselves Communists, they seem quite intent on creating the world's dominant capitalist economy. Plato wrote that the natural progression of government was from tyranny to oligarchy to democracy, and then came chaos, with dictatorship on its heels. China is now at the stage of moving from tyranny toward democracy, and those in charge probably have their sleep disturbed by dreams of the chaos that might follow that transition. By most accounts, however, even the Party's homegrown entrepreneurs—known as "red capitalists" by China scholars outside the country—are actually a conservative lot. Eager to protect their own wealth and status, they will not be much in favor of any radical democratic reforms too soon. They saw what happened in the USSR. These Party entrepreneurs may end up being democracy's Trojan horse—pushing for the kinds of economic and legal reforms that will make doing business easier and more productive and thus busting up the Marxist-Leninist foundations of the Party itself. Their success has already emboldened the tens of millions of small entrepreneurs and ambitious young people who want to get rich.

Unlike Russia, which had a feudal society before its Communist revolution in 1917, China, which opted for a Communist economy in 1949, has had a vibrant merchant class throughout much of its history; many are still alive who remember what capitalism was like before Mao Zedong's revolution. Many of those Chinese capitalists went abroad to Hong Kong, Taiwan, and elsewhere to pursue their business interests. Before the Communist revolution, Shanghai had the largest stock market in Asia and between London and New York, and it will again. Even after a half century of a strictly controlled Communist economy, the Chinese seem more culturally predisposed to capitalism than their Russian counterparts. They also have the habits of ready-made capitalists: The Chinese save and invest upwards of 40 percent of their income (Americans save barely 2 percent), and they have an incredible work ethic. The Chinese work and work to get the job done. I saw men and women working on highways late at night under floodlights. They demonstrate the kind of productivity and ingenuity that are required to build good companies.

The conversion from Communism to the world's most dominant capitalistic economy will not be instantaneous or smooth. In the meantime, China will have to settle for being the world champion in commodity consumption.

A GROWING ECONOMY WITH 1.3 BILLION PEOPLE NEEDS THINGS

The changes I have witnessed in China during the 10-year period after my first four visits and my fifth in 1999 were breathtaking. Building up steam in the 1990s in its production capacity, China headed into the first six years of the new millennium with an extraordinary boom in manufacturing, producing more refrigerators, television sets, mobile phones, and motorcycles than exist in the U.S. To make and house so many goods, China built manufacturing plants, office buildings, and houses at a feverish rate; it churned out more cars, trucks, and heavy machinery than ever before. The growth rate in production across the board, according to China's own figures, was a staggering 19.4 percent between April 2003 and April 2004 alone. Even those who might charge that such figures are simply self-serving cannot ignore the astonishing results of China's hard work:

- Its production of refrigerators, washing machines, air conditioners, color TVs, and video recorders had increased a hundredfold.
- Its output of mobile telephones and sound equipment is No. 1 in the world.
- Its growth rates of chemical fibers, plastic, and plate glass had at least doubled.
- Its machine-building industry was capable of churning out new

textile machinery as well as such advanced power-generating equipment as gas turbines and nuclear power sets.

- Its auto industry has been growing at an average annual rate of almost 20 percent.

Banks have fueled this production binge by lending money at ridiculously low rates. Entrepreneurs and state-owned enterprises have used this easy money to build more factories and houses (and to build political reputations along the way). Most urban housing was privatized in the late 1990s, and affluent Chinese, borrowing money for the first time in their lives, have been rushing into the housing market, pushing up prices. Real-estate speculators have used property deals as collateral for loans for manufacturing projects. An estimated 25 percent of those loans to state-owned enterprises may never be paid back.

All of that production requires material, stuff, commodities. According to China's National Board of Statistics and figures from international industry organizations, China accounted for 37 percent of the demand growth in oil in 2003 and another 30 percent in 2004. Cement and aluminum plants were going full tilt, and the Chinese were using steel at an amazing rate, consuming iron ore and coke to make steel even faster. China's National Board of Statistics reported that the nation's consumption of steel in 2003 alone was 260 million tons, which would account for 36 percent of the consumption of steel worldwide. China accounted for half of the world's consumption of cement, 30 percent of its coal, and 25 percent of its aluminum. Recent worldwide growth in iron ore (an essential ingredient in steel) is essentially due to China. China now imports 80 percent of its copper and all of its platinum. These statistics are phenomenal, unheard-of numbers—and they left mineral and metal producers throughout the world with increasing profits. (And if you owned stock in Rio Tinto, the multinational mining giant; BHP Billiton, the British-Australian mining company; and Alcoa, the world's leading aluminum producer, you were profiting, too.)

China has been fueling the commodity bull market for years now. And for a very simple reason:

Supply is tight, and China needs more raw materials than it has.

U.S. exports of scrap steel to China have tripled since 2002. The Chinese are also buying every bit of scrap metal available from European recycling plants. Throughout Asia and the former Soviet Union, entrepreneurs are stripping old army bases and industrial sites of scrap metal and shipping it to China to feed its demand for steel. China's scrap imports have almost doubled since 2000 and are likely to double again within the decade. In 2003, the country increased its total imports by $120 billion—half of it raw materials. In 2004, foreign bankers in Shanghai were betting that China would be spending $30 billion more. China is using more commodities than any other nation in the world and at a faster rate, making it the world's

No. 1 consumer of copper
No. 1 consumer of steel
No. 1 consumer of iron ore (to make steel)
No. 1 consumer of soybeans
No. 2 consumer of oil and energy products

According to the Commodity Research Bureau, which tracks these figures through international government and industry agencies, including the CIA, as well as through official Chinese sources, Chinese copper imports have risen by 25 percent since 2001, sending copper to a new all-time high in 2006. Aluminum imports roughly doubled between 2001 and the end of 2003.

Oil consumption went from slightly more than 2 million barrels a day in 1987 to 5.4 million barrels a day by the end of 2003. (The U.S. consumes roughly 15 million barrels a day, 18 percent of world production, with a fraction of China's population.) Consuming only 8 percent of the world's oil, China contributed 37 percent of the world's growth in oil consumption from 2000 to 2004. China's oil imports were 2 million barrels a day in 2003—up more than a third from the previous year. According to the Paris-based International Energy Agency (IEA), an oil-policy forum of 26 industrial countries, including the U.S., China's imports are likely to double to 4 million barrels a day by 2010. By then, according to the oil analysts at the Massachusetts-based Cambridge Energy Research Associates, China will be consuming 9 percent of the world's oil. The IEA forecasts that by 2030 China will be importing 85 percent of its total consumption of oil.

China has already been importing soy from as far afield as Brazil and Argentina. Its Dalian Commodity Exchange handles more soybean volume than any exchange in the world. The Chinese are eating more beef and chicken than ever before, and more fruit and vegetables. Yet their per capita soybean consumption is still nowhere close to the levels of China's more affluent cousins: Taiwan and Hong Kong. According to an estimate by the Chicago agricultural forecasting firm AgResource, if every Chinese sipped just one more teaspoon of soybean oil a year, the soybean oil trade would *double* worldwide.

With commodities already in short supply worldwide, China's rapid emergence as an insatiable customer has added an unprecedented dimension to demand. As I pointed out earlier, it takes time to increase production; even after you find the right metal deposit, for instance, it takes years to bring the metals to market. According to various analysts, all the expansions now planned by the world's largest iron-ore and copper producers fail to meet the projected 2010 demand in China for those materials.

On its way to becoming the No. 1 economy in the world during the next 20 years or so, China will increase its consumption in almost every category of commodities—and commodity prices will respond, over the long term, accordingly. With all that action in commodities, the volume at China's three commodities futures exchanges at the end of 2004 was a record high of $1.3 trillion and rising. The government has been cautious about allowing its own citizens to trade futures abroad and foreigners to trade on Chinese exchanges. That hesitation is likely to recede soon. The Chicago Board of Trade signed a deal with the Dalian Exchange in 2003 to share information with the prospect of developing products together. And there have been reports of executives from other U.S. exchanges visiting China to discuss ways that they, too, can get a piece of the trading action in China once restrictions begin loosening up more.

While China has been using up its own natural resources at an astonishing rate, it has one amazing resource that will never go away: the overseas Chinese. There are now at least 57 million Chinese living abroad in 60 countries, 85 percent of them in Southeast Asia. There are more than one million Chinese living in California alone. Most of them have done quite well. The Chinese control 70 percent of the wealth, for example, in Indonesia and the Philippines; they own 81 percent of the companies in Thailand. By one count, the overseas Chinese together make up the third-largest economy in the world.

More important, although 90 percent of the Chinese living abroad are naturalized citizens of their new countries, a majority speak Chinese, have family ties to the motherland, and are inclined to invest in China. China, in turn, welcomes their capital and expertise. In fact, 80 percent of all investment in China comes from the overseas Chinese. To encourage such economic patriotism, China will issue a passport to nearly anyone of Chinese descent.

THE NEXT WORLD CURRENCY?

The Chinese currency, the renminbi, has been extremely undervalued—by 20 percent or more, some experts contend. Even if its currency *doubled* in value against the U.S. dollar, China would still be competitive. (The Japanese yen has risen 400 percent against the dollar over several decades, yet Japan still has a trade surplus with the U.S.) The renminbi is one of the few currencies in the world whose value does not fluctuate completely freely although China began a managed float of its currency in 2005. It is pegged to a basket of foreign currencies at roughly 7.8 to the U.S. dollar, which has weakened in recent years against the euro and other currencies. The dollar's decreasing value means that Chinese goods and services are a lot cheaper than they ought to be in European and Japanese markets. The U.S. imports about $500 billion from China, but half or more of those imports are offshore production of U.S. firms for U.S. markets. U.S. politicians are worried that China's low prices will squeeze U.S. companies out of markets all around the world and have urged the Chinese government to "unpeg" its currency from the dollar.

Threats of protectionism have been tossed around in the U.S. and the European Union, whose members have suggested that the Chinese might consider the euro as an alternative reserve currency to the dollar. Most European politicians and their Asian counterparts tend to have fewer complaints about China, since they sell huge amounts of their goods there, and many of those nations have trade *surpluses* with China. Rarely does anyone complain about their best customers.

Historically, China's leaders have been afraid to let their currency float, presuming that its citizens would move money out of the country and the renminbi would collapse. A higher rate of exchange would also slow foreign investment and exports, another threat to the economy. The Chinese leadership still uses that argument as a means of refusing to revalue the renminbi. It would have had merit 20 years ago, but China is a much more attractive investment opportunity now. Let the currency go down, I say. If people want to dump the renminbi, go for it. I would be a buyer whether it declines or rises, and I doubt that I would be alone. Nor do I think that the overseas Chinese will stop sending money home or abandon investing in one of the world's largest and fastest-growing economies. I suspect that once the Chinese currency floats, even more funds will pour in. Capital is always more likely to go where it will not be trapped by currency controls. But the best argument against a fixed currency is that it has never worked and it never will. No fixed currency in history has ever been able to maintain its peg.

Another argument that should appeal to the Chinese leadership, which is extremely nationalistic and sensitive to the charge of sucking up to Washington, the capital of "capitalist roaders": The renminbi is in a possible position to take over as the dominant currency in the world, beating out the euro, the yen, and the dollar. Businesses around the world have long sought to sell to the American consumer. By 2004, China had passed nearly everyone as one of the world's largest importers of goods. Now, every businessperson in the world salivates as he or she calculates the current price of a product multiplied times 1.3 billion Chinese.

And though China is buying more stuff from the rest of the world than ever and has finally racked up a trade deficit with some countries, its vaults are filled with stacks of foreign currencies—more than $1 trillion worth, second only to Japan. China is a creditor nation. The U.S. became a debtor nation again in 1987 and has been the world's largest debtor nation since. The international debts of the U.S. are more than $9 trillion and growing, at the rate of $1 trillion every 15 months. For years, we have been financing our standard of living with other people's money, and one of our biggest bankers is China.

That dependency makes the renminbi a perfect candidate for a world currency—once its leaders allow it to be freely convertible and tradable on the world market. The sine qua non of free trade is that people can come and go with their money. When that will happen in China I do not know for certain. Surely, however, the Chinese have been feeling the pinch of buying commodities at high prices and selling goods at cheaper ones. One thing's for sure: China's leaders will not unpeg the renminbi to the dollar just because foreign politicians say they must. Ironically, when the Chinese pegged their currency to the dollar in 1994 the U.S. applauded it as a smart move. Now that we are begging them to unpeg it, they are bound to express their independence by letting the renminbi float in their own good time. China has been accepted into the World Trade Organization, which requires that its members have convertible funds. I suspect that the renminbi will be floating quite freely by the time the Olympic torch is lit in Beijing in 2008.

CHINA VS. INDIA

Since I returned from my 1999–2001 trip around the world, I have been invited to speak to audiences in North America, Asia, and Europe, and I have continued to make my case for China as the world's next major economic player. During the question-and-answer period, inevitably, someone will ask, "What about India?"

These days India looms large in the American imagination, mainly, I suspect, because most Americans now know that when they make a call to straighten out a billing problem or to buy a computer they're talking to someone in New Delhi or somewhere else in India, where American jobs have been outsourced. The media have also pointed to India as a great success story in modern capitalism—a nation of inconceivable poverty that has emerged as a force in the information-technology revolution that is helping to globalize the world's economies. India is also a democracy, which carries a lot of weight with the U.S. media, our politicians, and the public, who are still a bit skeptical of our old Cold War enemies Russia and China, which seem to have trouble shedding their authoritarian pasts. (Of course, the media seem to have forgotten that India was allied with the Soviet Union during most of the Cold War, and that its political outlook is still largely socialist.)

I am not one of those fans of India, at least as an investor. While I consider India to be one of the great places in the world to travel, a huge nation filled with beautiful people, exquisite cuisines, a dramatic history, depth of culture, and truly awe-inspiring sights, I looked for promising investment opportunities when I was there in 2001 and 2004, and I was disappointed. Sure, the country had liberalized its economy in the past 15 years, and the government had admitted that it needed outside expertise and capital. But the prevailing spirit in the India I visited was still anticapitalist. (And the 2004 return to power of the Congress Party of Nehru and his daughter, Indira Gandhi, now headed by Indira's daughter-in-law, the Italian-born Sonia Gandhi, is not encouraging.) That is not to say that there haven't been some great capitalist success stories there. But in a country of a billion people there are bound to be some successes.

In most important social and economic areas, however, India is no match for China. It doesn't even come close. Traveling around the country, we had to buy a different mobile phone in almost every city, while in China our cell phones worked everywhere. When we went shopping in Mumbai (Bombay) and Delhi, the most recent computers we saw were three-year-old American systems. In an effort to protect its own industries, India keeps the latest technology out of the country.

Furthermore, the nation's infrastructure is hardly world-class. It took us almost a week to drive coast to coast on the antiquated roads from Mumbai to Calcutta, a distance of no more than 2,000 miles. We were lucky to average 30 miles per hour—on two-lane highways that, though they were paved, we had to share with trucks, camels, and donkeys. Trans-India truck drivers do much worse, averaging 12 miles an hour. Their Chinese counterparts move across the best highways in the world at four times the speed. And while everyone talks about socialism as a thing of India's political past and about India's place in global capitalism, when I was there in 2001 I was astonished to learn that in 10 years the country had privatized only one company: a bakery.

India, of course, has some big companies, but I do not believe those companies will be competitive in the world market. While China now exports various goods and agricultural products, I have driven around the world twice and have seen very few Indian products along the way. With a government-protected home market of one billion people, India has not yet developed the concentration of capital or the expertise or the drive required to compete outside its borders.

More worrisome still is India's education system. Virtually all children in China finish primary school. In India, surveys have revealed that more than one half of the children aged 6 to 10 do not finish primary school. University education is still for the children of the elite and the well connected, and one of the reasons that so many Indians study abroad is that there aren't enough universities to meet the demand for higher and graduate education.

The Indians are quick to point out that, unlike China, their country is a democracy. But isn't that just one more mark against them—that a Communist dictatorship's economy is leaving them in the dust? India is also a democracy that from its very beginnings has been defined by political violence and instability, and where the social effects of an age-old caste system still linger. When I visited in 1988, you could not travel in some areas without a military convoy. And while it was much easier to travel there on my most recent visit, the Muslim separatist movement in Indian-administered Kashmir, where a never-ending struggle has cost tens of thousands of lives, still has the potential to push India and Pakistan into nuclear war. And in recent years India's Hindu extremists have displayed savagery toward their fellow citizens. Eastern India gets little press, but there are insurrections in nearly every state.

India is also a democracy that still treats its women more as property than as human beings. (Being "second-class citizens" would be a huge step up for Indian women.) More than half the women (54 percent) are illiterate, while in China less than half that number are unable to read. In every 100,000 births in India, 440 women die; seven times fewer Chinese women die in childbirth. In rural areas, women are still not allowed outside the home without a male escort. In one village, a man who thought nothing of placing his hand on my wife's bottom learned a quick lesson in feminism when she grabbed him by his shirt and slapped him three times, like Bogart shaping up Peter Lorre in *The Maltese Falcon*.

THE DOWNSIDE

China is a fragile giant—at once emboldened by its economic growth and afraid of the consequences. Its top leaders are cautious. Embracing the market without abandoning its Leninist principles, the Chinese government is learning how to live with its homegrown capitalism with trepidation. And while capitalists have been allowed to join the Party, there are still plenty of diehard Maoists who do not believe in the freedom to pursue profit and want to keep their business colleagues on a short leash. There are bound to be clashes of interests, mistakes will be made, and the rest of the world's economies will feel the pain.

· What else could one expect from the biggest and boldest experiment in free markets in history? Chinese leaders have become captains of a huge ocean liner who have had to learn on the job how to steer. In the 1970s, the Chinese premier Zhou Enlai, the most worldly and wily of Mao's deputies, announced the "Four Modernizations," aimed at unleashing the dormant commercial spirit of the Chinese people. When Zhou became ill, the administration of China's economic modernization fell to his deputy premier, another veteran of the Long March, Deng Xiaoping, whose commitment to restoring the Chinese economy in the late 1950s earned him the label "capitalist roader" and a stint as a worker in a tractor factory. Reinstated by Zhou as his deputy in 1973, Deng was purged again after his protector died in 1976. Within a year, he made a second comeback as deputy premier, proceeding to dominate the Party as the most powerful Chinese leader since Mao himself, devoting the next decade to loosening government control over the economy in an effort to promote development. "To get rich is glorious" became a popular slogan in the 1980s, when the Chinese began practicing capitalism in earnest.

I myself saw the results on my first visit to China in 1984, just eight years after the end of Mao's disastrous Cultural Revolution. In the countryside, people were building houses, and in the cities they were complaining about rising prices. The government's proposed solution was bonuses, which it financed by printing money. The economy eventually stalled. People got more upset, and began demonstrating their feelings in the streets throughout China.

Deng's liberalism did not extend to politics. He believed that the Party had to maintain tight control over the government and dissent. And when the demonstrations moved to Tiananmen Square in central Beijing in 1989, Deng authorized the use of military force, thus undercutting his own long efforts to make China an economic player in the world. Chinese officials are eager for the world to forget the Tiananmen massacre, and for good reason. In the minds of many Americans, for example, Tiananmen coalesced into a dramatic moment when the Chinese stood up, and were shot down, for democracy American style. Didn't we see those brave students under fire and being mowed down by government tanks?

We certainly did—and mainly because the Western media on hand could not pass up such a dramatic story. But it wasn't the entire story. Most of the people in the streets that spring didn't give a hoot about democracy. *They were there to complain about tight money.* The government was trying to cool an overheated economy. The economy was slowing, people knew it, and workers all over China were worried about their jobs. That's why the laborers, peasants, and Communist Party members, no fans of Western-style democracy, poured into Tiananmen Square. The students and intellectuals who had been demonstrating for weeks on behalf of democracy were not about to miss any opportunity to publicize their position, and they, too, headed for Tiananmen. The students became the story—and the target of government guns. Government officials quickly regretted their woodenheaded response, which even they have realized has been devastating to the image of a more open and modern China they were trying to project to the outside world. Tiananmen left the economy reeling, but the market reforms that Deng had put into place eventually began to do their work. Under his designated successor, Jiang Zemin, monetary and fiscal policies loosened up, and within a few years the economy was back in gear. On my next visit to China, in 1990, the entrepreneurs I had befriended on previous trips were doing fine.

By 1994, however, the economy was moving *too* quickly. The government had to put on the brakes once again, instituting the kind of austerity programs in which tough old Communists used to specialize. The result: urban areas littered with empty office buildings, half-built luxury town houses, deserted department stores. The state banks were left holding a bag of worthless loans. This economic cooling got out of control, too, and led to the currency devaluation of 1994.

Financial reforms were put in place to tame inflation; interest rates were raised to cut off easy money from local banks; and within another decade the Chinese economy was the hottest in the world. Too hot, in fact. It was shaping up as a classic investment bubble. Government statistics indicated that the economy was growing faster every year. In 2004, the reported rate of growth was 9.7 percent (some Western economists were saying it was really as high as 12 percent). China accounted for 15 percent of global growth for the year. Every sector of the economy had been going full speed ahead. The Chinese were building steel mills and manufacturing plants, investing in textiles, pharmaceuticals, and apartment buildings. Banks, big and small, were jockeying for market share of the loans to state-owned enterprises for real-estate projects that would increase local economic growth (and political careers). Overbuilding was encouraged by easy money. In late 2004, no one was even quite sure how many bad loans were out there; the government admitted to 20 percent, while more independent observers claimed that the banks weren't receiving timely payments on more than 40 percent of outstanding loans. Speculation was rampant, and so was bank fraud. The result has been extraordinary overinvestment. The fixed investment share of China's GDP was approaching 50 percent. The cost of living was going up across the board, particularly for food and transportation. With inflation also moving quickly past the 3 percent that government officials were willing to tolerate—independent bankers were putting real inflation at 7–8 percent—the country's leaders were looking for ways to slow this train down without the kind of crack-up they experienced in 1989 and 1994.

China watchers were hoping that Beijing had learned its lesson and that a lighter, more modern touch would prevent another hard landing—knocking growth down to below 7 percent, a level that would be injurious to other economies in the region that have boosted their own economies by exporting goods to China. After all, China has accounted for a third of all the growth in exports from Japan and South Korea. China also needs long-term foreign investment to grow, just as the U.S. did 100 to 150 years ago. Multinationals used to borrow from Chinese banks in the renminbi. But then they started borrowing in dollars and euros, betting that the Chinese currency would appreciate and make it cheaper for them to pay off their loans. The result has been lots of foreign currency pouring into China, whose huge reserves of cash have been estimated at well over $1 trillion. Chinese law gives companies the right to convert their currency back into dollars to repay debts. If something goes wrong in China, a lot of cash will head out the door. More worrisome still, much of that $1 trillion in reserves has been invested in U.S. Treasury securities. What happens if China wants its money back?

Rural areas have not participated as much in the boom. This inequality is no small problem. Sixty percent of China's population falls in the category of "rural poor." A study published in China about the conditions among the Chinese peasantry revealed that while wealth had risen in the cities, the incomes of the nation's 900 million farmers were not growing fast enough. Once a nation of peasants, China is now two nations—of increasingly affluent urban dwellers and farmers and other rural workers who are underpaid, if they have jobs at all. According to reports from independent financial analysts in China that have appeared in the world press, rural unemployment as well as underemployment is between 150 and 250 million people, leading the *New York Times* to note that China has "more unemployed people in rural areas than the entire American workforce." People looking for work have been flowing into China's cities, putting a strain on social services and sparking fears of social unrest. The government has initiated special "people first" programs to improve the lives of rural people. One of the plans is to move 300 million to 500 million people from the countryside into cities by 2020. (That target would increase the nation's urban population by 60 percent.)

The pressure on China's economic wizards will be daunting. They have to slow down growth—but not too much. By most estimates, anything lower than 7 percent growth will lead to a sharp drop in imports—bad news for neighboring economies whose growth has been fueled by selling stuff to China, as well as nations as far off as Brazil, which has been profiting hugely by selling loads of commodities to China, and struggling Argentina, which has been exporting soybeans. High urban unemployment is dangerous news for the stability of China itself. According to a study by the International Monetary Fund (IMF), China needs to create about 9 million new jobs a year in order to keep pace with the increase in the growing labor force of young workers, those who are laid off when old, inefficient factories get closed down, and peasants in search of their piece of the Chinese dream. To put that 9 million figure in perspective, in a good year the U.S. economy generates 3 million jobs. There have already been reports of labor unrest and peasant protests in the countryside, and the government has been ruthless in suppressing demonstrations, jailing dissident leaders and worse, which has only increased resentment and the prospect of such pockets of unrest turning into big bags full of trouble.

On a recent visit to China, in the summer of 2006, government officials, the IMF, and some foreign investment bankers were hopeful that China would be able to pull off a soft landing. The prime minister assured the rest of the world that his people would slow the money supply and bank lending that have accelerated growth. I did not share that optimism. Crashes will occur in those areas where investment has been wild, such as real estate and some manufacturing. Local officials with illusions of grandeur are still borrowing money for projects in the boondocks. Electric power shortages have been so bad that, according to the New China News Agency, an official government media outlet, China has begun importing power from Russia. And the government is still resisting letting the renminbi float freely.

When you factor in the millions of peasants who need work, the young people who cannot find jobs—not to mention an aging population that wants expensive social services—it's asinine not to expect some measure of unrest and turmoil in China. Chinese officials are learning about regulating markets on the job, and there are many smart people among them. But they are not infallible. More problematic, they are politicians and bureaucrats, and prone to all the liabilities of their profession.

I expect things to get out of control somewhere along the line as they did in 1989 and 1994, and if they do that will be the next buying opportunity for China and for commodities.

IMPERIAL AMBITIONS?

Historically, empires have looked around for opportunities in the world and taken them, usually through force of arms. At a time when the U.S. has adopted a policy of preemptive strikes, it is understandable for some people to worry that China might decide that it may be a lot cheaper to occupy a country than to buy its exports. Already, some have suggested that China is bound to be setting its sights on the Middle East. China is already the No. 2 consumer of oil in the world, and it is just a matter of time before it becomes No. 1. Will China decide that it wants to occupy an oil country? It already has oil interests in Sudan—and troops there protecting them. China's neighbors in Central Asia also apparently have lots of oil.

And then there's the problem of Taiwan's independence, any prospect of which seems to rile the otherwise rational Chinese into fits of hysteria. The current Taiwanese president is doing his best to provoke the mainland further for his own political reasons. He may shoot himself—and the rest of us—in the foot. Chinese generals have already threatened to regain Taiwan by force—foreign investment, economic growth, and the Olympics be damned. Consumed with concern about "weapons of mass destruction" in the Middle East or North Korea, U.S. politicians seem to have forgotten Beijing's 500 warheads aimed straight at Taiwan, an island only 100 miles away from the Chinese mainland. Taiwan's security blanket—that the U.S. would rush to its aid—turned a bit scratchy when U.S. forces were stretched in the Middle East, followed by reports from Washington that the Pentagon believed Beijing's forces could seize the island before the Americans could ride to the rescue.

I myself doubt that the Chinese government will wage war unless provoked. Throughout history, the Chinese have not been a very aggressive people, and my bet is that they are even less aggressive now. In 1980, the leadership initiated a national policy rewarding couples for limiting their families to one child. This one-child policy was terminated in 2002, but the damage was done. Tens of millions of families are likely to resist sending their only child or grandchild off to war.

That doesn't mean China won't avoid domestic violence or disruption. Plenty of variables could send the country straight toward more prosperity or on a more circuitous route to economic dominance—via labor unrest and peasant revolts, a military coup d'état, or outright civil war. To distract people from those problems, the Chinese may try to stir up tensions with Taiwan. I am dumbfounded that Taiwan and the mainland would pursue such a dangerous course. If they would only combine Taiwan's expertise and capital with the mainland's labor and markets, they would have an economic powerhouse. Unfortunately, history is full of politicians making absurd mistakes and leading countries into disastrous wars.

THE UPSIDE OF THE DOWNSIDE

China will stumble along the way, but those 1.3 billion–plus consumers aren't going away. The Chinese will be back saving their more than 30 percent and investing it. Millions of homegrown entrepreneurs will be looking for ways to get rich. People in the countryside—and those 300 million heading to the city—are bound to covet goods that their city cousins enjoy, such as electricity, running water, cell phones, computers, and labor-saving devices. Only 4 percent of the people, in cities as well as rural areas, have cars. Not even the Chinese can create steel or iron ore or copper or sugar or soybeans out of nothing. They will have to buy stuff, and that will give another boost to commodity prices.

The U.S. had several serious setbacks as it rose to power, glory, and riches. In 1907, for example, Wall Street's and the U.S. Government's finances collapsed—just as U.S. dominance of the twentieth century was about to begin. Japan is the great success story of the past 60 years, yet in 1966, just as it began rising as the richest country in the world, Japan's entire financial system collapsed. Selling investments in the U.S. or Japan owing to setbacks would have been a serious mistake. And should the Chinese slip, by the time they recover the Communist Party will be a relic. The capitalist genie has been too long out of the bottle. Those girls in Shanghai shopping at Armani and the local fat cats driving BMWs and soon Cadillacs care little about the Chinese Communist Party. The last demonstration I read about in Tiananmen Square involved a group of property owners complaining about getting ripped off by developers. The only Party slogan that young and ambitious Chinese are likely to utter is that line from the Deng Xiaoping years: "To get rich is glorious." When foreign entertainers tour China, one of the provisos is "Relevant departments will carry out strict reviews of performance clothing."

Talk about losing battles. Decades ago, hard-line Maoists warned that you can't separate foreign investment from the "poison" of capitalism and dreams of "bourgeois freedom." They were right—and the unintended consequences of China's capitalist turn are still hard to imagine. The smart investor, however, will be paying close attention for opportunities to cash in on China's excellent adventure in capitalism.

For the time being, the best way is to buy commodities—and particularly during times of correction and consolidation.

6

Goodbye, Cheap Oil

O N October 6, 1973, Egyptian and Syrian jets attacked Israeli positions on the eastern bank of the Suez Canal, the Sinai, and along Israel's northern border; on the ground Arab gun and artillery fire barraged Israelis. The date marked the most solemn day on the Jewish calendar—Yom Kippur, the holy day of atonement—and the Israelis were caught off guard and outgunned, no match for Egypt and Syria's array of Russian weapons and additional supplies from the Soviet Union. A few days after the attack, Israel sent word to President Nixon that the Jewish state verged on destruction. The White House airlifted supplies to the Israelis, who managed to hold off the Egyptian offensive in the Sinai with successful counteroffensives.

Ten days after the attack, the Organization of Petroleum Exporting Countries finally decided to use "the oil weapon," oft-threatened but never before employed, announcing oil-production cutbacks and an embargo on exports to the U.S. Gasoline prices soared 40 percent, cars lined up at gas stations, some of which were forced to post apologetic signs: "Sorry, No Gas Today." By December, oil, which had been selling for $2 a barrel in September, was going for $11.65. The economic effects were felt throughout Europe and Japan. Americans were stunned. It's hard to imagine now, but most hadn't even realized that the U.S. imported oil from anywhere, never mind from the Arabs.

The 1973–74 "oil crisis" still looms large in the American imagination. What most people seem to have forgotten (or never knew) was that the OPEC oil embargo had little to do with high prices. In the early 1970s, long before the war, oil supplies were already tighter than they had been for decades. The huge U.S. oil fields had already begun to decline. Oil producers no longer had the capacity to produce a surplus, while demand for oil was increasing. To stall inflation, the Nixon administration had put price controls on oil in 1971, discouraging investment in oil production or exploration while encouraging Americans to consume more oil. U.S. oil imports had more than doubled since 1970, and buyers and refineries began looking for as much oil as they could find, bidding up the price.

It was a seller's market, and OPEC had oil to sell. Its member nations had become the new Texans, and many of them were wondering why they shouldn't throw their weight around, stick it to the U.S., and get rich in the process. The cartel's most prolific producer, Saudi Arabia, had resisted "the oil weapon," but, before the war, in September 1973 the Saudis finally agreed at an OPEC meeting in Vienna to summon the world's major oil companies to confer about a price hike the following month in Vienna. In fact, when the war broke out the Saudi delegation were on a plane back to Vienna and didn't get the news until they landed. On October 8, OPEC and the oil companies convened to consider a hike in the price of oil, which was then $3 a barrel: The oil companies offered to increase the price 15 percent, about 45 cents a barrel; OPEC proposed a 100 percent increase. Within four days, negotiations broke down, and the oil executives asked for a couple of more weeks to make their case. But on October 18, at another OPEC meeting, in Kuwait City, the exporters decided to go it alone—and announced a 70 percent increase in price, to $5.11 a barrel. The Saudi oil minister told a fellow delegate, "We are masters of our own commodity."

He was wrong. The commodity—oil—was the real boss, which the events of subsequent weeks and months proved beyond any doubt. A cease-fire was declared within a week of OPEC's move. But that legendary October oil embargo was relaxed by December, and terminated in March. OPEC was not about to let politics get in the way of cashing in on those high prices. Egypt's pullout from the Sinai was negotiated in January 1974, and by the end of May, Israel and Syria had made a deal, negotiated by Henry Kissinger. And the price of oil kept going up for the rest of the decade. While many still insist on seeing the "big oil companies" or "the Arabs" (or a combination of both) behind every spike in oil and gasoline prices, oil has become bigger than the corporations and the nations that produce it. Everyone involved is at the mercy of supply and demand, and will continue to be, no matter who tries to control the market.

TODAY'S "OIL CRISIS"

In 2006, the price of a barrel of oil, which had been less than $10 as recently as eight years earlier, crested $70 for the first time ever; U.S. gasoline prices topped $3 a gallon—and politicians, once again, began screaming and pointing fingers at the oil companies and OPEC.

Both sides were living in a fantasy world. *In the real world,* oil production has been declining for years. *In the real world,* economies in the U.S. and Asia were growing faster than they had in 15 years, and oil consumption was already outpacing supplies. *In the real world,* only one near "elephant" oil strike had been made in the past 35 years, in the Caspian Sea off Kazakhstan in 1999, but for political and economic reasons it may never make a significant addition to the world's oil supplies. The newest refinery

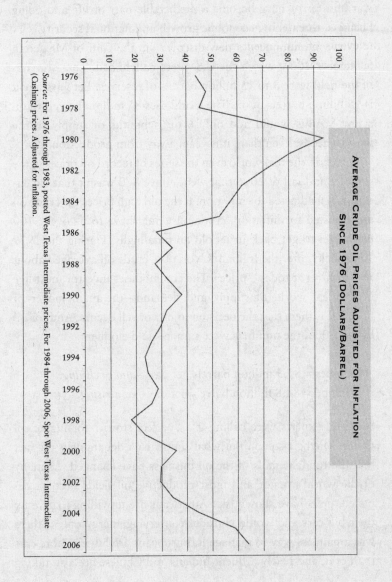

AVERAGE CRUDE OIL PRICES ADJUSTED FOR INFLATION
SINCE 1976 (DOLLARS/BARREL)

Source: For 1976 through 1983, posted West Texas Intermediate prices. For 1984 through 2006, Spot West Texas Intermediate (Cushing) prices. Adjusted for inflation.

in the U.S. is more than 30 years old, and companies are shutting down older ones. *In the real world,* the once "unpredictables" of war and terror have become a predictable part of life and doing business, threatening economic growth and national security.

Chevron announced a new discovery in the Gulf of Mexico in September 2006, which the U.S. press ballyhooed. The estimates of the field were 3 to 15 billion barrels of reserves. Let's assume it is 15 billion barrels of oil. The world uses 85 million barrels of oil a day, so this would add only 6 or 7 months of supply to the world's needs. Even then, it is years away from production.

In fact, in the real world even the series of record oil prices in the summer and fall of 2006 that went above $70 wasn't that expensive, when adjusted for inflation. If the old high prices for crude oil are adjusted for inflation, crude oil would have to be over $100 per barrel to get back to its old all-time highs. During the 1979 "oil shock" after the Iranian Revolution, crude oil averaged about $87 a barrel at today's prices. The commodities investor must live in the real world of supply and demand—the main mover of prices. It is there that the decision to buy or sell occurs. And for oil by fall 2006, the numbers were simple—and eloquent:

Supplies = 85.5 million barrels per day—*and declining.*
Demand = 84.8 million barrels per day—*and rising.**

Some oil experts were calling it a "perfect storm" for higher oil prices. Maybe a squall. But what simply isn't debatable is the fact that the fundamentals of the oil business have changed. As many of the world's major and most productive oil fields become depleted, polls have shown that Americans are unwilling to give up their big cars and would consider conserving energy only if there was a painless way to manage it. Europeans are buying more cars than ever, and newly affluent Indians and Chinese are also taking

*The International Energy Agency's update in August 2006 of previous forecasts for 2006 worldwide oil production and demand.

to the road while also enjoying the pleasures of newly available electricity in their homes powering new refrigerators and TVs. In a previous forecast, the International Energy Agency, the Paris-based watchdog of the global industry, reported that demand in 2004 had grown worldwide by 2.3 million barrels a day—the steepest annual increase since 1980. In its August report, the IEA had noted that OPEC members were already pumping at almost full capacity—with as few as 500,000 barrels a day of "effective" idle capacity (excluding Iraq, Nigeria, Venezuela, and Indonesia, where political problems and strikes blocked increased output). In 2002, OPEC supposedly had 7 million barrels a day of reserved capacity. That drop in capacity meant that even with oil-producing countries pumping oil as fast as they could, if only to take advantage of higher prices, the margin of error had become paper-thin between high-priced oil and much higher priced oil. The IEA laid out the bleak future with updated estimates:

Demand (2007) = 86.4 million barrels per day—*and still rising*.
Supplies (2006) = 85.5 million barrels per day—*and struggling*.

The IEA reported that non-OPEC producers might be able to increase their output another 1.2 million by the end of the year. Perhaps. But the figures clearly showed that even with all the oil-producing countries in the world pumping at maximum capacity, oil demand was outpacing supplies. Suddenly, the world was looking at the kind of extreme imbalance in supply and demand that produces a classic long-term secular bull market in any commodity. Let's take a closer look at both sides of the oil equation.

SUPPLY

In 1956, a senior scientist at the Shell Oil Company in the U.S. with the memorable name of King Hubbert delivered an academic paper to a group of geologists in which he predicted that the U.S. would peak as an oil producer by the early 1970s. Everyone thought he was crazy. The U.S. had been the biggest source of oil in the world for the past century. By 1970, the U.S. was pumping 9.6 million barrels of oil per day, while Saudi Arabia was producing less than half that. Oil was plentiful and cheap; King Hubbert had become a joke—that crazy guy who predicted that we'd be running out of oil by now.

But Hubbert had the last laugh. About the time everyone was making fun of "Hubbert's Peak," the former Columbia University professor's theory was in the process of coming true. U.S. oil supplies peaked in 1973, and by 1981 the nation's oil companies were pumping almost a third less oil in the lower 48 states. The Saudis had become No. 1 in oil production, while the U.S. had settled into the role of No. 1 in oil and gasoline guzzling. The U.S. now imports most of its oil, undercutting our national security and adding to an already worrisome trade deficit. U.S. production—Alaska included—continues to decline. In 1986, American oil fields were pumping an average of 8.68 million barrels per day. By 2001, the daily average was down 33 percent, to 5.8 million barrels. Alaskan oil alone was down more than 50 percent between 1988 and 2002. Those numbers make the U.S. extremely dependent on foreign oil. Extremely. By 2004, we were importing 13 million barrels a day, *more than 60 percent of the oil we use*—and almost twice as much as we imported in 1975. U.S. economic growth is now a hostage of foreign oil.

King Hubbert had made a prophetic call. What was even more surprising was that he seemed to be the only man in the world who noticed that U.S. oil supplies outside of Alaska had nowhere to go but down. Today, there is a small group of new King Hubberts in the world, professional geologists and a few energy analysts who are predicting that a *worldwide* peak is upon us. And, once again, no one wants to listen.

They aren't claiming that oil is about to vanish. The world will have oil long after man has figured out how to end his role on the planet. What they are saying is that *easy* oil—the stuff that just flows out when you tap into it—is declining. The other oil, what the industry calls "unconventional oil," is hard to find, difficult to pump, and expensive to turn into usable energy. The acclaimed "technological revolution" in oil drilling has not resulted in significant discoveries or production advances; in fact, the increase in newfangled drilling techniques may simply have managed to drain the easy oil faster.

No one knows precisely how much oil there is in the world today—or will be. It seems an extraordinary thing to say about something that the world's economies are so dependent upon. Yet no one in the American government or oil industry can put a finger on the total oil available to be brought to market for the next 20 years. The oil-producing countries report pumping capacities; the oil companies report how much they have "in reserve" (i.e., found oil that can be brought to market), along with how much they hope to discover, and the federal government gives us its estimates of supply and demand (based, of course, on what the oil countries and companies tell it).

In other words, "Trust us." The absurdity of that situation for a world supposedly run by grown-ups came to light in 2004, when the sixth-largest oil company in the world, Royal Dutch Shell, conceded that it had overreported its reserves by 20 percent—and then a few months later amended the figure to 22 percent. The company agreed to pay $120 million in fines to the Securities and Exchange Commission and another $31 million to Britain's Financial Services Authority. The Texas-based oil company El Paso also admitted that it, too, had overstated its reserves—by 40 percent. At least, Royal Dutch Shell and El Paso are accountable to shareholders and government watchdogs in the U.S. and Britain. When the Saudi oil minister tells us that the Saudis can keep pumping oil at their current capacity for decades, we have no independent source to verify it.

Independent evaluations of oil production tend to be a lot more gloomy. Between 2001 and 2003, for example, according to a study by Deutsche Bank reported in the *Financial Times,* only 6 of the world's 15 major oil companies have been able to replace all the oil reserves they have pumped. In fact, Deutsche Bank estimates leading oil companies have cut exploration by 27 percent.*

So the question remains: How much foreign oil is there, and will supplies be adequate for the future? Historically, when oil prices have risen the White House and Congress have looked to "our friends the Saudis" to save their skins by pumping more oil. The Saudi oil minister has become the energy equivalent of former Federal Reserve chairman Alan Greenspan: If oil prices go up, he turns on the spigot to create more supplies, pushing prices back down to reasonable levels; too much oil, the Saudis tighten production. Unfortunately the Saudis have been saying this for three or four years now, but the resulting production increases have not followed the rhetoric. This only increases the suspicions that the Saudis may have reserve problems they are hiding from the world. This "maestro" control may be approaching an expiration date. Some geologists and oil analysts now argue that the Saudi oil fields are in the process of succumbing to Hubbert's Peak.

THE SAUDI DEBATE

Geologists and oil analysts estimate that OPEC is sitting on top of more than half of the world's proven oil reserves, supplying more than a third of the world's oil. By fall 2004, OPEC was reporting that it had increased production from 23.5 million barrels per day to 26 million and was ready to pump even more. Saudi Arabia, the only oil producer claiming any significant spare capacity, maintained that it was producing 8 to 9 million barrels of OPEC's daily production. Saudi oil officials contend that within 48 hours they can ratchet production up another 2 million barrels a day and con-

---

* "Tough Choices for Oil Companies in the Quest to Head Off a Global Capacity Crunch," *Financial Times,* September 22, 2004.

tinue pumping that amount through 2009. They also claim that by 2015 they will have new fields on line and will be able to pump 2 to 3 million more barrels a day—and continue to do so for 50 years. In addition, the Saudis claim to have 260 billion barrels in proven crude reserves, more than a quarter of the world's total supplies.

The "reported" reserves of the major OPEC producers have raised eyebrows since the 1980s. At that time, Iraq reported a 174 percent increase in reserves (and we know how reliable Saddam Hussein's regime was), Venezuela weighed in with a 262 percent increase, the United Arab Emirates claimed its reserves had grown 202 percent, Iran reported a 62 percent growth, the Saudis 58 percent, and Kuwait 44 percent. According to British Petroleum's Statistical Review, the industry standard, between 1980 and 2002, the Middle East and Venezuela reported a combined 373 billion barrel increase in proven oil reserves—essentially accounting for roughly 70 percent of the oil growth in the entire world in 2002—raising the question: Why is it that OPEC's oil has been increasing, despite no major new finds, while the rest of world's reserves are becoming depleted?

The output for an average oil field, according to geologists, declines by about 4.8 percent a year. In 2000, oil production worldwide was about 77 million barrels a day. By 2010, existing fields will be producing 47 million barrels a day. The U.S. fields have been declining for 30 years; Britain's reserves are dwindling fast. In 2004, analysts were forecasting a net growth in non-OPEC oil (not counting Russia) of *zero*.

This zero-growth scenario has led some analysts to charge that the OPEC increases were phony—mere "paper barrels" of oil that existed only in the minds of oil producers. (Remember, OPEC production quotas are based on each member country's reserves, so everyone wants to report higher reserves.) More ominous still, a handful of geologists and analysts have invoked Hubbert's ghost by predicting that the peak of *world* oil production is nigh—literally now or within the decade. Colin Campbell, a retired British geologist who worked for major oil companies from 1957 to 1990, has predicted that production peaked around 2005. The British independent energy-analysis firm Douglas-Westwood warns that "the world is drawing down its oil reserves faster than ever and is facing a future of oil price increases." In the U.S., Ken Deffeyes at Princeton University has been updating Hubbert's work and is not optimistic. Henry Groppe of the Houston-based oil industry analysts Groppe, Long & Littell, who has been analyzing the oil business for more than 50 years, is convinced that worldwide oil production peaked sometime in the first five years of this century, i.e., between 2000 and 2005. PFC Energy, petroleum consultants in Washington, D.C., predicts peak production by 2015.

By far the most outspoken Cassandra in the oil business has been Matthew Simmons, CEO of Simmons & Company International, a Houston investment bank specializing in energy. In a series of interviews and speeches in recent years, Simmons, who was also an adviser to the Bush administration on energy issues, has made a well-researched case that the Saudi fields have already peaked. When the previous Western owners of Aramco left Saudi Arabia in the late 1970s, they announced Saudi had 245 billion barrels of oil—proven, probable, and possible.

We heard nothing again about the Saudi oil fields until 1988 when Saudi Arabia announced they had 260 billion barrels of oil. They did not say where they were, from where they came, or even how they knew. They just stated they had 260 billion barrels of oil.

Every year since then Saudi Arabia has announced they have 260 billion barrels of oil. It is amazing—it has been 260 billion barrels every year for 18 years since 1988. They have produced 69 billion barrels of oil since then, yet their reserves never go up or down for 18 years in a row. (I should qualify that slightly: In 2005 Saudi Arabia said they have 261 billion barrels of oil.)

I am not a geologist, and even if I were, I have never been to the Saudi oil fields. The Saudis do not let people go to their oil fields. The numbers do seem strange to me, though. When people now question the Saudis about these peculiar numbers, they answer, "You either believe us or you don't," and the conversation stops dead. "The entire world assumes Saudi Arabia can carry every-one's energy needs on its back cheaply," Simmons told an audience at the Center for Strategic Studies in Washington in February 2004. "If this turns out not to work, there is no Plan B."

Simmons does not share the conventional optimism that we can depend on the Saudis. While researching a book about Saudi oil, he claims to have read a few hundred geological reports from Saudi Arabia written over the past several decades, talked to everyone he could, and run his opinions past the world's oil experts. His conclusion is that the Saudi oil fields—like many others in the U.S. and elsewhere—are past their prime. For decades, oil executives have assured us that the "technical revolution" in oil drilling—3-D seisms, horizontal drilling, multilateral well completion, deep-ocean production techniques—would keep supplies growing easily. "Instead," Simmons claimed in his presentation (and repeated in several interviews), "the technical revolution created a monstrous decline rate." The days of the "easy flow" of oil are over, according to Simmons, "and no one has a clue how much work or money it will take to get what is left under the sand to make it useful." According to Simmons, "the world faces a giant crisis." His main arguments:

- The kingdom's five elephant wells, which were discovered between 1940 and 1965 and have delivered 90 percent of all Saudi oil from 1951 to 2000, are peaking. In fact, they would already have peaked if the Saudis hadn't injected water into them to drive oil to the wellhead. This easy flow is coming to an end.

- Ghawar, the "king" of the Saudis' giant oil fields and the largest oil reservoir in the world—and the source of between 55 and 60 percent of all the oil Saudi Arabia has produced—is 90 percent depleted.

- No independent, third-party inspector has examined the Saudi fields—what Simmons calls "the world's most important insurance policy"—for years. Aramco's last field-by-field proven reserve estimates for Ghawar was made in 1975.

• The next generation of Saudi oil fields will prove challenging and expensive to exploit and the results will not be risk-free because of issues of sand control, rising water cuts, low pressure, and other obstacles.

In an interview with Washington reporters later in 2004, Simmons further questioned Saudi output in even more alarming terms: "We could be on the verge of seeing a collapse of 30 percent or 40 percent of their production in the imminent future, and 'imminent' means sometime in the next three to five years—but it could even be tomorrow."

Not surprisingly, the Saudis have disagreed, vehemently. After Simmons's presentation at the Center for Strategic Studies, the customarily tight-lipped executives of Aramco, the government-owned Saudi oil company, publicly hammered Simmons's report—and continue to do so. Insisting that they still have the capacity to pump plenty of oil for decades to come, they also point to support from independent agencies. Cambridge Energy Research Associates' chairman Daniel Yergin, a historian of oil, according to Barron's, has stated that his organization's studies of new drilling technology counter the claims of Simmons and others that such methods tend to deplete existing oil quicker; according to Yergin, "the digital oil fields of the future" will actually be able to squeeze billions of barrels of oil from deposits that are not now economically feasible. (Dr. Yergin also predicted in February 2003 that oil prices would soon be declining significantly—just before they doubled in 28 months.) Both the U.S. Geological Survey and the U.S. Energy Information Administration, the number cruncher for the Energy Department, have issued statements indicating that they are comfortable with the OPEC and Saudi number. The USGS and the EIA have insisted that oil production can continue to rise for decades at current rates. Based on the USGS's estimate of what has been pumped and what will be, the EIA is arguing that supplies will not peak until 2037 and maybe even 2047. The EIA and the International Energy Agency have both predicted that Saudi oil output will double over the next 15 to 20 years.

Critics see those figures as "wildly optimistic," according to a 2004 report in *Barron's* on the debate over how soon oil will peak. Simmons waves a hand at the OPEC and Saudi data and also notes that the EIA and the International Energy Agency have an "awful" track record as prognosticators. He has called for a "new era of transparency" in reporting reserves according to field-by-field verified data. Simmons has also noted that the oil professionals of Exxon and Chevron who ran Aramco during the 1970s, when the oil fields were last checked using such valid techniques, have estimated Ghawar's reserves at 61 billion barrels and the total oil in all the fields to be 108 billion barrels. If they're on the mark, according to Simmons, "the end is in sight." And the modern-day King Hubberts aren't sanguine about the latest state-of-the-art "superstraw" drilling and pressurization techniques keeping production apace with demand. "We'll never be flush with oil again," T. Boone Pickens, the legendary American wildcatter and founder of Mesa Oil, has said repeatedly. "The worldwide decline will be so steep that whatever we put back will never allow us to catch up."

Whom to believe? Independent analysts and scientists who have broken with the conventional wisdom, T. Boone Pickens, who has 50 years in the oil business, the Saudis, or U.S. energy officials, who have been wrong many times in the past? Leaving aside my own suspicion of government officials, not to mention my discomfort with a medieval Middle East monarchy marked by rampant corruption and internal terror threats, I tend to make money when I bet against the conventional wisdom. In the future of U.S.-Saudi relations, oil will turn out to be a lot thicker than friendship. And when meeting U.S. oil demand gets tougher, which of the other OPEC members will rush to our aid—Algeria, Indonesia, Iran, Iraq, Kuwait, Libya, Nigeria, Qatar, United Arab Emirates, Venezuela—even if they have extra reserves? No "coalition of the willing" to help the U.S.

there. And if any one of them has to shut down oil production, we'll be facing higher prices. But, more important than politics, you do not need to be a geologist (or the Saudi oil minister) to know that even if the Saudis do have as much oil as they claim, the new oil they're drilling will be more and more expensive to get to market—and even then it may not be enough.

And I'm not even factoring in the prospect of more terrorist attacks on Saudi oil installations. When oil prices rose to $32 a barrel, analysts attributed it to a $10 "terror premium"; when oil hit $42, their analysis was the same; and when it went to $52, they insisted that spike, too, was due to the fear factor. In my opinion, that was their wish for $35 per barrel oil talking. And why wouldn't the Saudis agree? The threat of terror was a perfect excuse for them to keep the price of oil high.

But the real reason for the high price of oil, as always, was the supply-demand imbalance, which is not about to disappear soon. Remember: All the world's huge oil discoveries, except perhaps one, were made more than 35 years ago. Oil fields deplete. There are many who swear oil prices will soon decline and stay down. I always ask them: "Where will the oil come from to keep prices down?" So far there has been no reply.

WHAT ABOUT THAT OTHER "FRIEND" OF OURS—THE RUSSIANS?

The "bright spot" in the world's oil picture, according to most analysts, is Russia—additional proof, in my opinion, of how bad things really are.

By most accounts, Russia has plenty of oil, making it something of the great hope in saving Western nations from depending on the goodwill and security of authoritarian governments in the Middle East. Historically, Russian oil has had little effect on OPEC prices. During the Soviet regime, the Russians exported about 2 million barrels per day to the "free world"—a number that didn't change, according to Fadhil Chalabi, executive director of the Centre for Global Energy Studies in London, in spite of increased production between 1960 and 1988, when Russia was pumping 12 million barrels per day. According to Chalabi, "there was great wastage" in Russian oil consumption; prices were kept artificially low and there was a "high degree of inefficiency in fuel utilization." In short, the Communist leaders weren't very good oil executives. Exports barely increased after the fall of the Berlin Wall and the collapse of Communism. Under Vladimir Putin, however, massive investments were made in pumping capability and reported oil production increased 50 percent between 1999 and 2003.

Currently, Russia claims 6 percent of the world's reserves and pumps 10 percent of what the world needs. By 2004, Russia was exporting 4 million barrels per day. The Centre for Global Energy Studies has estimated that by 2010 exports could be as much as three times more. Some analysts have suggested that the Russians are sitting on enough oil to become the world's No. 1 oil producer. According to the respected *BP Statistical Review of World Energy*, Russia has 60 billion barrels of proven oil and natural-gas reserves—the equivalent of 280 billion barrels of oil. Auditors and analysts claim that strict U.S. Securities and Exchange Commission and Society of Petroleum Engineers have forced the Russians to report a lower percentage of their actual reserves when compared with Western counterparts. In 2004, after independent audits, two of Russia's largest oil companies reported that their reserves had increased by almost 6 billion barrels. The *Financial Times* reported that "Russia's oil reserves could prove to be three times higher than previously thought"—from 60 billion to 180 billion barrels. That would make Russia No. 2 in the world after Saudi Arabia; some predict that Russia will soon beat out the Saudis.

Such numbers have had oil execs in the U.S. and Europe licking their chops. After the September 11, 2001, attacks, U.S. officials were hoping the Russians would help U.S. firms "diversify their sources"—

i.e., get some oil that didn't come from the Middle East—and thus make U.S. oil imports less vulnerable. President Bush met with President Putin twice in 2002, discussing major energy cooperation between their two countries and the possibility of links between U.S. and Russian oil companies. There was talk about a pipeline from the Caspian Sea to Murmansk, a town in the Russian far north, where Russian oil companies could load supertankers for shipment to the U.S. Western oil companies were proposing huge investments in Russian firms. BP bought a 50 percent stake of one company, while ExxonMobil was licensed to join with the Russian oil giant Yukos in a $12 billion oil-drilling project in the icy Pacific and by 2004 was ready to invest $25 billion for a major stake in the Russian oil company. And then, suddenly, the U.S.-Russian "energy dialogue" went silent on the Kremlin end. First came President Putin's opposition to the war in Iraq, and then came an even more pragmatic factor—higher oil prices. In 2004, the Putin government ruled that no foreign firm would be allowed to control more than 50 percent of any Russian oil company. Oil and natural gas account for almost 25 percent of the Russian economy, and it is hardly surprising that President Putin isn't eager to become a wholly owned subsidiary of Western oil companies. Higher oil prices had Putin counting up the profits and reevaluating his position on what one U.S.-Russian analyst called "the global energy stage."

Are the Russians ready for the big time? They claim that their economy has been growing steadily since 1999, surging 7.2 percent in 2003, thanks in large part to higher oil prices. Oil exports continue to increase, and Yukos was shipping oil to China by rail. But the negatives have also been adding up, owing primarily to politics. Having spent his first term finding ways to increase oil exports, Putin, reelected by a landslide in 2004, seems more eager to keep wealthy oil executives in line and tax domestic oil to bankroll other economic changes rather than to develop the oil industry. This imbalance wasn't encouraging to foreign investors; neither was the Russian president's opposition to the Exxon deal. The Murmansk pipeline project to move oil more quickly to the U.S.

was history. Worse still, Putin threw the billionaire CEO of Yukos into jail for tax fraud. But after Putin froze company bank accounts and threatened to confiscate its assets to pay back taxes, Yukos counterpunched with a warning that it might have to stop exporting its oil, 1.7 million barrels a day, which is roughly equal to the size of the world's spare production capacity.

Such strong-arm tactics were hardly what U.S. officials had in mind when they were touting democratic and free-market reforms in the "new Russia." The Russian people have tasted democracy, and surveys have indicated a growing nostalgia for "order." But even if the state resists the temptation to intervene further in oil matters, the question remains whether the Russian oil industry will be motivated to make necessary investments in the kinds of infrastructure projects that will allow Russia to take its place as the world's biggest exporter of oil. By all accounts, Russian firms remain backward in oil technology and well management. Until they can do more exploratory work and drilling, all their oil will be sitting deep in Russian soil and oceans. And while they claim to be pumping as much as 9 million barrels a day, the current pipelines can handle only half that. New pipelines are reportedly years away. More worrisome, in spite of all the oil Russian companies are producing, hundreds of millions of dollars in profits are ending up in, as one report euphemistically phrased it, "places unknown to investors." In Russian, that translates as "Swiss bank accounts" and "villas on the French Riviera."

Higher oil prices will only increase the temptation among Russia's enterprising privateers and other outlaw capitalists to steal more oil money. Everywhere I went in the former USSR, new owners in every industry were stripping assets as fast as possible. Little maintenance of oil wells, rigs, and pipelines is in evidence. Efforts to pump more oil faster by injecting water and gas into wells will undercut the productivity of Russian reserves in the long-term. Genuine entrepreneurs and investors know the importance of long-term foresight; sadly, the oil barons in that part of the post-

Communist world will impede Russia's ability to establish de-
pendable oil supplies for the rest of the world.

SOME OTHER QUESTION MARKS

Investors and oil-industry experts who still have prospects of $28
oil dancing in their heads have been banking on relief from new
discoveries in West Africa and the former Soviet republics border-
ing the Caspian Sea, Azerbaijan, Turkmenistan, and Kazakhstan. I
am afraid that they may be disappointed.

CASPIAN SEA

The world's first great oil province was Azerbaijan. At the turn of
the twentieth century, half of the world's oil came from this region,
which was also a major oil producer under the Soviet regime. In
1994, Azerbaijan made a $7.4 billion deal with Western companies
to develop its oil fields in the Caspian Sea. I was in Baku in 1999 and
the only capitalism that I saw was "outlaw capitalism": Instead of
building infrastructure, local entrepreneurs were stripping all the
country's available assets. As I write, hopeful oil analysts are still
waiting for those supplies. My take: You'd have to be crazy to invest
there—or in any other of the former Soviet republics in Central Asia.

Two of the biggest claimed oil discoveries in the past 30 years
have occurred in Kazakhstan: the large Tengiz field (1979) and the
giant Kashagan (1999), an offshore reservoir reputed to have 40 billion barrels of oil and thus three times bigger than Tengiz. But only
6 to 9 billion of Kashagan are recoverable. The Russians did not
have the technology to develop Tengiz, the world's fifth-largest oil
field, and concentrated on easier oil in Siberia. Now Western oil
companies have a piece of the action at Tengiz and Kashagan, where
two successful wells have been drilled and production is expected by
2005, according to the U.S. Energy Information Administration.

None of this oil will do those countries or the rest of the world much good in the short term. (Almost three decades after its discovery, Tengiz is pumping less than 300,000 barrels per day.) In the long term, in my opinion, things are likely to get a lot worse than better. Ever since the fall of the Berlin Wall, I've been hearing how much things have improved in the former Soviet Union, but the only changes I've seen there are for the worse. In fact, the former Soviet republics of Central Asia are, as I said in my last book, "a disaster about to spiral into a catastrophe"—with enough disputes over borders, water, and oil pipelines to keep the various ethnic groups in the region at one another's throats for generations. Like the rest of the Caspian Sea oil, Kazakhstan's prize is landlocked. Billions have already been invested in pipelines to get the oil out—through mountain and desert terrain vulnerable to attack and earthquakes. Corruption has already erupted—muffled by the government, which is an unstable dictatorship.

WEST AFRICA

U.S. companies, with the support of the State Department, have also promoted the prospect of increased supplies from West Africa, especially Nigeria and Angola. Africa is reportedly sitting on proven oil reserves that constitute 9.1 percent of the world's total, and the rate of discovery in Africa surpassed all other regions of the world between 1997 and 2002, according to a U.S. State Department report. Companies have been drilling off the coast of West Africa for years, and some hopeful souls have predicted that by 2010 some 3 million barrels per day will be pumped from West African offshore deep-water reservoirs, an amount that could meet upwards of 25 percent of American oil consumption for the coming 10 years.

Don't hold your breath. That there is plenty of oil in the region is beyond doubt. The real question remains: Who would risk spending a cent to drill for it? On our way to Nigeria in the spring of 2000, after three months of driving down the West Coast of Africa from Morocco, everyone kept telling us, "You ought to avoid Nigeria; it will ruin your experience of Africa." Africa's most populous nation, with more than 130 million people, Nigeria has vast amounts of oil and is an official member of OPEC. The Nigerian people, however, have not benefited from their oil. Their leaders have stolen most of it. At the turn of the millennium, the son of a former dictator testified that he himself had taken $750 million in cash out of the country in boxes and bags for his family.

Nigeria has four oil refineries, but when we were there not one of them was in operation for lack of capital. And five years later they were still not running. A new government was in power. We were in Nigeria in the middle of parliamentary elections and witnessed for ourselves at least one distinction in which Nigeria was already world-class: political corruption. Members of Parliament increased their budget by a total of $200 million so that each could purchase a luxury car and take advantage of a $30,000 furniture allowance. We were out of there in three more days. In 2004, a Christian militia armed with automatic weapons and clubs demolished a Muslim market town, slaughtering scores of people. Within weeks, Muslims of the region retaliated and 20,000 Christians fled their homes. That same year, in a little-noticed move, the U.S. donated four warships to Nigeria to help scare off rampant theft of crude oil from its coastal fields.

Oil companies will not be rushing to spend shareholders' money in Nigeria—a place I doubt will survive as a nation. We also visited Angola, the site of a 30-year civil war. The capital, Luanda, was a hellhole with streets named after Karl Marx, Che Guevara, and Fidel Castro. The war has ended, and things have improved. Oil production has been on the rise. Will it be enough to offset declines elsewhere? I am bullish on Angola, but it will take time.

Even if we assume that all this African oil will someday flow smoothly and bountifully, it is years away and cannot arrive in time to prevent a bull market. Yes, the oil bull market will end someday. Based on historical precedent, as I have explained, the current commodity bull market will last until sometime between 2013 and 2022. Perhaps oil from Africa will be the catalyst to end the energy bull market and then the overall boom in commodities, where energy prices are such a major factor. It is important to remember that the last bull market in commodities did not end with even the discovery of huge fields in Alaska, the North Sea, and the Gulf of Mexico. Time is on the commodities investor's side. It takes a long time to bring all this stuff to market.

VENEZUELA

Another OPEC member, Venezuela claims to produce 3 million barrels a day at maximum capacity, making it, after Saudi Arabia and Iran, OPEC's No. 3 oil producer. Oil revenue accounts for one-third of the country's GDP, half of the government's revenue, and 80 percent of exports. The U.S. imports more than 12 percent of its oil from Venezuela—a country now run by a populist left-wing ticking time bomb named Hugo Chavez, who was elected by a landslide in 1998. (President Chavez actually called President Bush an [expletive deleted] for supporting an aborted coup against him in 2002.) A former army officer and a big fan of Fidel Castro, Chavez tightened his control of Venezuela's state oil firm in 2003 after 18,000 employees went on strike to protest his oil policies, disrupting oil production. Chavez fired the strikers and replaced them with soldiers and others loyal to his government.

Ex-managers contend that the 3 million a day figure is inflated. Chavez has also restricted foreign investment in the Venezuelan oil industry, which is bound to cripple further production. The U.S., which imports more oil from Venezuela than it does from Saudi Arabia, was still feeling the effects of this 2003 Venezuelan slowdown more than a year later. In 2004, with Venezuela awash in profits from record oil prices, Chavez was more focused on diverting oil money into social and other development projects to boost his image, reportedly causing more slippage in actual oil capacity. I wouldn't count on Venezuela to keep oil prices down. The country is certainly in no position to increase production for years, even if it can maintain present rates.

IRAQ

The U.S. was hoping that Iraqi oil would not only ease prices but generate sufficient profits to help pay the costs of reconstruction in a country that has been torn to bits by wars with Iran and the U.S. So far, neither has happened. In 2006, Iraqi pipelines were sabotaged several times, disrupting supplies and contributing to price increases. It will be years before Iraq returns to the 2.5 million barrels a day it used to claim. Political stability may be even more difficult, and those Iraqi pipelines are likely to remain prime targets for the enemies of U.S. policies in the Middle East and whatever government rises out of the ruins of Iraq.

Some fear the worst—political chaos and even civil war, disrupting the flow of oil, as happened before the war, when the Saddam Hussein regime was under United Nations sanctions, and during the Iran-Iraq war. I wouldn't count on Iraqi oil making much of a dent in demand. Neither does OPEC, evidently. In the International Energy Agency's June 2005 report on OPEC production, capacity, and spare capacity, Iraq was literally off the chart; the OPEC "total" had a footnote, conceding "Figures don't include Iraq."

CANADA

It comes as a surprise to most Americans to learn that the U.S. imports almost as much oil from Canada as it does from Saudi Arabia. For years, the Canadians have been claiming that there may be more oil in the province of Alberta than under the deserts of Saudi Arabia—1.6 trillion barrels of oil, which would be a third of the world's oil supplies. The potential takeaway of real oil is 311 billion barrels, and in 2003 the *Oil & Gas Journal* declared that some 180 million barrels of that can be produced at a price low enough to be economically viable.

All that Canadian oil so close to the U.S. is good news, to be sure. The bad news is that to get it oil engineers have to literally squeeze oil from stone. The oil is trapped in the Athabasca tar sands of northeast Alberta, 650 miles from the Arctic Circle. To get it to the surface and usable is a complicated procedure and has already cost oil companies $23 billion. Engineers are now using the multidirectional wells favored in deep-water drilling—one to inject steam into the ground to push the energy-rich bitumen to the surface, the other to extract it. The process is so labor-intensive that a plant opened by Royal Dutch Shell and its partners in 2003 employs 10,000 people—all of whom are paid premium wages to work in the Arctic wilderness. The tar-sand oil is also extremely carbon-intensive, and even Shell concedes that the Alberta stuff emits 25 percent more greenhouse gases than Saudi oil. Unlike the Saudis, Canada is a signatory to the Kyoto Protocol Treaty on climate change, which imposes a limit on how much greenhouse gases governments can allow. Shell claims that over the next decade it will be able to cut the greenhouse gas per barrel. Worse still, powering all that steam required in the extraction process demands huge amounts of natural gas.

All that money, natural gas, and fuss produce a total of some 740,000 barrels a day from the Alberta oil sands—a true drop in the bucket and hardly the solution to growing world demand. Those companies are spending billions to expand, and I own tar sands shares. Certainly it would be fabulous if they could produce huge quantities of oil, but not even the bulls expect it. The biggest optimists hope for an extra one million barrels a day by 2012 and two million additional by 2018. The world uses 85 million barrels per day with most oil fields already declining.

DEMAND

The U.S. economy is growing; so are the economies of Europe, Asia, and the Middle East. That has meant bigger cars and homes in the U.S. and Europe and more motor scooters and cars in China and India, along with better-equipped houses that consume more heating oil and electricity, also generated by oil (and natural gas). From 1980 to 2001, U.S. oil consumption grew 20 percent, with large trucks accounting for two-thirds of that increase. During the same period, conservation and a decline in U.S. manufacturing have kept consumption under control in industrial, commercial, and residential electric-power generation. But even with conservation the Bush administration has estimated that a new power plant would have to be built *every week* in order to meet rising demand, estimated to increase 29 percent by 2020. After years of recession, the people of Japan, South Korea, and other Asian countries have been feeling more confident about their futures; consumption there, too, has picked up. With a population of 3.6 billion, Asia's oil use in 2004 was 20 million barrels a day, up 2 million barrels per day from the previous year. (The U.S., with a mere 270 million people, uses 15 million barrels.) According to trends in demand over the past 10 years, Asia's demand will *double* within the next 6 to 12 years.

The International Energy Agency has noted that economic growth in the world has sped up the demand for oil faster than at any other period in the past 15 years. This speedy recovery worldwide seemed to catch both the IEA and OPEC unawares. One wonders how officials whose job is to think about oil every day could possibly miss the increased need for oil in a region as big as Asia. Economic slowdowns are bound to occur in the world in the next decade or so, but does anyone really believe that Asians will rip out their new electricity, throw out their television sets, stop taking buses or riding their scooters, and return to walking and bicycling in order to save energy? Growth may slow or even decline a bit, but nowhere near enough to make up for the declining supply of oil that's heading down at a clip.

China now consumes only 8 percent of the world's oil, but it accounted for 37 percent of the growth in consumption during the first four years of the new millennium. Since 1992, China's consumption of oil has more than doubled, to more than 5.4 million barrels per day according to IEA data. Various estimates project that by 2010 China's consumption could be as little as 7 million or more than 10 million barrels per day. That would translate into a compound annual rate of 3.8 percent or 9.2 percent. This voracious demand for oil will make China the decisive player in international oil markets: When China is thirsty, the price will go up, and when China hiccups, so will the oil markets.

The demand for oil in China—and in the rest of Asia—will re-arrange world politics. The Chinese aren't likely to leave them-selves at the mercy of OPEC or the Russians, for that matter. The prospect of China's interests running up against ours in the Middle East or against Russia's in Central Asia will give the oil market—and the politicians—plenty to worry about.

THE ALTERNATIVES TO OIL?

High oil prices in the 1970s shocked most Americans into giving energy costs at least a second thought. People bought more energy-efficient cars, drove at slower speeds on highways, and turned home heating down. Affordability trumped comfort. The govern-ment even provided tax breaks for improvements to make homes and buildings more energy-efficient and for investing in solar, wind, and geothermal technologies.

So why are we in another oil crisis, without any popular wide-spread renewable energy alternatives to fossil fuels? Politics is one answer. The major parties and everyone in between (or on their ex-treme margins), along with industry and environmental groups, differ on the desirability of alternatives. For instance, nuclear al-ternatives to fossil fuels in the U.S. vanished after the accident at the Three Mile Island nuclear plant in Pennsylvania in 1979. Other nations—France and Canada, for example—have depended on nuclear power for decades. The province of Ontario has three such plants on the shores of Lake Huron in sight of the state of Michigan and is considering building a new one—the first in North America since Three Mile Island.

The U.S. currently gets about 10 percent of its electricity from hydro plants, which convert the water flowing from rivers and reservoirs into hydroelectric power. But environmental groups claim that hydro plants damage river water and impede the migra-tion of fish, and that the decaying vegetation in large reservoirs behind hydro dams may give off as much greenhouse gases as the energy sources they're trying to replace.

The high upfront costs of these alternative renewable energy technologies may present an even bigger obstacle than politics. Existing financial incentives have been no match for the huge price tag on developing alternative energy sources paired with the low cost of oil during the 1980s and 1990s.

Brave and enterprising souls, however, have taken some steps forward to free us from hydrocarbon addiction, including corporations that have built "green" factories and office buildings that conserve and recycle energy. The Ford Motor Company is renovating Henry Ford's famous Rouge assembly plant in Dearborn, Michigan—an icon of the American industrial revolution—into a "factory of the future," with such renewable energy sources as solar and fuel cells (along with a 500,000-square-foot roof that will hold several inches of rain and increase the area's watershed, and grounds full of natural plants that rid the soil of contaminants). But these steps are rare, and such alternatives have not yet won over the public.

Here's a brief roundup of what has been happening in the world of alternative energies:*

SOLAR POWER

The sun generates an average of 200 megawatts of energy on the earth each day—enough energy to power the current population of the world for the next 27 years. Effective technology to harness solar energy has been around for years. As long ago as 1994, 83 percent of the households in Israel had solar collectors, and in Japan 4.2 million buildings were using solar hot-water systems in 1992. There are essentially two kinds of technology:

---

*I have learned a great deal from alternative energy experts, particularly the various industry associations, the Renewable Energy Policy Project, and the U.S. Department of Energy.

- *Photovoltaics* (PVs), which create electricity from sunlight (photons) and are most commonly used in buildings. A beam of ultraviolet light strikes one part of a pair of negatively charged metal plates, freeing the electrons. These electrons are then attracted to the other plate by electrostatic forces, thus creating an electrical current.

- *Solar thermal technologies,* which use the sun to generate heat. Mirrors and lenses focus sunlight on receivers that convert it into heated fluid, which is then sent through pipes to a steam generator or engine, where it is converted into electricity.

Such solar power devices, which convert radiation from the sun into electricity, can range in size from a small portable solar stove to huge centralized solar power plants using acres of mirrors to generate electricity. Once such plant in Barstow, California—Solar Two—has a 10-megawatt capacity, capable of powering 10,000 households.

The manufacture of solar panels and big electricity-generating plants is growing—but not enough. Although the operating costs of such devices are low, upfront costs are steep. Solar Two, which opened in 1996 to replace a less efficient solar plant, was developed by a consortium of 10 organizations led by Southern California Edison in partnership with the Department of Energy. The total cost: $48.5 million. That level of long-term investment is scary for private business and entrepreneurs. Yet without adequate financing entrepreneurs cannot improve the technology, and without better technology it is impossible to produce cheaper energy.

The Japanese have reportedly spent more than 10 times as much as the Americans to commercialize PV technologies and have plans to build solar plants with 4,600 megawatts of sun power by 2010. So far, the push toward solar energy from Washington has been half-hearted. Residential tax credits for solar use have been around since 1978, and the latest Energy Policy Act passed by Congress in 1992 offers a 10 percent tax credit to businesses that install solar equipment. There are a couple of new bills in the works that would refund upwards of 50 percent of the costs for new residential solar equipment, such as solar water heaters and other equipment that converts sunlight into electrical power. So far, American consumers have not gotten serious about solar energy. And until more consumer demand emerges, private entrepreneurs will struggle for financing.

WIND POWER

As old as the sails made from animal skins that powered ancient boats and the windmills that Don Quixote mistook for giants, wind power, ironically, has been the fastest-growing source of electricity in the world, according to the U.S. Energy Department, growing an average of 25 percent a year since 1990. Germany, the U.S., Spain, Denmark, and India account for 84 percent of the wind energy in the world. The U.S. accounts for about 18 percent of that total, with power generated mainly in Texas and California (most famously in the California desert off the highway into Palm Springs, where you can see an eerie "wind farm" of modern windmills [or turbines] that sit on the landscape like long-stemmed flowers with their three petals spinning in the wind).

As light as air might seem, it does have mass, and moving air creates kinetic energy that can be converted into electricity by turbines. A small increase in the speed of a wind turbine generates significantly more power. Efficient and environmentally pure, wind is not about to get depleted. A one-megawatt wind turbine operating for one year, according to one estimate, results in 1,500 fewer tons of carbon dioxide in the world—along with 6.5 tons of sulfur dioxide, 3.2 tons of nitrogen oxides, and 60 pounds of mercury. Fourteen percent of the land area of the U.S. is amenable to such wind farms (also known as wind parks), and some estimates suggest that 43,000 square kilometers of land could supply upwards of 15 percent of the total U.S. demand in electricity.

This alternative has enormous potential. Yet not every town is eager to give permits to wind farms, and locations far from a given power grid would require prohibitively costly transmission lines to get the power to the grid. Like other renewable energy sources, producing more energy from the endless supply of wind available requires large capital outlay upfront and benefits from economies of scale. There are also environmental objections, along with claims that wind turbines kill birds, produce noise, and so on.

What cannot be ignored, however, is that wind is becoming a competitive energy source with the price of oil over $50 a barrel. The U.K. has mandated that wind provide a significant percentage of its energy by 2010, from virtually nothing now. In late 2004 the U.S. re-established the tax credit for generating electricity by wind power, a big boost to the industry. You might consider windmill stock instead of oil futures.

BIOENERGY

Estimated to be the fourth-largest energy resource worldwide after coal, oil, and natural gas, bioenergy is stored in any *biomass* resources or any renewable organic matter from plants. Biomass includes trees, plants, and dedicated energy crops such as sugar and corn for ethanol, agricultural crops and residue, wood and animal wastes, aquatic plants, and methane from landfill and energy wastes. From biomass, electricity, heat, steam, and fuels can be generated through different conversion processes.

"Biopower technologies," according to the U.S. Department of Energy, "are a proven electricity-generation option in the U.S., with 10 gigawatts of installed capacity." That existing capacity comes from "direct-combustion technology"—generating electrical power via boiler and steam turbines. More efficiency, however, is vital, and improved technology will make that possible, including co-firing of biomass in existing coal-fired boilers and new systems that can turn it into gas ("gasification"), along with fuel cell systems. Biomass can produce a number of different *liquid* fuels, including ethanol, methanol, and biodiesel, as well as *gaseous* fuels such as hydrogen and methane. Bio-based products also have potential—"green chemicals," renewable plastics, and natural fibers. These products could replace those customarily derived from petrochemicals.

The world's biomass resources are widespread, with a potential of decades of energy use. Standing vegetation in the U.S. alone has been estimated to be between 65 and 90 billion tons of dry matter that add up to between 14 and 19 years of primary energy use, at current U.S. levels. Biopower will also energize, as it were, and add substantial value to the U.S. agricultural industry. *But* (it's an ever-present word in the renewable energy field), as the Energy Efficiency and Renewable Energy section of the U.S. Department of Energy concedes, "new and improved processing technologies will be required." By 2004, according to USDE estimates, bioenergy accounted for 3 percent of the nation's primary energy use.

GEOTHERMAL POWER

Hot water and steam, trapped in the earth's core in permeable rocks under a layer of impermeable rocks, creates a geothermal reservoir. The heat from this subterranean goo can be tapped and converted into geothermal energy. The geothermal energy potential in the top six miles of the earth's crust is estimated to be equal to 50,000 times the energy of all known oil and gas resources in the world. The geothermal resources of the U.S. alone have been estimated to be equivalent to 750,000 years of total primary energy supply at current rates of consumption.

That energy is but a dream, of course, because harnessing much of that potential is neither technologically nor economically feasible. As of 2000, only about 8,000 megawatts of geothermal electricity-generating capacity was in use worldwide (less than a quarter of overall global electrical-generating capacity). And in 2001 geothermal energy in the U.S. accounted for about 10 percent of the renewable generating capacity not produced from hydroelectric sources—enough to meet the needs of about 1.7 million households. A drop in the bucket, of course. But, according to Geothermal Energy Association estimates, current technology could generate as much as 23,000 megawatts of electricity daily. Better technology would increase this amount significantly.

But getting to the source of all this energy is difficult and expensive. Geothermal energy production in the U.S. is only a $1.5 billion industry. Drilling one geothermal well can cost upwards of $4 million, and a geothermal field may consist of between 10 and 100 wells. And, like exploratory drilling for oil, there is always the chance of digging into a dry hole. Experts also warn that though a geothermal plant's lifetime is typically 30 to 45 years, it is not likely to be profitable for the first 15 years. After that, with no fuel costs, overhead can drop by half, covering mainly operations and maintenance. According to industry sources, the maximum capital cost of building a geothermal plant is about the same as for a nuclear plant. The plants require relatively little land, they aren't subject to pollution, and they don't produce waste. And they do save a lot of oil. The Philippines, which began developing geothermal sources during the last oil crisis, claims that by the mid-1980s it had reduced its dependence on foreign oil by almost half. Geothermal plants in Nevada, according to state energy officials, produce as much electricity annually as 3 million barrels of oil. On the negative side, emissions can create a sulfurlike smell that may not be popular among neighbors downwind. And there is evidence that withdrawing geothermal fluids from the earth's core at high rates can cause ground and building instability.

Alternatives to oil certainly exist, but all of them are still many dollars and many years away. And, while these areas might offer some interesting investment opportunities down the line, none of these alternatives are about to strike fear into the hearts of OPEC oil ministers. Even with a major incentive to develop an alternative agency—e.g., oil prices suddenly go to $150 tomorrow—it would take years for the world to gear up the switch to alternative sources. Renewable energy alternatives to fossil fuels will not make so much as a dent in the price of oil for at least a decade.

OIL PRICES AND THE WORLD ECONOMY

According to the bears, the price of oil will tumble during the next recession. There will surely be corrections and consolidations in the price of energy over the next decade. Nothing goes straight up every month. China or who knows what may cause a setback. Harder times do not necessarily affect the price of oil. Let me remind you that in the 1970s, when the economies of the U.S., Europe, and many other countries around the world went sour, the price of oil rose *15 times*. The U.K. was one of the five largest economies in the world—and then it went bankrupt. The International Monetary Fund had to fly to the rescue and bail out the British. Yet the supplies of oil were so low that prices kept rising.

And remember, too, that supplies of oil were down despite stupendous technological breakthroughs in oil drilling and production in the 1960s. Geologists knew there was oil offshore, but it was impossible to drill in deep water. Even on land, existing technology couldn't get below 5,000 feet. And then the diamond drill bit was invented. By the 1970s, oil companies were pumping from wells 25,000 feet deep, and massive oil rigs dotted the seas of oil-rich nations around the world. And yet even with new oil in Alaska, the North Sea, and the Gulf of Mexico, with revolutionary oil exploration and drilling taking place, oil prices rose phenomenally between 1968 and 1980. In the history of oil prices, supply-demand imbalances trump even poor economies and technological revolutions.

And history is repeating itself. Oil capacity is, once again, not keeping pace with consumption. The reasons are as simple as they are perennial:

> *Underinvestment in the capacity to pump, refine,*
> *and transport oil AND a supply-demand imbalance*

The industry itself is partly to blame for not tending to the business of infrastructure. In 1997, OPEC met in Jakarta and raised the output quotas of its member nations—just as the Asian economies were heading into a tailspin. With markets brimming over with oil, prices plunged to less than $10. Predictably, oil companies slashed inventories and tightened spending on exploration and new capacity. Meanwhile, investors, much too distracted by watching their money grow exponentially in the stock market, never considered investing in projects to improve the infrastructure of the energy business.

The next stage was familiar to those of us who had gone through the oil shocks of the 1970s. While the oil industry was failing to invest in its capacity to find, pump, refine, and transport oil to market, the world went on consuming oil, and soon voraciously, because the stuff was dirt cheap. The U.S. economy grew, the Asian economies began to improve, and China spurted out of the box at a rate of growth more than triple that of the U.S. Suddenly, before OPEC and the International Energy Agency could say "$40 a barrel oil"—there was not enough oil.

The IEA has estimated that the oil industry will have to invest $69 billion a year in exploration and production during the next decade, developing new sources of oil, building refineries, maintaining pipelines, and building new tankers to meet world demand. That's an enormous number, and oil producers so far have been more eager to acquire other oil producers than to spend money on finding more oil, developing what is already there, or improving infrastructure. Even if they do decide to invest some money, it will be years before we see the results. Meanwhile, existing fields continue to be depleted.

And the consumption of oil will keep increasing. In 2006, $70-plus oil had not affected consumption significantly in the U.S. India and China will continue to need more oil. Where will it come from? As the experts try to answer that question, you can buy a hybrid car, turn down your thermostat, stockpile some new sweaters for the winter, and go solar. But the best hedge against increased oil prices is to buy some oil—which, by the way, is still a lot cheaper than a barrel of Perrier or Coca-Cola.

7

GOLD—MYSTIQUE VS. FUNDAMENTALS

O IL may be the commodity that dominates the news, not to mention the commodity indexes, but no other asset has the mystique and popular appeal of gold. It has been this way since the beginning of time.

The ancients valued gold for its rarity, its durability, and its ornamental appeal. Some even believed that gold had magical properties. The Egyptians mined gold before 2000 B.C., and in 1352 B.C. they buried young King Tutankhamen in an exquisite 2,448-pound gold coffin fashioned in his image. In the sixth century B.C., King Croesus of Lydia, the Aegean kingdom in what is now Turkey, ordered the first pure-gold coin to be minted. The Romans issued their first gold coin in 50 B.C., though the *aureus,* as it was called (from the Latin for *golden*), was used only sporadically during the republic and did not become Rome's common currency until the era of the Roman emperors that began with the rule of Augustus in 31 B.C.

The pre-Columbian Incas used gold in their art and for decor on virtually everything: Each Incan emperor took his stock of gold with him to his tomb, leaving his successor to amass his own collection. When Spanish explorers returned with reports of all that decorative Incan gold, the yellow metal fired the imaginations of many in the late Middle Ages. At the turn of the sixteenth century, Spain's Ferdinand and Isabella sent galleons to the New World to find gold, and they returned laden with deposits for the royal treasury, inspiring Spain's golden age.

The ancient Alchemist's Dream to turn lead into gold took over many fine minds from the third century B.C. into the Middle Ages. And lest you think that all of those alchemists were uneducated cranks, consider that Isaac Newton, a man who had revolutionized physics by the age of 24, put his notebooks aside in 1666 and proceeded to devote the next 20 years of his research to alchemy.*

Today's gold maniacs are the Goldbugs, investors who believe that this ancient precious metal is the only currency with lasting value and that an explosion in its price is ever nigh. A gloomy bunch, the Goldbugs buy gold and hold it as insurance against corporate stupidity, a real-estate crash, a stock-market meltdown, or the collapse of the U.S. dollar, not to mention worldwide financial chaos. Disturbed by visions of their children living in a future shantytown in a deserted area once known as Wall Street, the Goldbugs' solution is to buy more gold, at any price.

This attachment to gold is certainly fascinating from a psychological point of view, but following an obsession is not the best investment philosophy. With a little historical research of the price of gold through the centuries, surely the Goldbugs would have noticed that many things besides gold have been used as "the ultimate money," from cattle and ivory to sea shells and pretty beads.

---

*Newton played another major role in the history of gold. In 1717, Britain adopted the gold standard, and the price of gold was set by the master of the London Mint—Isaac Newton. That mint price lasted for the next 200 years, until the gold standard was suspended in 1914, because of World War I.

To be sure, gold has had its moments, but so have silver and many other less glamorous commodities, such as copper, sugar, wheat, and lumber. History also shows that for long periods of time gold has decreased in price and stayed there.

When I started out on Wall Street in the late 1960s, gold was $35 an ounce. And while it rose to its historic high of $850 an ounce in 1980, the undeniable fact is that for the next 25 years the metal was in a bear market. In fact, gold has been worth a fraction of the price of a Mickey Mantle bubble gum card and has been nowhere near as stable in price. (Current price of a mint 1952 Mantle Topps card on eBay, $1,200; a 1963 version can be had in the $252 range.) Yes, in 2003–04, gold prices got a kick upward from a weakened dollar and threats of inflation, while anxiety over the war in Iraq and the constant threat of terror at home increased the Goldbug population. But even in the $600 range the price of gold is far below that all-time high of $850 (an estimated $1,933 an ounce in 2004 dollars); and compared with the bullish behavior of most other commodities since 1999, gold has been relatively lethargic. More sobering still, the realities of supply and demand cut against gold's performing as well as other commodities in the near future.

As much of a fan of commodities as I am right now, gold is not my favorite. I own some gold personally, as does my baby girl, and gold also makes up 3 percent of the Rogers International Commodity Index. But other commodities will do much better in this bull market. In fact, the supply of nearly every one of the world's major commodities has been allowed to dwindle, gold being the exception. While most mining exploration has been on hold for decades, gold mining production has continued to expand—even with gold prices down. And when other metal prices escalated during the early 2000s, *half* of the mining exploration done worldwide was still for gold. In 2003, the search for gold reportedly accounted for 75 *percent* of the total ongoing exploration for the world's largest mining companies.

It is as if mining professionals were as gaga over gold as the general public.

Investors ignore supply and demand at their peril. And nowhere else do emotions and other psychological factors get more in the way of seeing those fundamental forces clearly than on the subject of gold. The commodities investor must try to look at gold as just one more commodity among many whose prices might rise or fall, depending on the forces of supply and demand. To gain this perspective, it also helps to see gold in its own historical context, which in the U.S. has been both complex and colorful. History shows that gold has not always been the best investment. By some estimates, more money has been lost over the past century or so in gold shares than in any other industry, and that includes railroad and airline companies. Those poor investors should have listened to Mark Twain, who once said that a gold miner was a liar standing beside a hole in the ground.

U.S. GOLD

The English colonists who settled in Jamestown and Plymouth claimed to be seeking a spiritual refuge rather than treasure-houses of gold. The millions of immigrants who followed came in search of the promise of vast expanses of farmland; their primary dream was to step out of poverty. And while the idea of America was bound to include land speculators, flimflam artists, and plenty of industrious entrepreneurs eager to make a greenback, the people who built America were hardly in gold's thrall. The U.S. did not even enact its first federal mining statute until 1866—18 years after hundreds of thousands of miners began prospecting for gold on federal lands in California, where gold was first discovered in 1848. When after intense national debate the U.S. decided to back its currency with gold in 1900, Congress set the conversion price of gold—the "gold standard"—at $20.67 an ounce, where it re-

mained until President Franklin Delano Roosevelt debased the
dollar against gold in response to the economic and currency crises
of the Great Depression.

Many Americans are still steamed over FDR's position on gold.
In 1933, Roosevelt banned the export of gold, halted the convert-
ibility of U.S. dollars to gold, and made it illegal for individuals to
own gold for investment purposes, even abrogating all government and private contracts based on gold. Why? "It's for your
own good," the government said, without further explanation, as
if it were recommending more spinach in the nation's diet. The
U.S. raised the price to $25.56 for 1933, moved it up to $34.95 for
1934, and that year the president proceeded to fix it again, at $35.
Why $35? FDR evidently just picked a round number. Govern-
ments around the world that held dollars applauded the move, as
they could convert their dollar reserves into gold. And everyone
who owned gold could cash in—for a 67 percent premium. Everyone, that is, except U.S. citizens. World War II suspended international economic trade, and the demand for gold disappeared.

From 1935 through 1970, gold remained at $35, eventually a
very low price. With gold so undervalued, who was going to invest
in the extremely capital-intensive task of exploring for gold at
depths of more than 3,000 meters and bringing a major mine on
line? Understandably, gold production kept decreasing. Until 1970,
when the supply-and-demand equation had grown too imbalanced,
and with the price of such a versatile metal so cheap, manufacturers were soon trying to dream up ways to use the stuff. Soon more
gold was being used in dentistry and electronics, and as demand increased so did the price. Meanwhile, the U.S. had been living off
trade deficits since the 1950s and printing money. Instead of dealing with a badly valued currency and those nagging deficits, the
government tried to prop up the dollar with price- and currency-
exchange controls. The U.S. economy turned shaky, and so did the
dollar. By the early 1960s, there wasn't enough gold in reserve to
cover the nation's liabilities to other countries. Other countries, es-

pecially the French, turned up waving their U.S. dollar reserves demanding gold. There was a run on Fort Knox.

President Nixon finally got the message—and promptly changed the rules. In 1971, he announced that the U.S. would no longer convert dollars into gold, in effect, defaulting on the nation's obligation to allow Europeans to redeem their dollars for gold. Demand for gold increased. While governments around the world tried to hold the price at $35, dollar holders were showing up to exchange them for gold. It was crazy, but then the central bankers around the world always seem to be trying to support artificial prices in currencies, metals, and other commodities, whether up or down, while the smart investor knows to go the other way. With gold in demand and the supply reduced by decades of artificially low prices, the only smart thing to do was buy gold at $35.

Except that American citizens couldn't legally own gold. At the time, the Swiss could own gold, as could the Germans, the French, and the Japanese. But in "the land of the free and the brave" it was still against the law for Americans to have their own stash of the yellow metal. In 1973, the Nixon administration removed the dollar from the gold standard, allowing gold prices to float freely— straight up to $120 an ounce. At the end of the following year, Congress decided that American investors were grown-up enough to own gold, and in anticipation of Americans entering the gold market the price shot up to $200 but soon headed back down toward $100 as the rest of the world dumped gold onto the Americans, who had not been allowed to own gold earlier when it had been cheap—"for our own good," of course. The foreigners made a killing at our expense.

What happened next is a story told quite well in a graph of gold prices for the past 35 years. After 1976, gold prices went through the roof. With inflation higher than ever before in U.S. history, investors were convinced that paper money would lose its value. The Iranian Revolution in 1979 and the subsequent American hostage

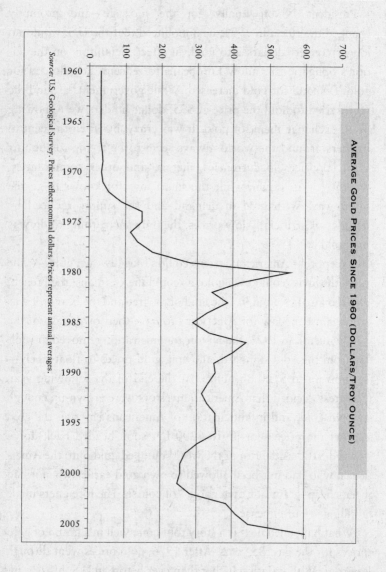

AVERAGE GOLD PRICES SINCE 1960 (DOLLARS/TROY OUNCE)

Source: U.S. Geological Survey. Prices reflect nominal dollars. Prices represent annual averages.

crisis seemed only to confirm the anxieties of the doomsayers. And a huge suppressed demand entered a market in which supply had been constrained for decades. In January 1980, gold hit that phenomenal $850 price. But eventually the hostages were released, the new U.S. president, Ronald Reagan, announced that it was now "morning in America," inflation was tamed, and the dollar survived.

Not surprisingly, the charts also show that in 1980 worldwide gold production began to pick up for the first time since the Great Depression. With record-high gold prices, every mining company in the world seemed to be looking for the metal. For the next 20 years, the world kept producing more gold nearly every year than the year before—and during that same period, with a few ups and more downs, gold lost 70 percent of its value. The mystique of gold could not safeguard against this collapse. There was too much of it around. The price of gold, like anything else, was subject to pure supply and demand.

Then came the dot-com crash, beginning in 2000, and then September 11. The U.S. economy went into reverse, a much reported budget surplus turned into a deficit even before all the tax cuts kicked in and the war in Iraq grew more expensive. Suddenly, everyone seemed to be looking at the world through the prism of a Goldbug. The price of gold began to rise. By the start of 2004, the global economy was feeling better, the Chinese economy began to sizzle, while the dollar was experiencing persistent weakness. Add all that to what Wall Street likes to call "a highly uncertain geopolitical climate"—what you and I know as war in Iraq, threats of terror at home, attacks in Saudi Arabia, an election year in the U.S.—and gold was looking appetizing again to investors diving for cover. Japanese demand increased as bank-account guarantees in that country were modified. The Chinese were once again allowed to own gold after a decades-long ban. The price rallied upwards of $430 per ounce, a 16-year high, before consolidating and renewing its run to over $700 in 2006 before consolidating again into 2007.

Some investors tend to go for the gold when the dollar struggles. In my opinion, in the long term the dollar is likely to continue moving downward. There are too many factors lining up against it, not the least being the intentional efforts of Dr. Bernanke & Co. to keep the dollar weak by printing as much of it as they want. War is expensive, so is the fight against terror, so are those U.S. troops that have been posted in more than 100 nations. And then there's that nasty trade deficit. As difficult as it might be for an American to stomach, the reality is that we are the largest debtor nation the world has *ever* seen. Our foreign debts exceed the foreign debts of every other nation in the world—combined. As much as we Americans love being "No. 1," this debt is one area where I would prefer to come in last place. We owe the world more than $9 trillion. Our international debts are increasing at a rate of $1 trillion every 15 months.

And in spite of what the Fed keeps saying about "inflation being under control," that is not the case in my neighborhood. I don't know about your costs, but mine keep going up. Gold has been a favorite inflation hedge for some, and with the dollar likely to continue weakening over the next few years, I can see gold continuing to climb, which is why I own some. But you may do a whole lot better buying other commodities that will be making much more impressive moves. You should also be aware that the continual fascination with gold flies in the face of the realities of supply and demand.

SUPPLY

Gold inventories are the highest they've been in the history of the world. Unlike most other commodities that get used up, gold is virtually indestructible. All the gold that has ever been mined is still out there in one form or another. Gold Fields Mineral Services has estimated that at the end of 2003 the "aboveground stocks" totaled roughly 150,500 tons, 61 percent of that mined since 1950. The central banks of the world are sitting on a little more than one billion troy ounces of gold—or roughly $600 billion worth (at 2006 prices of $600 an ounce). The U.S. holds the most in reserve, reportedly roughly 262 million troy ounces, followed by Germany (112 million troy ounces) and France (97 million troy ounces). The U.S. reserves are worth roughly $150 billion, which means all the gold in Fort Knox is a paltry supply when put up against the total U.S. debt or the dollars outstanding—evidence of the insignificant role that gold now plays in backing up the dollar, a fact that drives the Goldbugs to distraction. So does the fact that the world's central banks seem eager to sell their gold. Whether the central bankers are right or wrong, there is plenty of gold in the world. (Precisely how much is another matter. No one really knows, for example, how much gold the U.S. actually owns. There has been no outside audit of the gold in Fort Knox for several decades, despite many calls for verification.)

Gold, in fact, is mined on every continent, except Antarctica, where an international moratorium on mining has been in effect for decades; the original Antarctic Treaty was reinforced by the Madrid Protocol of 1991 designating Antarctica a "natural reserve devoted to peace and science." According to the research for the *2004 CRB Commodity Yearbook*, production from the world's mines fell by 0.5 percent in 2004, to 2.430 million kilograms (from 2.550 million in 2001). The world's champion gold producer was South Africa (16 percent of world production); the U.S. (12 percent) was second, followed by Australia (11 percent), China (7.5 percent), Russia (6.2 percent), and Canada (5.8 percent). The production of U.S. mines was also down slightly in 2004 over the previous year.

In spite of this recent dip in production, mining companies are hardly about to run out of gold anytime soon. In fact, while investment in base metals mines and exploration has been down across the board for years, more than half the existing metals exploration in recent years has been for gold. Newmont Mining, the world's biggest gold company (and the only one in the S&P 500), with roughly 100 million ounces in reserve, found more gold in its mines in the U.S., Peru, Australia, and Indonesia in 2003 than it sold that year. The Denver-based company expects rising production into 2007, particularly in Peru and a new find in Ghana in West Africa. Other companies keep looking for gold, and new gold mines elsewhere in Africa will be coming on stream, as will mines in other parts of the world, from Canada to Sardinia.

DEMAND

Gold has become a bit like an aging movie star—the glamour is still there, but there's not as much work as there used to be. Gold remains a staple in jewelry, particularly on the subcontinent of India, where Indian brides get a dowry of gold, typically in the form of jewelry, and wedding guests also give the couple lucky gold coins, and in the Middle East, where oil-rich Arabs show off their wealth with gold watches and jewelry for their wives. Throughout the Middle East, gold souks with dozens of shops are major attractions. In the U.S., however, gold jewelry seems to have lost some of its cachet. The consumption of gold used in jewelry and other fine arts in the U.S. has decreased so much since 1987 that the *CRB Commodity Yearbook* hasn't reported figures on it since 1995.

These days, industry and dentistry are the biggest consumers of gold—about 11 percent of total demand (or an average of a little less than 400 tons a year between 1999 and 2003), according to an estimate by Gold Fields Mineral Services, the London-based precious metals consultancy firm. Malleable, exceedingly resistant to corrosion, and superior in conducting heat and electricity, this ancient metal is essential to the manufacture of such icons of modern technology as televisions, computers, and rocket engines. Gold's resistance to tarnishing also makes it a reliable electrical conductor for switches. In computers, for example, the fine, thinner-than-a-human-hair wire that connects the circuits to the semiconductors (or "computer brain") are made of gold; each computer key strikes gold circuits that relay data to the machine's microprocessor. Similar hair-thin gold wires are found in the microcircuitry of televisions and video recording machines. The cables between your TV and VCR are also gold-coated for a clear relay of the TV signal. The diaphragm of every telephone that is crucial in transcribing voice vibrations into electric current contains gold. You are able to unplug your phone from one jack and use it in another without experiencing lots of static because of the gold coating on the contacts, which neither tarnishes nor corrodes, assuring a reliable signal.

That same malleability and resistance to corrosion have made gold a natural for dentistry, dating from as early as the seventh century B.C., when the Etruscans fastened false teeth with gold wire. Nontoxic and biologically inert, gold still has an appeal for modern dentists. The metal's softness, however, must be bolstered by platinum, silver, and copper alloys. Whenever the price goes up, cheaper alloys are bound to be preferred. Higher gold prices have also made government and private insurance companies less likely to pay for gold dental work, and advances in techniques for creating ceramic crowns have cut the demand for gold in dentistry considerably.

Gold has been used to treat rheumatoid arthritis since the 1920s, in the form of gold salts that are either injected or taken in pill form, to help reduce the swelling and pain of the afflicted joints. The kind of advanced lasers used in medicine and industry employ gold coating on their interior surfaces to control the focus of their powerful light beams. Gold vapor lasers are now used to seek out, select, and destroy cancerous cells without injuring healthy neighbors. Battlefield medics are now armed with lightweight lasers that can seal wounds, improving the soldier's chances of survival. Surgeons use gold instruments to unblock clogged coronary arteries and inject microscopic gold pellets into the prostate to retard that cancer that is so common among men.

According to the CRB Yearbook, U.S. consumption of gold was flat between 2003 and 2004 (from 183,000 to 185,000 kilograms). Demand, however, rose by more than 4 percent in 2003, mainly as a result of investment in gold by speculators. Worldwide average annual demand, according to Gold Fields Mineral Services estimates, has been down for the period beginning in 1999 through 2003 across the board. "Industrial and other uses" of gold were down 17,300 tons, gold jewelry demand was minus 76,800 tons, and the amount of gold in private hands was down 23,600 tons.

PRICES

The gold standard for gold prices among the Goldbugs and other gold hopefuls was that 1980 historic high of $850. That price will eventually be exceeded during the bull market, but who knows when—outside an economic collapse so awful that we will all be fighting one another to buy gold.

Since the stock-market bubble burst in 2000, gold prices have been inching up to periodic highs. The biggest price drivers have been anxiety over the war in Iraq, terror at home, the weakness of the U.S. dollar, the slumping stock market, and a growing loss of sleep among investors of all stripes everywhere about the exponential rise in U.S. deficits. Not nothing, to be sure—but also not much to do with the fundamentals of supply and demand. It seems that when the going really gets tough, many investors have a bit of the Goldbug in them, and instead of reaching for a piece of chocolate cake to make them feel better they put in an order for some gold bullion or coins.

In 2006, prices ended at over $600 an ounce, and fueling that rise was an improving U.S. and world economy, and increased industrial demand for gold, and the persistent weakness in the dollar, which was falling substantially against the euro and other paper currencies and also against gold. Measured in euros, gold prices really went nowhere.

There was lots of "bullish" talk about gold in the press, where memories are short on what a real gold bull market looks like. Those of us who have been around since Nixon allowed gold prices to float in 1971 know that, while gold may be up more than 1,000 percent since then, the prices of just about everything else are up much more over that same period. For the past 30 years, gold hasn't done all that great compared with other assets. If you bought a house in a decent spot in the New York City, Boston, or Los Angeles areas in the 1970s, it might now be worth more than 20 times your original investment. Over the same period, the S&P 500 is up more than 3,000 percent (reinvested dividends included).

In my first book, *Investment Biker,* published in 1994, when gold was averaging about $384 an ounce, I was even less bullish on gold. But I did predict, "Gold will have its day again, and that day is getting closer, but it will be based on supply and demand—not hope or mysticism." That will not change. I also noted that inflation or a currency crisis could kick prices upward. That, too, has been happening, and my bet is that the dollar will continue to fall on hard times, giving the Goldbugs reason to keep buying. Gold will someday see new all-time highs along with other commodities.

But no wise investor should buy gold only in anticipation of the Apocalypse. Own some perhaps as an insurance policy, as many around the world do—including me. I'm not about to rule out the possibility of an economic crisis in the U.S. and/or the world in the next decade or so. The world might panic and turn to gold as a desperate last resort. In the meantime, there are too many other more attractive opportunities in the commodities arena. Lead, for example, is at its all-time high and has been outperforming gold (75 percent of its all-time high) for the past 30 years. I am thus inclined to counsel a new Alchemist's Dream for the current commodities bull market: The person who figures out how to turn gold into lead is the one who's going to get richer than Croesus—at least until the Apocalypse arrives.

8

A HEAVY METAL WITH THE POTENTIAL TO BE A HIGH FLIER

No commodity has had worse press than lead. One of the first metals utilized by man, with 5,000 years of known use, lead has been branded a poisonous killer literally since the beginning of history. Abundant and malleable, lead (*plumbum* in Latin) was the perfect material for Rome's legendary water system, easily fabricated by the city's *plumbarii* (and thus our English word *plumbers*) into water pipes. Contrary to the popular theory that too much lead in the diet caused the decline and fall of the Roman Empire, historians have found written evidence that the authorities in Rome were well aware that lead was toxic: "Water from clay pipes is much more wholesome . . . because lead is found to be . . . hurtful to the human system," wrote the Roman architect Vitruvius (90 B.C.–20 B.C.) in his famous treatise *De Architectura,* a fascinating description of Greek and Roman architecture and building techniques written at the time when the Emperor Augustus was in power. According to recent historical research, the water moved too quickly through Rome's aqueducts, whose pipes were encrusted with limestone deposits, thus protecting the water further from lead contamination. The water passed into cisterns through the safer terra-cotta pipes, which reportedly gave it a sweeter taste. Pliny railed against "poisonous" fumes from lead furnaces, and unfermented grape juice used to sweeten wine and fruit was boiled in leaden cauldrons. Romans did get ill from ingesting too much lead; but if lead were knocking off massive numbers of Romans, these same writers would surely have mentioned it.* The Roman Empire declined and fell, as every empire tends to do, more likely as a result of occupying too much territory too far away with too many troops, a difficult and extremely expensive undertaking— and a history lesson that the U.S., with troops now in more than 100 countries, might contemplate.

For centuries after Rome's fall, lead's usefulness—malleable, ductile, dense, and corrosion-resistant—encouraged short memories of its dangers. Lead was a favorite material for the builders of the cathedrals and castles of Europe. In nineteenth-century America, the metal was used in ceramic glazes, pewter, brass, leaded glass, burial vaults, paints, pipes, water lines, and, of course, bullets. Lead was also a prime participant in the revolutions in electronics, communications, and automotive engineering that took place in the twentieth century. After World War I, lead use increased, mainly in electrical cable covers and solders. As the motorcar came into vogue, demand for lead rose with the introduction of the starting-lighting-ignition (SLI) lead-acid storage batteries and metal gas tanks. As Americans prospered and took to the road, they bought more cars—and more batteries. Lead additives were put into gasoline for better engine performance. New uses of storage batteries emerged in industry and mining as well as stationary

---

*I am no ancient historian, but for more on this debate see "The Myth of Lead Poisoning Among the Romans: An Essay Review," John Scarborough, *Journal of the History of Medicine and Allied Sciences* 7 (1984): 53–60. And "Lead Poisoning and the Decline of the Roman Aristocracy," Lionel and Diane Needleman, *Classical Views* 4,1 (1985): 63–94.

power sources for hospitals, communications, and computer networks. As the U.S. population and economy expanded in the 1950s and 1960s, so did the demand for these lead-filled products.

Inevitably, the health and environmental effects of all that lead came to light, again (albeit some 2,000 years after the Romans warned of lead's dangers to the "human system"). Millions of small children were found to have high levels of lead in their blood, typically from eating chips of oil lead paint in decrepit urban buildings; the unluckiest suffered brain damage, even death. By the 1980s, government agencies had banned the use of lead in paint, solders, and gasoline. The lawsuits followed. In 2002, the 84-year-old Lead Industries Association, Inc., filed for bankruptcy and closed its doors owing to a "lack of insurance to cover litigation," which the company had faced for the past 14 years.*

In recent years, lead poisoning has been reported in towns near mines and smelters in Peru and Africa. In 2000, hundreds of people living near two large lead smelters in Australia filed what was believed to be the first class-action suit against industrial pollution in that country. In 2003, half the children in a town in Zambia, near what was once one of the largest lead mines in Africa, were reported to have lead poisoning. If there is an existing smelter or mine any place in the world, or a plan to build one, there is likely to be legal resistance from environmental groups. In 2004, the U.S. Consumer Product Safety Commission recalled 150 million toy bracelets, rings, and necklaces sold around the nation in vending machines; the toy jewelry was found to contain dangerous amounts of lead.

Lead is not a popular business in which to be. And for that reason, among others, lead prices are likely to rise. The metal has been undergoing a classic supply-demand imbalance, with mine and metal production going down every year around the world, while demand has been increasing, mainly in Asia and particularly in

*U.S. Geological Survey Minerals Yearbook—2002.

China, where more people are abandoning their bicycles in favor of motor scooters and cars that depend on lead-acid batteries.

SUPPLY

Lead production in the U.S. peaked in 1999. In 2002, according to U.S. Geological Survey statistics, U.S. mine production fell to a six-year low of 440,000 metric tons. In 2003, the figure was only 450,000 metric tons. Seven lead mines in Missouri were responsible for 96 percent of U.S. production, according to the USGS and the 2006 CRB Yearbook. The rest was produced in Alaska, Idaho, and Montana. In 2005, recycled scrap metal produced almost twice as much lead as mines—but the total lead recovered from scrap (known as "secondary production") remains flat. The USGS reported a slight increase in scrap production for 2003 (1.1 million metric tons)—one million tons of it from used batteries.

Lead production from mines worldwide was down by 4 percent in 2001 and another 1.2 percent in 2002, the most recent figures available from the U.S. Geological Survey. Australia was the world's largest producer of lead, with 700,000 metric tons, unchanged from 2000. China's reported 600,000 tons was second—down 10 percent from the previous year; No. 3, with 450,000 tons, is the U.S., where mine production has been declining steadily since 1999. The other major lead-producing nations are Peru, Mexico, Canada, and Sweden. The largest lead (and silver) mine in the world is Australia's Cannington mine, in Northwest Queensland. Owned and operated by BHP Billiton, one of the largest mining companies, Cannington, opened in 1997, is the only major new lead mine in decades and has been expanding capacity gradually since start-up.

In 2002, smelter production of lead worldwide from mines and scrap fell 1.2 percent from the previous year's total. The largest smelter producers in the world were reportedly the U.S. (21.6 percent) and China (20 percent), followed by Germany (6.1 percent). The largest lead smelter in the U.S. is in Herculaneum, Missouri, 30 miles south of St. Louis on the Mississippi. Owned by The Doe Run Company, a St. Louis firm that is the world's largest primary producer of lead, the Herculaneum smelter is 112 years old. In 2002, a state study based on blood samples from 935 residents of the area found that one-quarter of the children living close to the smelter had high levels of lead in their blood. The U.S. Environmental Protection Agency eventually relocated about 100 families, mainly with children 6 years old and younger, while crews cleaned up the contamination. In 2004 Doe Run announced the closing of its Viburnum No. 28 lead mine in Missouri after 41 years of operation. There are only three smelters processing primary lead in the U.S.: the Herculaneum plant, the Buick Mine and Mill, also in Missouri, and another operation in Montana. The Buick Mine and Mill is the most recent smelter to be built in the U.S.—in 1969— and it was later acquired by Doe Run.

In summary, lead supplies are down worldwide.

DEMAND

As environmental restrictions have increased around the world, lead has disappeared from many products. According to a 2004 study by the International Lead and Zinc Study Group, 15 percent of paints contained lead 30 years ago; today lead compounds are found solely in paints used for outdoor applications, such as road paints. The study predicts that "by 2006 it is likely that lead compounds will no longer be used anywhere as gasoline additives." It adds, "Phase-out is now under way in Africa and Eastern Europe."

The ancient metal, however, is an essential component to SLI vehicle batteries—a market that already consumes more than 70 percent of the world's lead and is likely to get only larger. Not only is there that growing automobile market in China and India, but, as I noted in my analysis of oil, large trucks were responsible for *two-thirds* of the 20 percent increase in oil consumption between 1980 and 2001. Big trucks don't just guzzle lots of oil; they also need big lead-acid batteries. In addition, according to the industry, government agencies, and the London Metal Exchange (LME), where lead has been traded since 1903, lead is used in industry for non-SLI batteries that power forklifts, airport ground equipment, mining equipment, and load-leveling equipment for electric utility companies. Computer and telecommunications networks also use lead, as do special electrical power systems for hospitals that are not subject to interruption; and the metal is also used to prevent the emission of harmful radiation from television, video, and computer monitors, as well as from X-ray machines. Three percent of lead production continues to be used in ammunition, oxides in glass and ceramics (3 percent), casting metals (2 percent), and sheet lead for roofing (one percent), along with smaller amounts for solders, bearing metal, cable covers, caulking lead, wheel weights, and a few other applications. But by the beginning of the new millennium, according to the U.S. Government Survey of minerals, 88 percent of the apparent U.S. lead consumption was in lead-acid storage batteries of all types.

Demand for replacement batteries for cars in the U.S. and Europe is likely to go down over the next several years, largely because improved quality has extended the lives of batteries and car production in Western Europe has declined. Increases in auto, truck, and motorcycle production in Eastern Europe, South America, and Asia will more than compensate. And, once again, the China factor is dominant. The Chinese are manufacturing more vehicles every year, while U.S. and European carmakers have been establishing their own beachheads in China. The Western automakers are not just looking for the compact car market. Mercedes, BMW, and Cadillac are all in the China game. And little wonder. In 2004, only 4 percent of China's more than 1.3 billion people had cars. There were 4 million cars made in China in 2003, up 750,000 from the previous year. The potential for car sales among China's increasing plutocracy, not to mention its future middle class, left Western automotive executives dizzy with expectation. But they cannot be as happy as the world's battery-makers.

Or lead-producing companies. There is another bright spot on the horizon for lead demand, again tied to China. The cathode-ray tube found in television sets also uses lead. China is already the No. 1 producer of TVs in the world, and, better still, according to the International Lead and Zinc Study Group's special report, sales there are rising 20 percent. Even when digital television drives the cathode ray tube into extinction the Chinese will be watching TV on their computer monitors—which use lead to block radiation.

Worldwide demand for lead is up and increasing.

PRICES

Few commodity prices have been hotter in recent years than lead. After zigging and zagging from 2000 to the middle of 2003, lead headed up—along with the rest of the metals sectors—from about $500 a metric ton to about $1500 by 2005, roughly triple and way above the previous all-time high of $668 in 1979.

But, as we have seen, lead is hardly just going along for the ride with the other metals. Decreased supplies and increased demand result in scarcity. Of course, what is unfortunate for battery-makers around the world watching their profit margins tighten is good news for lead traders, not to mention lead producers.

By 2005, lead prices were about $1500 a ton. It is instructive to compare this bull market in lead, in which there was a clear imbalance between depleting supplies and increasing demand, with the previous all-time high of $668 in 1979, when prices spiked

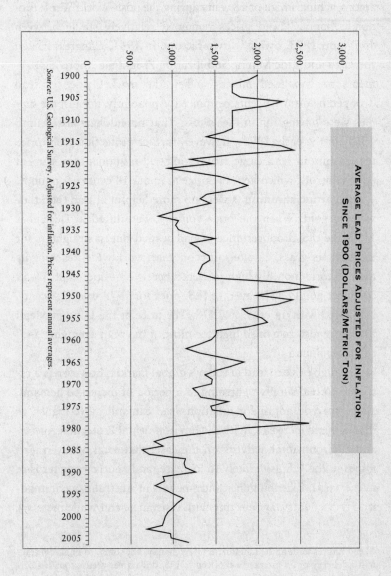

AVERAGE LEAD PRICES ADJUSTED FOR INFLATION
SINCE 1900 (DOLLARS/METRIC TON)

Source: U.S. Geological Survey. Adjusted for inflation. Prices represent annual averages.

after being artificially restrained for years. From the early 1900s to 1959, the price of lead went from 4 cents a pound to 12 cents, after reaching a high of 18 cents during the post–World War II economic boom.* Lead prices remained relatively stable between 1959 and 1973, owing to two factors: In 1961, Congress passed the Lead and Zinc Mining Stabilization Program authorizing payments to "qualified miners" when the market price of lead dropped below 14.5 cents per pound. Apparently, not just the hippies were having fun in the 1960s. That boondoggle lasted until 1969. In the early 1970s, however, further protection from price movements in lead came from good old-fashioned government price controls, which kept the price at about 14 cents per pound.

Such artificial restraints were no more helpful in lead than they were in gold. When the price controls were lifted in December 1973, the U.S. producer price of lead headed almost straight up for the next six years, despite soft economies worldwide, reaching its then historic monthly high in December 1979—quoted at 57–59 cents per pound. (The average U.S. price for 1979 was 52.8 cents, compared with 34 cents in 1978. The price at the London Metal Exchange also remained high for most of the year, averaging 54.7 cents per pound.)

The high price of lead in today's global market, however, is a response to real supply tightening in a period of increased demand. And once you adjust for inflation, lead can still move higher, as that demand increases. With the Environmental Protection Agency and environmental activists on the case, that total of seven lead mines in the U.S. isn't likely to increase, and another smelter isn't in the cards. Existing mines and smelters in Australia, a commodity-savvy country, are meeting with resistance, and while there are

---

*Lead futures trade at the London Metal Exchange. The standard single contract is for delivery of 25 metric tons, priced in U.S. dollars per metric ton. Historically, lead prices were listed in *cents per pound*. But in 1993 the LME began listing its lead data in dollars per metric ton. I use the following historical prices not to confuse but to show the effects of artificial price restraints.

reports that Ivernia West, an Irish company, is considering developing a major lead deposit in Western Australia and an Australian company is "evaluating" a deposit in the Northern Territory, I'll believe it when both companies come on stream. According to recent U.S. Geological Survey reports, there is drilling going on in Canada, Sweden, and Peru; in addition, a Chinese construction company has been developing a lead-zinc deposit with a Pakistani mineral company near Karachi. Even if all these efforts pan out—an unlikely prospect—it will be years before they get any lead out of the ground and to market.

In the meantime, existing mines continue to deplete.

CODA: THE IRONY OF LEAD— AND A LESSON IN COMMODITIES

Even though the lead industry has lost two of its largest markets in the past two decades—paint and gasoline—lead prices are making all-time highs. Lead is a perfect example of how there can be a huge bull market even when demand declines. The lesson is clear: Decreased demand or even a slowdown of economic growth does not necessarily mean a bear market—not if supplies are decreasing faster.

9

SEARCHING FOR THE
NEXT SUGAR HIGH

WHEN I was one of the lone voices talking up commodities and China heading into the new millennium, I ran into much skepticism among the press. The writers, reporters, and anchors around the world, the so-called business media who ought to have known better, were more likely to raise an eyebrow or even turn hostile when I wanted to talk about oil, lead, and sugar more than about the "next big thing" in stocks. I must admit that I find the press's behavior curious. They interview people like me because we're supposed to know things that they don't know, and then when we hand them news they can use they turn contentious.

Occasionally, I like to tease these media types. During one breakfast interview in a Paris hotel, a congenial writer from a French business magazine who was much more eager to discuss the falling dollar and the surging euro—for obvious reasons (*Vive la France!*)—asked me what I would recommend for an ordinary investor like her. I plucked a wrapped sugar cube from the bowl on the table and handed it to her. She looked at me as if I had gone

mad. "Put this in your pocket and take it home," I advised, "because the price of sugar is going to go up five times in the next
decade."

She laughed, eyeing her sugar with skepticism. I told her that the
price of sugar that day was 5.5 cents per pound, so cheap that no
one in the world was even paying attention to the sugar business.
I reminded her that when sugar prices last made their all-time
record run—soaring more than 45 times, from 1.4 cents in 1966 to
66.5 cents in 1974—her countrymen were planting sugar all over
France. There was even a famous French movie about that sugar
boom (*Le Sucre*, or "The Sugar"), starring, as all French films
seem to do, Gérard Depardieu as a wily speculator who persuades
a naïve tax inspector to invest his wife's savings in sugar. The guy
gets extremely rich, but, before he can spend his newfound wealth
he loses his chemise when sugar prices plummet, as they did in the
real world soon after setting that record high. She nodded—"Supply and demand," she said—and pocketed her sugar. But I suspect
that she has not put any of her money where her mouth—or her
pocket—is.

No one had for years, which, of course, was my point. Sugar
prices were so low for so long that it was the last business enterprising souls around the world would be likely to enter in the
1990s and early 2000s. If you are an ambitious young farmer in
Brazil (or Germany or Australia or Thailand, also major sugar-
producing nations), do you choose to produce sugar at 13.8 cents
a pound or soybeans at $6 a bushel, just below an eight-year
high? Even in the U.S., which has its own protected domestic
sugar market at two to three times the world price, only the most
efficient producers are surviving. According to the American
Sugar Alliance, an industry group, a third of all sugar-beet processing mills have shut down since 1996. Government subsidies
are often the only incentive keeping many American and European producers in the game. These producers, too, may be an en-
dangered species.

For years, international pressure has been building on the U.S. and the European Union to end their subsidies for agricultural products, including sugar. The roughly $5 billion the U.S. pays out and the $2 billion by the EU is a frivolous economic drain on their economies, forcing their consumers to pay two to three times the global price for sugar. In 2004, the World Trade Organization finally ruled that the subsidies the EU pays its sugar farmers encouraged overproduction and artificially depressed international prices. The ruling has been appealed, but it was good news for the sugar industry.

But other positive, more immediate events and trends in the sugar business bode well for higher sugar prices. Sugar has had its boom times in the past—that 1974 record, and another spike in 1981 during the last bull market in commodities. And if I'm right and we're in another long-term bull market in commodities, we're likely to see another sugar high. Historically, nearly everything goes up in every kind of bull market, whether it's company shares, commodities, or apartments on Park Avenue. And with world sugar prices at 80 percent or so below their all-time high, the chances of moving higher are strong. To those of us who have been there before, it is promising to note that similar supply-and-demand imbalances are shaping up that could push sugar prices upward over the next decade. You could even sum up sugar's story in three words: Brazil, China, oil.

THE CHANGING GLOBAL SUGAR MARKET

Those white crystals in the sugar bowl, as many will remember from high-school chemistry, are the organic chemical compound sucrose ($C_{12}H_{22}O_{11}$). And in these days of high-carbohydrate consciousness, everyone knows that sugar is a calorie-packed carbohydrate, characterized by its sweet taste, along with the other sugars: glucose, dextrose, fructose, and lactose. Sugar also conjures up images of sweating workers in the field swinging machetes at stalks of sugarcane, the perennial grass (from the genus *Saccharum*) believed to have originated in New Guinea thousands of years ago, and now cultivated in hot, wet regions of the world located more or less between the Tropics of Cancer and Capricorn. Chopped and shredded, the sugarcane is then crushed to extract the juice, which, through an evaporation process, turns into crystalline sugar.

What is less well known is that sucrose also exists in a slightly higher concentration in sugar *beets*, accounting for 25 percent of the world's sugar production. The sugar is found in the root of the beet and is identical to sugar from sugarcane when refined. Seed-grown annuals (planted in the spring and harvested in the fall), sugar beets can grow in temperate and colder climates, prefer a more equal distribution of rain than sugarcane, and can be stored for longer periods without deterioration. Produced primarily in Europe, the U.S., China, and Japan, sugar beets also have the advantage of being harvested by machines rather than by hand. The beets are washed and diffused at high temperatures to produce a juice that is part sucrose, which is further refined into pure sugar. According to the *2004 CRB Commodity Yearbook*, the production trend has been moving more toward sugarcane, which does not seem to be as responsive to price movements as beets, since it is a perennial plant with a longer production cycle.

For the past 20 years, however, the most significant change in the global sugar markets has been the shift in the center of production from the Northern to the Southern Hemisphere. Replacing the old major contenders—Cuba, the U.S., and the EU—are Brazil and fellow southerners Australia, South Africa, Zimbabwe, and Swaziland. Production has also picked up in Guatemala as well as in four Asian countries: India, Pakistan, Thailand, and China. But, as a special report from the Foreign Agricultural Service division of the U.S. Department of Agriculture, "Changes in the World Sugar Situation," has noted, over the past 20 years,

"The star of the Southern Hemisphere production and trade is Brazil. All the other performers are the supporting cast."

Before its rise to sugar stardom, the Brazilians grew sugar mainly for domestic consumption and for ethanol, the gasoline substitute. Since being deregulated in the 1999–2000 sugar season, what the FAS report refers to as the "modernized, low cost" Brazilian sugar industry, the undisputed largest producer of sugar in the world began to supply the world with sugar big time—and quickly became the world's largest *exporter* of sugar. With oil and gasoline cheap and the Brazilian currency weak, it made economic sense for Brazil to move more into the export business, where, according to the FAS report, the advantage of its cheaper currency allowed it to ship sugar at cheaper rates in the Far East, making it difficult for Australia to compete in markets that it had once dominated in Indonesia, Taiwan, the Philippines, and Malaysia. In 2002–03, Brazil accounted for 43 percent of the raw-sugar exports in the world (more than double the Brazilian exports of 18 years earlier).

One other significant change was also in store for the world's sugar markets: While Brazil was a bit player during the previous bull market in sugar prices, the next one is pretty much Brazil's to make—or break.

SUGAR'S PAST UPS AND DOWNS—AND WHYS

The prices of a commodity usually move for a good reason, and the savvy commodities investor must be familiar with past trends and have an eye out for new ones, along with potential glitches, fundamental changes, and anything else that might affect the price of sugar. Between 1966 and November 1974, sugar made the astonishing climb, as I have noted, from 1.4 cents to 66.5 cents. How do sugar prices go up more than 45 times?

By the end of 1972, there had been four straight sugar seasons with record crops. Yet consumption actually *outpaced* supplies in

1972, literally eating into sugar inventories over the next year. The 1973–74 sugar season began with extremely tight supply conditions worldwide; demand continued to rise. There was evidence that some big industry users were stockpiling sugar in anticipation of higher prices. Soon people were grabbing sugar off the shelves in armloads to offset rising prices. Others were grabbing cubes off restaurant tables for home use. Dinner guests were arriving with five-pound bags of sugar instead of the traditional bottle of wine or bouquet of flowers. Even people who had never given the sugar futures markets a moment's thought knew something was up when they walked into the local coffee shop and noticed that the sugar had vanished from the table. Quite simply, global demand for sugar had exceeded supply, and before long the price of sugar headed for the roof.

Everyone had a theory for the high prices. Sugar traders had no idea where prices might be when the U.S.'s long-standing price supports expired at the end of 1974; some blamed the high prices on a "scarcity of cheap labor to harvest sugarcane"; others pointed to the failure of the European sugar-beet crop. Others even suspected that both the Soviet Union, which had just suffered two bad production years in a row in its own sugar crop, and "Arab oil money" (remember that oil crisis of the 1970s?) had moved into the sugar futures markets, along with a rise in speculation by others looking to make money from rising prices.

Significant, too, was the fact that Americans had come to see cheap sugar as a birthright. Even those consumers (and food and beverage companies) who might have turned to the newest artificial sugar substitute, cyclamate, and thus decreased demand, quickly returned to the real thing when the FDA pulled cyclamate off the market in 1969 after reports that it might cause cancer. Over the next few years, companies put sugar back into their products, boosting demand.

U.S. consumption did not slow down much until September 1974, when the reality of high prices finally kicked in. Soft-drink prices increased and candy bars got smaller. But before the White House published the "Presidential Proclamation" of 1975 protecting U.S. sugar producers with the same duty rates and establishing a global quota for sugar imports into the U.S., prices were heading back down.

And once again, the controlling factor was those two politically incorruptible economic players supply and demand. People had been planting sugarcane and sugar beets all over the world to cash in on those high prices. As a result, the 1975–76 world sugar crop broke records. But sugar lovers everywhere, still reeling from high prices, were trying to kick the sugar habit, depressing consumption. The 1976–77 season was another bumper crop.

By December 1976 and January 1977, world sugar prices were ranging between 7 and 9 cents a pound—figures that were, according to the *CRB Commodity Yearbook* report at the time, "below their reported cost of production in some countries." And many, many Johnny-come-lately sugar speculators lost their money—proving, once again, the perils of rushing into a market where prices are rising 45 times, whether it's sugar or dot-coms. The forces of supply and demand put hysteria in its place, once again.

While three straight bumper crops assured plenty of sugar in the world—prices averaged 7.81 cents per pound in 1978—the next season saw a few glitches in the supply chain, as a result of events around the world. With so much sugar on the market in previous years, Australia decided to reduce production by about 10 percent. A major typhoon struck some large sugar-producing regions in the Philippines. And with sky-high oil prices persisting, Brazil decided to divert about one-third of its cane crop to ethanol production.

In the 1979–80 season, production deteriorated below the previous year's numbers. The Soviet Union's crop fell below normal, as did Thailand's and India's, and so prices kept rising through 1979 and 1980 toward a mini-boom in sugar. Prices hit a monthly average of more than 40 cents a pound in 1981, up 400 percent from just 8 cents four years earlier. Hopeful European producers planted more sugar beets. But higher prices, coupled with slow economic growth, soon led to lower consumption as well as moves around the world by governments of major sugar-using nations to ration the stuff or at least reduce its availability. Soon sugar was plentiful again, and sugar prices headed downward.

And so it went. For the next 20 years—during a bear market in commodities—sugar remained plentiful, with bearish prices zigging and zagging at the low end with a few minor spikes, as typically happens in bear as well as bull markets. Gradually, sugar had gone from a respectable commodity that fed the world and supported entire economies to a victim of changing fashions in diet and health: sugar was bad for you; it made you fat, it made kids hyper, and it rotted their teeth. Meanwhile, in labs all over the world chemists were looking for substitutes, preferably noncarcinogens. In 1981, the U.S. Food and Drug Administration approved the artificial sweetener aspartame, and in a flash this newcomer replaced sugar in cookies, cakes, and other favorite snacks sold around the world. It seemed that every weight-conscious person in sight was tapping aspartame into their coffee and cereal from little packets labeled "NutraSweet" and "Lo-Cal," different brands of aspartame. Diet colas were becoming more popular because they had less sugar, and if the sugar's competition had not become tough enough, in 1983 the major soft-drink companies started using literally millions of tons of high-fructose corn syrup to sweeten their beverages. Bad for sugar. (But good for corn, and a great example, by the way, of how researching one commodity might turn up some moneymaking possibilities in a different one.)

By 1985, the price of sugar had made it all the way down to 2.5 cents. No one wanted to be in the sugar business. They were giving away seats on the sugar exchange at the New York Board of Trade. I know, because I bought one on the cheap, and because I wasn't interested in going to the sugar exchange every day I leased it out to someone who was. When sugar prices eventually went up,

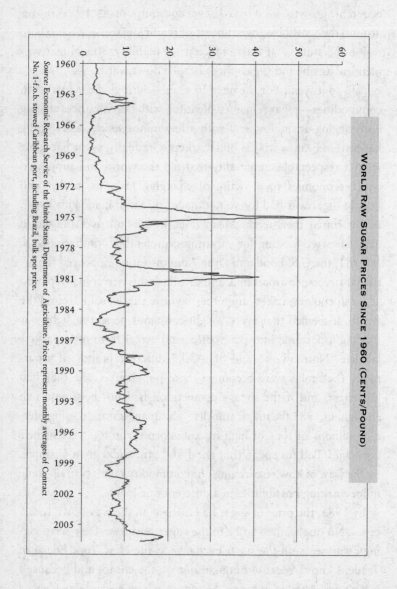

WORLD RAW SUGAR PRICES SINCE 1960 (CENTS/POUND)

Source: Economic Research Service of the United States Department of Agriculture. Prices represent monthly averages of Contract No. 1-f.o.b. stowed Caribbean port, including Brazil, bulk spot price.

I sold my seat for a tidy profit—and thus revealed another way of benefiting from the rise of commodity prices.

Sugar prices stayed in a bear market for the next 19 years, and were still bearish that day in early 2004 when I was teaching the French business writer about her future as a sugar baroness. World production of raw sugar had reached a record level in the 2002–03 season, and the next season produced almost as much. Brazilian exports were also at a record high. That French writer had reason to be skeptical: The price of sugar, after all, at 5.5 cents per pound at the time was not that removed from the 1.4 cent figure of 38 years earlier and a lot closer to that 2.5 cent number of 1985. In fact, most prognosticators were saying, as one analyst for the Australian and New Zealand Banking Group put it at the end of 2003 in a brief report about the market that I read, "sugar prices were likely to remain under downward pressure."*

So why was I, a few months later, confidently telling someone to buy sugar? Supply and demand. Or to translate that into better English—Brazil, a growing Asian sweet tooth, and the price of oil. Of course, I was already a firm believer in the fact that a bull market in commodities was under way, and if, as I've noted, the history of past bull markets tells us that nearly everything makes a new all-time high, why not sugar? For the most likely answer to that question (certainty, remember, doesn't exist in the smart investor's world), let's take a look at more recent trends and events affecting world sugar supply and demand.

SUPPLY

In discussing supply trends in sugar, it's tempting to write "Brazil" and leave it at that. (Come to think of it, Brazil is also a pretty

*Frank Foley, "The World Sugar Market—Focus on Brazil," *ANZ Industry Brief,* October 20, 2003.

good answer to the question "What about demand?" And we'll see why later.) Brazil has learned to play the sugar market cleverly, and the sugar speculator must know how the Brazilians play. In 1992, Brazil had an 8.4 percent share of the world's market in sugar; in 2004, according to a report on sugar demand in the regular "Commodities Corner" column in *Barron's,* Brazil's share was up to 31 percent.* Global sugar production increased 35.4 million metric tons between the 1986–87 and the 2002–03 seasons—an average of 2.2 million tons a year (or a 2.1 percent annual increase).† Brazil was responsible for most of it. According to that Foreign Agricultural Service report, "Changes in the World Sugar Situation," between 1984 and 2003, Brazilian production has increased 144 percent—but with all that increase coming after 1993–94.

As the world's largest producer and exporter of raw sugar, Brazil knows that inundating the world market will push prices down and ultimately hamper the nation's sugar producers with high storage and shipping costs. In response, the Brazilian government devised a clever solution: Simply increase the amount of sugarcane diverted into ethanol production. During the commodity bear market in the 1980s and 1990s, with sugar prices hovering in the 5 to 8 cents range with the usual temporary spikes in a long market, Brazil, according to the Economic Research Service of the U.S. Department of Agriculture, diverted 65 percent of its annual sugarcane crop for ethanol while using the rest for sugar.

Brazil turned a lose-lose situation into a win-win. Until, however, the inevitable happened: Ethanol inventories got too huge in 1998 and 1999. With oil so cheap for years, Brazilian drivers had no incentive to purchase gasohol rather than gasoline, and the Brazilian sugar industry adapted swiftly. The government ceded its

---

* "Sugar Rush," "Commodities Corner," by Susan Buchanan, *Barron's,* May 24, 2004.
† According to a special analysis in the *2003 CRB Commodity Yearbook,* "Understanding and Analyzing the Sugar Market," by Walter Spilka.

control over ethanol production and distribution, allowing Brazilian producers to set up their own enterprise for managing ethanol
supplies—Brasil Alcool S.A.—and in an effort to centralize and
stabilize their domestic market, they also founded the Brazilian Alcohol Exchange. (The government kept a hand in the sugar bowl
through its power to regulate the percentage of ethanol added to
gasoline.)

The ethanol-sugar producing ratio shifted closer to 50–50, increasing Brazilian sugar supplies and potential exports. Poor economic conditions in Brazil also increased the incentive to export
more sugar. To shove the economy into forward gear, the government devalued its already suspect currency in April 1999, cutting
the real's purchasing power by a third. The devaluation made
Brazilian sugar more competitive as far away as Asia, and, even
with low sugar prices, exporters would be earning hard foreign
currency from sugar sales, while selling it on the depressed domestic ethanol market would bring in only depreciated *reals*. The
Brazilians certainly had plenty of sugar to sell, after a record crop
in 2002–03 and almost as much in the 2003–04 season. Production in Australia, China, India, Mexico, Thailand, and the U.S.
was also up, due, in large part, to favorable weather.

And thus the price of sugar was going nowhere fast; between
1998 and 2003, the average price of sugar was only 8 cents. With
prices at 85 percent or so below its all-time high and the world flush
with sugar, investors and analysts saw no real promise in the sugar
market. But then a funny thing happened in 2004: Oil prices made
all-time highs. More promising still, record oil hit at about the same
time China recognized that it needed to import more sugar.

DEMAND

World sugar consumption has been rising steadily for the past
decade. In fact, in both the 2000–01 and 2001–02 seasons, de-

mand almost caught up with supply.* Demand increased the following season and might have passed supply if there hadn't been a record sugar crop. Significantly, however, ending inventories (or stocks) of world sugar for 2003–04 were reported to have dropped by as much as 6.9 percent. That *Barron's* "Commodities Corner" cited earlier reported that "world sugar demand should outpace production this [2004–05] season." This prediction was based on forecasts by a French brokerage firm that showed 2004–05 supplies at 144.2 million tons and consumption at 147.6 million.

I tend to take "forecasts" in the commodity business with, in this case, a grain of sugar. The researchers who compile the information are often barely out of college, and when sugar supplies are counted forecasts have often been off by several million tons. But the French analysts pointed to a dry season in India, plus a pest infestation that was likely to keep the Indian crop smaller than usual and increase the likelihood for imports. India is the world's largest consumer, but it's generally self-sustaining. The Indians are also using more of their sugar for ethanol. But even ignoring India, should the weather turn against sugar during the next few years— major droughts dot sugar's history—undercutting world production and forcing those inventories to dwindle further, demand could zip right by supply.

Then there's the inevitable China effect. In recent years, China has talked a good game about becoming "self-sufficient in sugar." In fact, China has been importing sugar in increasing amounts in the early 2000s. Importing 672,000 tons in 2003, the Chinese government announced that it would be importing more than 1.2 million tons in 2004.† The reason? Jiao Nianmin, secretary-general of

*In 2000–01, total world production of sugar was, according to figures reported by the Foreign Agricultural Service of the USDA, 130.495 million metric tons; total world consumption was 130.164 million. In 2001–02, total production was 134.888 million metric tons; total consumption was 134.790 million.
†The China Sugar Association reported imports of 672,000 metric tons in 2003; the 2004 CRB Yearbook cites 600,000 tons for the same year.

the China Sugar Association, which oversees the domestic industry, reported, according to the country's only English-language newspaper, the Beijing-based *China Daily*: "The main reason for the possible surge in imports is that the estimated *domestic sugar supply falls short of market demand*" (italics mine). He cited a disastrous sugar-beet crop—down 50 percent from the same period for the 2002–03 season—and a drop in sugarcane production in the south as a result of droughts, creating a market gap of 1.5 million tons that had to be filled with imports.

China's increasing demand is very good news for sugar. Already the world's third largest producer *and* consumer of sugar (mainly homegrown), the Chinese are developing a sweet tooth, which means more imports and increased demand. China's per capita sugar consumption has always been small and steady—about 7 kilograms a year (compared with the "globally accepted levels" of 25 to 30 kilograms; U.S. per capita consumption is 45.3 kilograms [or 100 pounds] a year).

Multiplying even the smallest increases by that 1.3 billion–plus Chinese population is a favorite pastime of the world's sugar exporters who are eager to capture a share of the Chinese market. And while Chinese tastes have traditionally resisted a lot of sugar in the diet, evidence from around the world, including Asia, indicates that there is a direct correlation between increasing affluence and sugar consumption regardless of culture. I suspect that China's growing middle class will be no less susceptible to soda pop, iced tea, candy, cakes, and other pastries. The news from the China Sugar Association seems to bear this theory out: Eleven million tons of sugar were consumed in China recently (last year, U.S. consumption was slightly more than 9 million tons).

One more factor is likely to increase demand: oil. Sometimes it seems that economists (and government officials) blame every rise in prices on the "high price of oil." In the case of sugar prices, they might have a point. During the last oil crisis in the 1970s, the Brazilians turned a third of their sugar into ethanol for gasoline—

helping to fuel the bull market in sugar. Producing far more sugar in the 2000s, Brazil is now in the position to make—or break—a bull market. It all depends on how much sugar Brazilians decide to export or put into their gas tanks.

With oil prices moving to record highs, Brazil's choice was a no-brainer. With the price of gasohol 40 percent less than for gasoline, Brazilian drivers suddenly became more fuel-efficient. The São Paulo Sugarcane Agro-Industry Union (UNICA) predicted that 60 percent of all the cars manufactured in Brazil by Volkswagen, Fiat, and General Motors in 2005 would run on ethanol—and that 50 percent of the 2004–05 crop was likely to end up in gas tanks. The government also announced that it was increasing the levels of ethanol to be added to gasoline.

The more sugar that goes into the gas tank, the less there will be for export. In fact, the growth opportunities in the Brazilian sugar industry are now in exporting ethanol. Brazil already exports ethanol to countries in the Caribbean, which redistill the stuff and ship it to the U.S. at low rates of duty. Sweden is also a customer. According to another report, Brazil shipped $170 million worth of ethanol in 2002—more than half of it to South Korea, Japan, and the U.S. (which also produces ethanol, though it's made mostly from corn). And once the Kyoto Protocol to reduce greenhouse gases goes into effect in 2012, Japan, a Kyoto signatory, is likely to become an even bigger ethanol customer. And what about China? The Chinese make their own ethanol—but from corn, which is much needed these days as feed for livestock to meet the nation's increasing demand for chicken, beef, and other protein. Nevertheless, according to the Barron's "Commodities Corner" sugar report, the head of UNICA has already visited Beijing to make the pitch that new cars in China should be running on Brazilian sugar.

And thus the simplicity of it all: Sugar was 85 percent below its all-time high; oil was at an all-time high. Sell sugar at low prices or turn it into gasohol and take advantage of high oil prices? The answer, of course, is likely to reduce supplies of sugar on the market.

It was news and trends like those from Brazil, China, and the oil market that had me pressing free cubes of sugar into the hands of surprised journalists. Am I saying that the price will return to that record high of 1974 or even that most recent high of 1981? No. But I am not saying that prices *cannot* go that high, either. As I have said many times (but it bears repeating), the history of bull markets tells us that when a long-term secular bull is under way, nearly everything reaches its all-time high. In the last commodity bull market, sugar performed accordingly. But this book isn't about hot tips on what to buy. It's about how to think about the commodities markets—by looking at the big picture over decades, keeping history in mind, especially the history of the markets (bulls and bears), and paying attention to the news. That's the way I have invested in commodities, and everything else.

For instance, the news about the World Trade Organization's efforts to rid the European Union of sugar subsidies is the kind of thing you cannot ignore. It was a ruling on a complaint brought by Brazil, which charged that the EU was allowing more subsidized exports than were allowed under world trade agreements, distorting the market and depressing prices artificially. Of course, the European sugar producers will fight back. But not only is getting rid of such subsidies the right thing to do—the Brazilians claimed they were losing $500 million to $700 million in exports as a result—also it is in the economic interest of the EU. The union will save $2 billion a year, while European consumers will not have to pay two to three times the world price for their sugar.

Of course, it will put most of those 60,000 European sugar-beet producers out of business. But that would be a good thing, in my opinion. In fact, to avoid more wrangling at the WTO or in the courts, I would advise a solution that I have often offered in public to the economic absurdities of the roughly $5 billion a year that the U.S. government hands over to the nation's 5,000 or so American producers (about $1 million per grower). According to the

Rogers Plan, we should instead offer them $100,000 a year for life, a condo at the beach, and a Porsche, the only stipulation being that they can never plant sugar again. It would a much better investment of $5 billion, and we ordinary American citizens would all come out way ahead over time.

That's not likely to happen. But "Bravo!" to the WTO solution, which is a step toward a real free market in sugar (and other commodities, too) that would cut production in advanced nations, forcing more imports that would give those poor farmers in Latin America an opportunity to improve their lives by selling more sugar and other agricultural products to rich countries. Brazil has estimated that if the EU subsidies are tossed, global sugar prices would rise almost 20 percent. According to at least one academic study that I've seen, if "all trade and domestic production and consumption distortions" were removed from the global sugar market, prices could increase by 47 percent through a 10-year period ending in 2012.* (A 47 percent rise sounds ominous for consumers, but remember, the rise would still be for *world* sugar prices. U.S. and European consumers would then be paying only *half* of what they are paying now as a result of these absurd protectionist policies.)

I'm not holding my breath. But it is an amazing future to contemplate (during a bull market in commodities)—when we speculator-capitalists will be in a position to actually do extremely well by doing good. In the meantime, anyone interested in commodities ought to be watching very closely how the sugar trio of Brazil, China, and oil is likely to rearrange the fundamentals of the world sugar market.

---

*Amani El-Obeid and John C. Beghin, "Policy Reforms in World Sugar Markets: What Would Happen?" *Iowa Agricultural Review* (spring 2004), Center for Agricultural and Rural Development at Iowa State University.

10

CAN COFFEE PERK UP?

I ENJOY a double espresso as much as the next person trying to get through a busy day. But I must confess to being confounded by those customers at Starbucks—or one of the many other cafés that seem to have prospered in U.S. cities and around the world over the past 15 years—sipping their $3-plus half-caf, decaf, no-fat lattes while complaining about the "high price of coffee." In fact, in the early 2000s coffee prices were at their lowest in decades.

And especially on the floor of the world's coffee exchanges.* The U.S. consumes more coffee than any other nation on the planet, yet I would bet that most American coffee drinkers, whether they stick to their basic cup of joe or sniff coffee beans at specialty food stores with the care of a wine connoisseur, have no idea that coffee is a commodity traded around the world, just like

---

*Coffee futures are traded at the Bolsa de Mercadorias & Futuros (BM&F) in Brazil, the Tokyo Grain Exchange (TGE), the London International Financial Futures and Options Exchange (LIFFE), and the Coffee, Sugar and Cocoa Exchange Division (CSCE) of the New York Board of Trade (NYBOT).

oil or copper or the sugar (and the milk) they might add to their favorite morning beverage. In fact, at certain times coffee has been
the second most important cash commodity in the world, surpassed in value only by crude oil.

Business, however, has been awful for coffee producers for
years. To research the situation in the world coffee markets is to
read a lot of reports with the word "crisis" in the headlines. According to Commodity Research Bureau historical figures, in 2001
and early 2002 coffee prices were at their lowest since the 1970s.
The all-time *contract* low of 41.50 cents occurred in December
2001. At the time, some grades of *cash* coffee prices dropped to
levels that hadn't been seen since the 1960s. Prices rallied in 2003,
but remained in the 50 to 70 cents range on the nearest futures
contract. Even the average retail price of a can of coffee at your
local grocery store was down 65 cents in the 10-year period between 1994 and 2004.

With the price of coffee below the costs of production for years,
coffee growers in the 14 or so major coffee-exporting countries
around the world have been quitting the business in droves. Coffee farmers in Brazil, the world's largest exporter, have responded
to the low prices of recent years by tearing out their trees and
planting more profitable sugarcane and soybeans. Those struggling to stay in the coffee business were cutting back on workers
and skimping on fertilizer for their trees and other maintenance in
order to save money. Colombian coffee growers have been tearing
out their coffee trees to replace them with coca plants, the source
of cocaine. To coffee producers (not to mention veteran speculators), coffee's all-time high price of $3.25 a pound in 1977 seems
like the most impossible of dreams.

Will coffee perk up? Coffee has definitely lagged behind many
other commodities in the early stages of this current bull market.
The best thing in its favor is that coffee prices have been in the cel-
lar for years now. Also in coffee's favor is the fact that prices go up
and down mainly because of dramatic changes in world supplies,

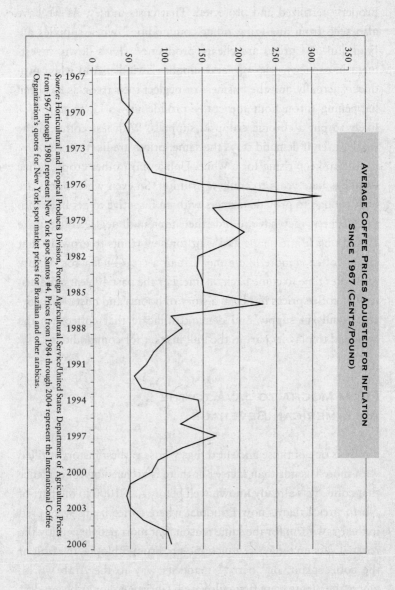

AVERAGE COFFEE PRICES ADJUSTED FOR INFLATION
SINCE 1967 (CENTS/POUND)

Source: Horticultural and Tropical Products Division, Foreign Agricultural Service/United States Department of Agriculture. Prices from 1967 through 1980 represent New York spot Santos #4. Prices from 1984 through 2004 represent the International Coffee Organization's quotes for New York spot market prices for Brazilian and other arabicas.

which are largely affected by coffee's special characteristics as a crop. Like most agricultural crops, productive coffee trees must be properly fertilized and protected. That costs money. As we have also seen from analyzing other commodities, when supplies are bountiful and prices are cheap, production slows down, investment in capacity dries up, and supplies dwindle. And when producers actually quit the business or neglect their trees, as has been happening throughout the coffee-producing world, that, too, is likely to put a chronic crimp in supplies. With less coffee in the world, even if demand stays the same, prices are likely to rise.

And to keep rising for a while. Unlike most other crops, coffee seedlings take years to come to fruition. So even when prices are high enough to provide farmers with an incentive to get back into the business, they have to bide their time until neglected trees are brought back into shape and wait for new plants to grow. In that sense, coffee is more like a metal than a crop—it's a commodity that takes time to come back on line. For the past 40 years, the history of coffee prices has been a story of booms and busts. The current trends in supply and demand indicate that coffee has the potential to play its part in the bull market for commodities.

FROM MOCHA TO JAVA TO THE ALL-AMERICAN BEVERAGE

Coffee is one of those ancient things whose earliest history is filled with more legends than facts. But there is archaeological evidence that coffee was already known well before A.D. 1000 in the part of North Africa that is now Ethiopia, where coffee beans were used in their raw form for the same reason that most people employ the roasted version today: as a pick-me-up. From Ethiopia, the fruit of the coffee plant, or "berry," made its way to the Arab world, where the plants were first cultivated. Christian monks began drying berries to carry them to far-off monasteries around the Mediterranean, which turned them into a kind of wine that gave those faithful servants of God the second wind they needed to get through their long days of prayer. By the fifteenth century, according to some accounts, Arabs were drinking a beverage made from roasted coffee beans. Venetian traders brought coffee to Europe around 1600, when the pope soon declared it to be a good Christian beverage. Before long, coffee had conquered Europe. The first coffeehouse opened in London in 1652; 20 years later, the French followed suit.

The English probably brought the first coffee beans to the New World when they landed in Jamestown in 1607, creating the first permanent British settlement in America. In 1690, as coffee lore has it, Dutch traders smuggled a coffee plant from the Arab port of Mocha to their colony of Java in Ceylon. A French naval officer stole a seedling and brought it to the French colony of Martinique in the Caribbean. Soon a new coffee industry flourished there, spreading throughout the tropical climates of Central and South America. Coffee-drinking became a national pastime among colonial North Americans even before the official birth of the USA. To protest that notorious tax on tea imposed by King George III, the Continental Congress declared coffee the national drink. Perhaps as a result of that early start (and the addictive agents of caffeine), more coffee is consumed in the U.S. than anyplace else in the world.

Few agricultural products require more effort between planting and marketing than coffee. Two species of coffee beans dominate the world market, robusta and arabica, which produces a less— now you know where this word also comes from—robust coffee with the milder flavor that Americans and others have traditionally preferred. (Arabica also has half the caffeine of its robusta cousin.) The beans grow on trees—more precisely, evergreen shrubs that grow in tropical areas of the world where there is lots of rain and an average temperature of 70 degrees Fahrenheit (21 degrees Celsius) year-round. It takes three to five years for a coffee plant to start yielding beans. The typical tree is kept at about 10 feet high so that the "cherries" can be picked easily by hand, and is generally replaced after 15 years, when its bean production tends to peak. The arabica beans grow mostly at higher altitudes of more than 3,000 feet in Brazil and Colombia, their largest producers. Arabica accounts for 70 percent of the world's green coffee-bean production. The largest producers of the cheaper robusta beans are Vietnam, Indonesia, West Africa, and also Brazil.

A coffee tree first flowers in clusters of white blossoms; a few days later, the small green cherries appear and ripen to a reddish color, darkening to an almost black hue within six to nine months, when the cherries are picked for processing. There are two methods of harvesting the actual seeds or coffee beans: the "dry" method, where the cherries are dried in the sun or special dryers and the fruit and bean are separated by mechanical huskers; and the "wet" process, which requires soaking the cherries to remove the various skins that encase the two green coffee beans. Most coffee undergoes the dry method, though the more expensive wet method is said to produce a better flavor, and higher price.

The resulting green beans are dried and sorted, graded and selected, generally by hand; the fresh beans are then bagged and shipped to roasters around the world, who will produce the coffee beans of various shades of brown and aromas beloved by coffee drinkers. According to coffee producers, it takes 2,000 cherries (or 4,000 beans) to make a pound of coffee, and the average tree produces only *one to two pounds* of roasted coffee per year. Coffee is transported in 60-kilogram (132-pound) bags—or as many as 66 trees' worth of coffee each. With world coffee production averaging about 106.6 million bags a year for the past decade, that's a lot of coffee trees.

And hard, manual labor. Once you actually understand what it takes to get a marketable commodity out of a coffee planting, you'll begin to forget about how much you pay for your cappuccino and start rooting for the poor coffee grower. Of course, coffee growers know about the hard work when they start out, and the risks. The coffee bean is the original middle-roader—not too hot, not too cold, just the right amount of rain. But Mother Nature plays her own brand of extreme games, and many a speculator has lost a bundle on coffee trying to second-guess the weather. Good weather is likely to increase production and thus depress prices. Really bad weather can send coffee prices into the stratosphere. After a major drought in Brazil during the summer of 1985, the next year's production fell by almost 58 percent. Too much rain, however, will knock flowers off the trees, also causing a weak crop, which is exactly what happened that same season in Colombia, producing a much smaller crop than in the previous two seasons. Prices moved higher, from a bit more than 80 cents to $1.40 a pound—until the rains returned to Brazil by the end of the year.

Then there are the freezes that attack the arabica trees in their high altitudes, resulting in the kind of severe damage that inevitably weakens the next harvest and even the one after that. According to a research study done by Salomon Smith Barney, in the twentieth century, there were 17 "major freezes" in Brazil, or one about every six years, all occurring between June and August, which are, of course, winter months in the Southern Hemisphere. Coffee prices tend to react to the news of frost in Brazil in the form of spectacular price spikes. As this crucial period approaches, both producers and traders turn into meteorologists, and prices tend to move according to what kind of weather is heading for those Brazilian arabica coffee trees. In 1994, for example, Brazil suffered a famous "double frost"—back-to-back freezes that did major damage to coffee trees. Swiftly, the market turned bullish, sending coffee prices from about $1.00 a pound to nearly $3. And for good reason, evidently. During the following season, the U.S. Department of Agriculture figured that coffee production declined by 40 percent. And in the mid-1970s coffee soared from 75 cents to its all-time high of $3.25 in 1977 because of another devastating frost that had struck Brazilian trees in July 1975. The 1976 harvest, which had been estimated at a potential 28 to 30 million bags, produced only 9.5 million—"unquestionably the worst [crop] in living memory in terms of area covered and number of trees affected," the analysis by the Commodity Research Bureau for that year reported. That famous frost kept Brazilian coffee production low for the next few years, assuring those equally famous high prices in 1977.

Let's take a closer look at coffee's current trends and what they might tell us about the direction of future coffee prices.

SUPPLY

For the past decade, there has been plenty of coffee in the world. Between 1995–96 and 2002–03, the world coffee crops grew significantly every year except one, averaging a total of 106.639 million bags per year. The 2002–03 harvest was predicted to be a record-breaker, and it was; production was confirmed at 120 million bags by the International Coffee Organization (ICO), a London-based intergovernmental coffee group that represents the world's major coffee producers. Bountiful coffee harvests led to buildups in inventories in coffee-producing countries in the 1998–99 season and the 1999–2000 season; in September 2001, world inventories were up 15 percent from the previous year. Given consumption levels during those years, global stocks composed almost a five-month supply. Analysts wondered when all that inventory would begin dwindling.

Brazil is the biggest producer and exporter, and Vietnam has now replaced Colombia in the No. 2 position—in production *and* exports—having bypassed the former Asian coffee power, Indonesia, with a record 1998–99 crop and then outpaced Colombia the following season. Vietnam's coffee production increased in 1999–2000 by more than half, generating, according to the Foreign Agricultural Service of the U.S. Department of Agriculture, slightly more than 11 million bags of coffee and thus more than 10 percent of the world's total production.

As a result of such bountiful supplies, prices were stuck in low gear. Unable to make enough money even to cover their production costs, Brazilian coffee farmers were leaving the business to grow sugarcane for domestic gasohol or soybeans for China. That meant fewer trees in production. And those who stayed in business couldn't afford to maintain their trees or hire enough labor, which was also bound to hurt the next crop.

In 2003, the U.S. Department of Agriculture announced that stocks would be down 24 percent from the previous year-ending stocks of 28.4 million bags. That put some smiles on the faces of speculators, as they bid prices up to levels not seen in three and a half years. The reason? It looked like a classic example of a commodity glut depressing prices as well as investment, which inevitably causes supplies to dwindle. Sure enough, the 2003–04 harvest came in at about 15 percent less than the previous year's 120 million bags, according to the International Coffee Organization. By all accounts, the drop was, as the *2004 CRB Commodity Yearbook* report put it, "in part, caused by the neglect of groves during the long period of weak prices." The crop was further hurt by heavy rains during the first four months of the growing season.

According to ICO figures, the level of Brazilian arabicas was down as much as 40 percent. Brazilian exports also decreased by 17 percent, according to USDA figures. In fact, so did exports from Colombia, where so many farmers had walked away from coffee-growing that previously "marginal" coffee-growing regions had stopped growing the crop altogether.

Supplies had finally dropped, and prices moved up, with a boost from the weak dollar. By mid-2004, the National Commodities Supply department of Brazil's Agricultural Ministry was counting on good weather and estimating a better crop for the 2004–05 season. It did not, however, explain how all those neglected or ex-coffee trees were supposed to meet increasing coffee demand.

And how long will the weather cooperate? If you explore the history of coffee prices for the past 30 years or so, you will notice that in every decade there has been a bout of bad weather, drought, heavy rains in Central America, or a nasty frost that devastates the arabica crop in Brazil, cutting supplies for a season or two. The last frost in Brazil was in the 1999 season, but it was a relatively brief attack and didn't hurt production as much as expected. Prices dropped back down. Two hurricanes hit the Mexican crop in 1997–98; drought hurt the crop in Guatemala as well as Brazil. Supplies dropped, and in 1997–98 coffee consumption outpaced demand. The coffee market is still waiting for this decade's really bad weather.

DEMAND

The U.S. remains the largest consumer of coffee in the world, importing virtually all of its coffee (21 million bags' worth) and consuming 27 percent of the world's exports. (The state of Hawaii produces some coffee, including the famous Kona brand, but it's a drop in the world's coffee bucket.) Most Americans would probably be surprised to learn that coffee is not as popular in the rest of the world. Only 20 percent of the world's population consumes coffee, and they tend to live in the U.S., Europe, and Japan. The second-largest coffee importer is Germany (17 percent), followed by Italy, France, and Japan (9 percent each).

According to the ICO, world coffee demand has been increasing by an average annual rate of 1.3 percent for the past decade. But supplies during the same period increased by 3.6 percent a year. Low prices, however, have already led to a shift in coffee's supply-and-demand dynamic.

Consumption for 2002–03, for example, was 114 million bags, according to USDA estimates, up about one percent from the previous year. As we saw above, the 2003–04 crop suffered a 15 percent decline from the previous year's 120 million bags, which led to production of 108 million bags—*a number that threatened to drop below the amount of coffee consumed during 2004.*

And so coffee demand might soon be in a position to outpace supply. If coffee demand simply increases at its 10-year average of 1.3 percent a year, it is likely to stay ahead of supplies for several years. You need coffee trees to produce coffee, and prices will have to move up higher—and stay there for a while—to persuade farmers to enter the business or return to cultivating coffee trees. That's three to five years before there can be new or even improved production, and, by all accounts, growers are still quitting the business.

WHAT ABOUT CHINA?

Like other commodities producers, the coffee pros have China on the brain. But unlike other commodities, coffee is something that China, a nation of inveterate tea drinkers, has not yet realized that it needs.

Of course, the International Coffee Organization has targeted China as part of its campaign to get that other 80 percent of the world to drink coffee. But the ICO has been running campaigns since its inception in 1963, without really making a big difference in coffee demand. The organization claims that coffee imports to China have doubled since 1998. But when you double minuscule imports you end up with minuscule imports. Before Nescafé and Maxwell House, for example, introduced their instant coffees into China in 1995, coffee-drinking there was virtually unheard of. And in rural areas, where most Chinese still live, that is probably still the case. Annual per capita consumption of coffee in China has been estimated at about .20 kilograms—less than half a pound. In comparison, the Swiss manage to consume more than 50 times as much, about 10.1 kilograms of coffee per capita. Americans drink 20 gallons a year.

There is some anecdotal evidence that coffee is picking up a little glamour in China, at least among China's young people and growing urban middle class. Using statistics from the China Market Database, ChinaDaily.com.cn, the Web site of the national English-language newspaper, has reported that "Chinese people with higher education are most likely to drink coffee." But evidently not all that much more than their less affluent fellow Chinese. In 2004, ChinaDaily.com reported that the country still represents only *one percent* of world coffee consumption.

Starbucks has been in China since 1999, and now has over 184 stores (including 51 in Beijing and 72 in Shanghai). But there are hardly lines running out the door. Even the cheapest coffee drinks, at $1.50 or so, are too expensive for the young upwardly mobile office workers who are attracted to such fashionable spots. Competitors from Hong Kong and Taiwan have also jumped into the urban coffee market, but all the cafés seem to be competing for the same customers—literally person by person. Rather than advertising, Starbucks has tried to win new customers with discount-coupon offers and visits to office buildings.

Hopeful coffee producers point to Japan, another traditional tea-drinking nation, which is now the world's third-largest consumer of coffee. That transformation, however, took decades to accomplish.

THE OUTLOOK FOR COFFEE

All the classic elements are lining up for a bull market in coffee: low prices, fewer growers, fewer trees, less coffee—and continued demand. The growing bull is also likely to get a further boost from bad weather.

And then some other classic things are likely to happen that the well-educated coffee speculator will keep an eye out for. When the next bull move in coffee happens, and prices stay high for a while, bullish investors will start dreaming about all those new buyers in China—and India and Russia. They will be putting out reports and showing all sorts of numbers about increases in demand, and why "this move in coffee is different." Some of those numbers may even be true, but the state of coffee prices will *not* be different— any more than the claim in 2000 that the dot-com rally had produced a "new economy" or the one in 1989 that Japan was going to dominate the world, or that oil prices after 1980 would continue to head into triple figures.

That is, as we have seen, classic bull-market hysteria. And when it happens in the coffee market, recognize it for what it is, take your profits, and look for value elsewhere.

CONCLUSION

I F stocks, bonds, and commodities were part of the same family, commodities would be the sibling who never measured up, the black sheep—the brother-in-law, perhaps, who got wiped out in soybeans. Commodities have never gotten the respect they deserve, and it's been something of a mystery to me why.

More than three decades ago, as a young investor searching for value wherever I could find it, I realized that by studying just a commodity or two one began to see the world anew. Suddenly, you were no longer eating breakfast but thinking about whether the weather in Brazil would keep coffee and sugar prices up or down, how Kellogg's shares would respond to higher corn prices, and whether demand for bacon (cut from pork bellies) would go down during the summer months. (Consumers prefer lighter fare for breakfast.) Those headlines in the newspaper about oil prices or agricultural subsidies were no longer just the news; you now knew why OPEC prefers higher oil prices than Washington and why sugar farmers in the U.S. and Europe have a different opinion about price supports than do their counterparts in Brazil and elsewhere in the Third World.

But knowing about the commodities markets does much more than make you interesting at breakfast; it can make you a better investor—not just in commodities futures but in stocks, bonds, currencies, real estate, and emerging markets. Once you understand, for example, why the prices of copper, lead, and other metals have been rising, it is only a baby step toward the further understanding of why the economies in countries such as Canada, Australia, Chile, and Peru, all rich in metal resources, are doing well; why shares in companies with investments in metal-producing countries are worth checking out; why some real-estate prices are likely to rise; and how you might even be able to make some money investing in hotel or supermarket chains in countries where consumers suddenly have more money than usual.

Of course, I've made a much bolder claim in this book: that a new commodity *bull market* is under way and will continue for years. I have been convinced of this since August 1, 1998, when I started my fund, and have been making my case for commodities ever since. I have written about commodities and given scores of speeches around the world filled with experienced investors and financial journalists. I have met with bankers and institutions. I have even been asked to confer with some mining companies to explain why I think they're going to do so well. But, as kind and hospitable as my audiences have been, some seemed no more eager to invest in commodities when I finished talking.

It was as if the myths about commodities had overtaken the realities. For most people, when you mention the word *commodities,* another word immediately comes to mind: *risky.* Worse still, when investors who are curious about commodities raise the subject with their financial advisers, consultants, or brokers at the big firms, the "experts" are likely to flinch in horror—as if Frankenstein himself had just stepped into the room. And then they launch into sermons about the dangers of such "risky" investments or that colleague who specialized in commodities but "is no longer with the company."

It's weird. From my own experience, I knew that investing in commodities was no more risky than investing in stocks or bonds—and at certain times in the business cycle commodities were a much better investment than most anything around. Some investors made money investing in commodities when it was virtually impossible to make money in the stock market. Some made money investing in commodities when the economy was booming and when the economy was going in reverse. And when I pointed out to people that their technology stocks had been much more volatile than virtually any commodity over time, they nodded politely and kept looking for the next new thing in equities.

One of the main reasons I wanted to write this book was to open the minds of investors to commodities. I was eager to point out that every 30 years or so there have been bull markets in commodities; that these cycles have always occurred as supply-and-demand patterns have shifted. I wanted people to know that it took no measure of genius on my part to figure out when supplies and demand were about to go so out of whack that commodity prices would benefit. How hard could it be to make the case that during bull markets in stocks and bear markets in commodities, such as the most recent ones in the 1980s and 1990s, few investments are made in productive capacity for natural resources? And further, if no one is investing in commodities or looking for more resources, no matter how much of a glut there is, how difficult is it to understand that those supplies are bound to dwindle and higher prices are likely to follow? The next step is as clear and logical as anything in economics can be: that if, in the face of dwindling supplies, demand increases or even just stays flat or declines slightly in any fundamental way, something marvelous happens, and it is called a bull market.

But even with the formidable forces of supply and demand on my side, I couldn't *prove* beyond anyone's doubt that without commodities no portfolio could be called truly diversified. I could make my arguments, cite examples from my own experience, point to historical and current trends. Still, I hadn't done the heavy lifting, the professorial analysis and detail, to *prove* academically, with charts and graphs, how commodities performed vis-à-vis stocks and bonds. I was an investor, not a professor. But then I got lucky. As I was deep into the writing of this book, two professors who had actually done the research and analysis of how commodities investments performed relative to stocks and bonds reported their results.

And that is why I am of the opinion that the 2004 study from the Yale School of Management's Center for International Finance, "Facts and Fantasies About Commodity Futures," is a truly revolutionary document. Professors Gary Gorton, of the University of Pennsylvania's Wharton School and the National Bureau of Economic Research, and Professor K. Geert Rouwenhorst, of the Yale School of Management, have finally done the research that confirms that:

- Since 1959, commodities futures have produced better annual returns than stocks and outperformed bonds even more. Commodities have also had *less* risk than stocks and bonds, as well as *better* returns.

- During the 1970s, commodities futures outperformed stocks; during the 1980s the exact opposite was true—evidence of the "negative correlation" between stocks and commodities that many of us had noticed. Bull markets in commodities are accompanied by bear markets in stocks, and vice versa.

- The returns on commodities futures in the study were "positively correlated" with inflation. Higher commodity prices were the leading wave of high prices in general (i.e., inflation), and that's why commodity returns do better in inflationary times, while stocks and bonds perform poorly.

- The volatility of the returns of commodities futures they examined for a 43-year period was "slightly below" the volatility of the S&P 500 for the same period.

- While investing in commodities companies is one rational way to play a commodity bull market, it is not necessarily the best way. The returns of commodities futures examined in the study were "triple" the returns for stocks in companies that produced those same commodities.

Therefore commodities are not just a good way to diversify a portfolio of stocks and bonds; they often offer better returns.* And, contrary to the most persistent fantasy of all about commodities, investing in them can be *less* risky than investing in stocks.

This is dramatic news. I call it "revolutionary," because it will change in a major way how financial advisers, fund trustees, and brokers treat commodities. To dismiss investing in commodities out of hand will now be liable to criticism and reproach—backed up by a reputable academic study. In the late 1970s, there was an academic study that examined one of the more controversial financial instruments ever devised, the junk bond, which bestowed credibility on investing in junk bonds and turned them into an acceptable asset class. I recall another academic report in the late 1960s, after stocks had been suspect for decades, giving a boost to buying shares in companies again. It helped reinvigorate the stock market. This Yale report will do the same for commodities.

Frankenstein is dead.

But please keep this in mind: Even in a bull market, few commodities go straight up; there are always consolidations along the way. And not all commodities move higher at the same time. Just because it's a bull market doesn't mean you can throw a dart at a list of things traded on the futures exchanges around the world

---

*See the Correlation Index in the Appendix (p. 225), which demonstrates the power of commodities as a diversification tool.

and hit a winner. You might, for example, hit copper, and copper may already have peaked. In the last long-term bull market, which began in 1968, sugar, as we have seen, reached its peak in 1974, but the commodity bull market continued for the rest of the decade. A bull market by itself, no matter how impressive, cannot keep every commodity on an upward spiral.

Every commodity, as we have seen, is guided by its own supply-and-demand dynamic. Not all commodities in a bull market will reach their peak at the same time—any more than all stocks do during their own bull market. Some company shares will soar in one year and others might make their highs a year or two or three later. That is also true of commodity bull markets.

During the question-and-answer periods after my speeches, some-one usually pipes up to say, "So I invest in commodities, and it is a bull market. When do I know it's over?"

You will know the end of the bull market when you see it, and especially once you have educated yourself in the world of com-modities and get some years of experience under your belt. You will notice increases in production and decreases in demand. Even then, the markets often rise for a while. Remember that oil pro-duction exceeded demand in 1978, but the price of oil skyrocketed for two more years because few noticed or cared. Politicians, ana-lysts, and learned professors were solemnly predicting $100 oil as late as 1980. Bull markets always end in hysteria.

When the shoeshine guy gives Bernard Baruch a stock tip, that's high-stage hysteria, and time to get out of the market. We saw it again in the dot-com crash. In the first stage of a bull market, hardly anyone even notices it is under way. By the end, formerly rational people are dropping out of medical school to become day-traders. Wild hysteria has taken over—and I am shorting by then. I usually lose money for a while, too, as I never believe how hys-terical people can get at the end of a long bull market. Remember all the giggling and drooling over dot-coms on CNBC in 1999 and

2000. Of course, no one ever admits that they never saw it coming. If I had told you in 1982–83 that a bull market in stocks was under way, you would have laughed at me. Everyone knew back then stocks were dead—except that over the next seven years the S&P 500 almost tripled. Had I advised you then to put all your money in stocks, you would have hooted me out of the room: Surely, no rational being would believe that stocks could continue to rise after already tripling in a few years. But between 1990 and 2000, the S&P 500 continued upward, almost quintupling—while the Nasdaq composite rose tenfold.

The commodities version will come in its own form of madness. Instead of CEOs and VCs in suspenders, you will see rich, smiling farmers and oil rigs on the covers of *Fortune* and *Business Week*. CNBC's "money honeys" will be broadcasting from the pork-belly pits in Chicago, and the ladies down at the supermarket will be talking about how they just made a killing in soybeans. Small cars will be the norm, homes will be heated five degrees below today's preferred room temperature, and there might be a wind farm on the outside of town as far as the eye can see. When you see all that, then it's time to get your money out of commodities. The bull market will be over.

Those days, in my opinion, are a decade away, at least. It is now up to you. Consider this book the beginning of your new expertise as a commodities investor. Do your homework and keep learning. Luck always follows the prepared mind.

COMMODITY INDEX COMPONENTS

Rogers International Commodities Index

Created to be an effective measure of the price action of commodities on a world-wide basis, the RICI is the largest existing commodities index, featuring 36 commodities that reflect the current state of international trade and commerce. Listed according to their weightings, the components are:

Crude Oil	21.000%	Heat Oil	1.800%
Brent Oil	14.000%	Platinum	1.800%
Wheat	7.000%	Gas Oil	1.200%
Corn	4.750%	Lumber	1.000%
Cotton	4.050%	Lean Hogs	1.000%
Copper	4.000%	Cocoa	1.000%
Aluminum	4.000%	Nickel	1.000%
Soybeans	3.000%	Tin	1.000%
Gold	3.000%	Rubber	1.000%
RBOB Gasoline	3.000%	Bean Meal	0.750%
Natural Gas	3.000%	Canola	0.670%
Bean Oil	2.000%	OJ	0.660%
Live Cattle	2.000%	Oats	0.500%
Silver	2.000%	Rice	0.500%
Sugar	2.000%	Azuki Beans	0.500%
Coffee	2.000%	Palladium	0.300%
Lead	2.000%	Barley	0.270%
Zinc	2.000%	Wool	0.250%

ROGERS INTERNATIONAL COMMODITY INDEX (RICI)
WEIGHTINGS BY GROUP—7/1/06

Grains and Oilseeds	% Total	Cume
Red Wheat		
Wheat	7.00%	
Corn	4.75%	
Soybeans	3.00%	
Soybean Oil	2.00%	
Rice	0.50%	
Azuki Beans	0.50%	
Barley	0.27%	
Canola	0.67%	
Oats	0.50%	
Soybean Meal	0.75%	
Total	19.94%	19.94%
Energy		
Crude Oil/WTI-NYMEX	21.00%	
Heating Oil/NYMEX	1.80%	
Unleaded Gas	3.00%	
Natural Gas	3.00%	
Brent Crude/IPE	14.00%	
Gas Oil/IPE	1.20%	
Total	44.00%	63.94%
Softs		
Cotton	4.05%	
Coffee	2.00%	
Sugar	2.00%	
Cocoa	1.00%	
Wool	0.25%	
Orange Juice	0.66%	
Total	9.96%	73.90%
Precious Metals		
Gold	3.00%	
Silver	2.00%	
Platinum	1.80%	
Palladium	0.30%	
Total	7.10%	81.00%
Industrial Metals		
Aluminum	4.00%	
Copper	4.00%	
Zinc	2.00%	
Lead	2.00%	
Nickel	1.00%	
Tin	1.00%	
Total	14.00%	95.00%
Livestock		
Live Cattle	2.00%	
Feeder Cattle		
Live Hogs	1.00%	
Total	3.00%	98.00%
Other		
Rubber	1.00%	
Lumber	1.00%	
Total	2.00%	100.00%

Agricultural Sector RICIA

Wheat	20.057%	Cocoa	2.865%
Corn	13.610%	Rubber	2.865%
Cotton	11.605%	Bean Meal	2.149%
Soybeans	8.596%	Canola	1.920%
Bean Oil	5.731%	OJ	1.891%
Live Cattle	5.731%	Oats	1.433%
Sugar	5.731%	Rice	1.433%
Coffee	5.731%	Azuki Beans	1.433%
Lumber	2.865%	Barley	0.774%
Lean Hogs	2.865%	Wool	0.716%

Metals Sector RICIM

Copper	18.957%	Zinc	9.479%
Aluminum	18.957%	Platinum	8.531%
Gold	14.218%	Nickel	4.739%
Silver	9.479%	Tin	4.739%
Lead	9.479%	Palladium	1.422%

Energy Sector RICIE

Crude Oil	47.727%	Natural Gas	6.818%
Brent Oil	31.818%	Heat Oil	4.091%
RBOB Gasoline	6.818%	Gas Oil	2.727%

Dow Jones-AIG Commodity Index

No single commodity in this index can constitute less than 2 percent of the total or more than 15 percent. And no group of commodities (e.g., Energy, Livestock, etc.) can make up more than 33 percent of the total. All the data, in both the liquidity and production calculations, is averaged over five years. This index includes 20 components (weightings are as of January 1, 2006):

Natural Gas	12.32%	Copper	5.88%
Crude Oil	12.78%	Zinc	2.70%
Unleaded Gas	4.05%	Nickel	2.66%
Heating Oil	3.85%	Gold	6.22%
Live Cattle	6.09%	Silver	2.00%
Lean Hogs	4.35%	Sugar	2.97%
Wheat	4.77%	Cotton	3.16%
Corn	5.87%	Coffee	2.93%
Soybeans	7.77%	Cocoa	0.00%
Aluminum	6.85%	Soybean Oil	2.77%

Because of the method of constituting the index, the actual weightings percentages will vary according to price fluctuations in the market. In fact, the weightings have differed significantly between 1999 and 2006, as can be seen in the following historical chart from Dow Jones-AIG:

DOW JONES-AIG COMMODITY INDEX (DJ-AIGCI)
HISTORICAL WEIGHTINGS

Commodity	1999	2000	2001	2002	2003	2004	2005	2006
Natural Gas	5.07%	6.01%	7.30%	9.18%	10.39%	11.61%	12.28%	12.32%
Crude Oil	14.17%	14.31%	14.75%	14.37%	13.77%	13.19%	12.81%	12.78%
Unleaded Gas	5.08%	5.10%	5.01%	4.62%	4.46%	4.20%	4.05%	4.05%
Heating Oil	5.75%	5.59%	5.24%	4.83%	4.38%	3.99%	3.85%	3.85%
Live Cattle	5.88%	5.49%	5.22%	5.34%	5.70%	5.87%	6.15%	6.09%
Lean Hogs	3.20%	3.14%	3.30%	3.58%	3.91%	4.11%	4.39%	4.35%
Wheat	4.25%	4.47%	4.50%	4.64%	4.81%	4.89%	4.87%	4.77%
Corn	6.10%	6.30%	6.33%	6.39%	6.05%	6.07%	5.94%	5.87%
Soybeans	9.08%	8.83%	8.62%	8.50%	7.88%	7.41%	7.60%	7.77%
Aluminum	4.97%	5.31%	5.75%	6.28%	6.99%	6.94%	7.06%	6.85%
Copper	7.33%	6.98%	6.56%	6.01%	5.92%	5.81%	5.89%	5.88%
Zinc	2.00%	2.00%	2.00%	2.00%	2.10%	2.36%	2.67%	2.70%
Nickel	2.00%	2.00%	2.00%	2.00%	2.00%	2.23%	2.61%	2.66%
Gold	9.69%	9.03%	8.48%	7.33%	6.36%	5.89%	5.98%	6.22%
Silver	3.86%	3.79%	3.41%	2.89%	2.48%	2.14%	2.00%	2.00%
Sugar	2.11%	2.07%	2.04%	2.27%	2.55%	2.72%	2.93%	2.97%
Cotton	2.81%	2.91%	2.87%	2.99%	3.16%	3.16%	3.23%	3.16%
Coffee	2.65%	2.68%	2.63%	2.77%	2.99%	2.94%	3.02%	2.93%
Cocoa	2.00%	2.00%	2.00%	2.00%	2.00%	2.00%	0.00%	0.00%
Soybean Oil	2.00%	2.00%	2.00%	2.00%	2.11%	2.46%	2.67%	2.77%

Sources: AIG Financial Products Corp. and Dow Jones

Goldman Sachs Commodity Index

The components in this index are weighted according to world production—"the quantity of each commodity in the index is determined by the average quantity of production in the last five years," according to GSCI's own description. That means that the GSCI is bound to be most heavily weighted toward energy. It also means that the index weightings increase when a particular commodity rises in price. The GSCI currently includes 24 commodities across the sectors of energy, industrial metals, precious metals, grains, and other foodstuffs or "softs." The weightings constantly change, but recently, those components are:

Crude Oil	28.60%	Silver	0.20%
Brent (UK) Crude Oil	13.35%	Wheat	2.96%
Unleaded Gas	8.35%	Red Wheat	1.29%
Heating Oil	8.42%	Corn	2.91%
Gas Oil	4.43%	Soybeans	1.76%
Natural Gas	9.34%	Cotton	1.14%
Aluminum	2.90%	Sugar	1.37%
Copper	2.28%	Coffee	0.65%
Lead	0.31%	Cocoa	0.25%
Nickel	0.76%	Live Cattle	3.62%
Zinc	0.46%	Feeder Cattle	0.80%
Gold	1.87%	Lean Hogs	1.99%

By the end of 2005, 75.7 of the GSCI consisted of energy products. But the world-weighted method of composition also creates shifting percentages in the other subsectors. It also means that this index contains more of the things that have been rising—a peculiar way to invest. Here is GSCI's own chart for its component weightings between 1988 and 2006:

GOLDMAN SACHS COMMODITY INDEX (GSCI) HISTORICAL WEIGHTINGS—% OF TOTAL

Contract Group	Year 2006	2005	2004	2003	2002	2001	2000	1999	1998	1997	1996	1995	1994	1993	1992	1991	1990	1989	1988
Energy	70.1	75.7	71.1	66.8	67.3	58.6	66.8	60.3	46.9	55.3	61.5	53.5	48.8	39.6	48.9	48.0	57.5	52.2	44.4
Livestock	4.6	5.0	6.6	6.3	7.7	11.2	8.7	10.5	12.0	11.1	10.1	10.6	19.6	26.4	24.0	22.7	22.0	23.0	24.6
Grains	8.6	6.7	8.5	12.6	12.0	14.1	10.5	11.7	18.6	15.1	13.0	18.4	12.4	17.7	13.0	15.2	10.0	13.3	17.0
Softs	3.1	3.5	3.7	4.5	4.9	5.5	5.6	6.4	9.5	8.8	6.6	6.8	8.4	7.0	5.7	5.9	5.9	6.7	7.7
Industrial Metals	11.2	7.2	7.8	7.4	5.6	7.8	6.4	8.5	9.2	7.2	6.4	7.9	8.2	6.3	6.1	5.9	2.3	2.3	3.4
Precious Metals	2.2	2.0	2.2	2.5	2.5	2.8	2.0	2.6	3.8	2.4	2.4	2.6	2.6	3.0	2.4	2.4	2.2	2.5	2.9
Total	100.0	100.0	100.0	100.0	100.0	100.0	100.0	100.0	100.0	100.0	100.0	100.0	100.0	100.0	100.0	100.0	100.0	100.0	100.0

Source: Goldman Sachs

Reuters-CRB Futures Price Index

Begun in 1956 as the CRB Futures Price Index, it has been revised ten times to reflect market structure and activity. The last change was in 2005. I wonder if they will ever get it right. For example, aluminum is now 600 percent more important than wheat to them for some reason.

Crude Oil	23%	Copper	6%
Heating Oil	5%	Live Cattle	6%
Natural Gas	6%	Lean Hogs	1%
Corn	6%	Cocoa	5%
Soybeans	6%	Coffee	5%
Wheat	1%	Orange Juice	1%
Cotton	5%	Sugar	5%
Gold	6%	Aluminum	6%
Silver	1%	Nickel	1%
		Unleaded Gasoline	5%

REUTERS-CRB INDEX WITH HISTORICAL WEIGHTINGS

	1957	1961	1967	1971	1973	1974	1983	1987	1992	1995	2005
Aluminum											6%
Barley	3.57%	3.70%	3.57%	3.70%	3.57%	3.70%	3.70%				
Broilers				3.70%	3.57%	3.70%					
Cocoa	3.57%	3.70%	3.57%	3.70%	3.57%	3.70%	3.70%	4.76%	4.76%	5.88%	5%
Coffee											5%
Coffee "B"	3.57%	3.70%	3.57%								
Coffee "C"	3.57%	3.70%	3.57%	3.70%	3.57%	3.70%	3.70%	4.76%	4.76%	5.88%	
Copper	3.57%	3.70%	3.57%	3.70%	3.57%	3.70%	3.70%	4.76%	4.76%	5.88%	6%
Corn	3.57%	3.70%	3.57%	3.70%	3.57%	3.70%	3.70%	4.76%	4.76%	5.88%	6%
Cotton	3.57%	3.70%	3.57%	3.70%	3.57%	3.70%	3.70%	4.76%	4.76%	5.88%	5%
Cotton (Spot)	3.57%	3.70%	3.57%								
Cottonseed Oil	3.57%	3.70%	3.57%								
Crude Oil								4.76%	4.76%	5.88%	23%
Eggs	3.57%	3.70%	3.57%	3.70%			3.70%	4.76%	4.76%		
Eggs, Shells					3.57%	3.70%					
Flaxseed	3.57%	3.70%	3.57%	3.70%	3.57%	3.70%	3.70%				
Gold							3.70%	4.76%	4.76%	5.88%	6%
Grease Wool	3.57%	3.70%	3.57%	3.70%	3.57%	3.70%	3.70%	4.76%	4.76%	5.88%	
Heating Oil								4.76%	4.76%	5.88%	5%
Hogs				3.70%							
Hides	3.57%	3.70%	3.57%	3.70%							
Lard	3.57%	3.70%	3.57%	3.70%							
Lead	3.57%	3.70%	3.57%								
Lean Hogs											1%
Live Cattle	3.57%	3.70%	3.57%	3.70%	3.57%	3.70%	3.70%	4.76%	4.76%	5.88%	6%
Live Hogs	3.57%	3.70%	3.57%		3.57%	3.70%	3.70%	4.76%	4.76%	5.88%	
Lumber							3.70%	4.76%	4.76%		

REUTERS-CRB INDEX WITH HISTORICAL WEIGHTINGS (cont'd)

	1957	1961	1967	1971	1973	1974	1983	1987	1992	1995	2005
Natural Gas										5.88%	6%
Nickel											1%
Oats	3.57%	3.70%	3.57%	3.70%	3.57%	3.70%	3.70%	4.76%			
Onions	3.57%										
Orange Juice				3.70%	3.57%	3.70%	3.70%	4.76%	4.76%	5.88%	1%
Platinum				3.70%	3.57%	3.70%	3.70%	4.76%	4.76%	5.88%	
Plywood				3.70%	3.57%	3.70%					
Pork Bellies			3.57%	3.70%	3.57%	3.70%	3.70%	4.76%	4.76%		
Potatoes	3.57%	3.70%	3.57%		3.57%	3.70%	3.70%				
Rapeseed						3.70%	3.70%				
Rubber	3.57%	3.70%	3.57%	3.70%	3.57%	3.70%	3.70%				
Rye	3.57%	3.70%	3.57%	3.70%	3.57%	3.70%	3.70%				
Silver	3.57%	3.70%	3.57%	3.70%	3.57%	3.70%	3.70%	4.76%	4.76%	5.88%	1%
Soybean Meal	3.57%	3.70%	3.57%	3.70%	3.57%	3.70%	3.70%	4.76%	4.76%		
Soybean Oil	3.57%	3.70%	3.57%	3.70%	3.57%	3.70%	3.70%	4.76%	4.76%		
Soybeans	3.57%	3.70%	3.57%	3.70%	3.57%	3.70%	3.70%	4.76%	4.76%	5.88%	6%
Sugar											5%
Sugar No. 4	3.57%	3.70%	3.57%	3.70%							
Sugar No. 6	3.57%	3.70%	3.57%	3.70%							
Sugar No. 10					3.57%						
Sugar No. 11						3.70%	3.70%	4.76%	4.76%	5.88%	
Unleaded Gasoline									4.76%	5.88%	5%
Wheat	3.57%	3.70%	3.57%	3.70%	3.57%	3.70%	3.70%	4.76%	4.76%	5.88%	1%
Wheat (Spot)	3.57%	3.70%	3.57%								
Wheat (MGEX)						3.70%	3.70%				
Wool Tops	3.57%	3.70%	3.57%								
Zinc	3.57%	3.70%	3.57%								

Source: Reuters/Jeffries CRB

CORRELATION INDEX

Commodities do not correlate to other asset classes. Some would use the following chart as a case for using commodities as a perfect diversification tool for portfolios. I am not a fan of diversification, but many are and many have to diversify. This table shows that commodities are the perfect diversification anchor for a portfolio since they are not going to do what your other holdings will do.

BCNDX   Barclay CTA Index
GHSNDX   Barclay Hedge Fund Index
DJI   Dow Jones Industrial Average
FTSE   FT-SE 100 Index
SALWG   JPMorgan World Gov't Bond Index

SLHTB   Lehman Brothers L. T. Treasury Index
NASDQ   NASDAQ Composite Index
NIKEI   Nikkei 225 Index
RICI   Rogers Intl Commodity Index (RICI)
SPTR   S&P 500 Total Return Index

	BCNDX	GHSNDX	DJI	FTSE	SALWG	SLHTB	NASDQ	NIKEI	RICI	SPTR
BCNDX	1.00	-0.07	-0.27	-0.25	0.41	0.33	-0.20	-0.11	0.23	-0.26
GHSNDX	-0.07	1.00	0.61	0.61	-0.06	-0.17	0.80	0.61	0.30	0.71
DJI	-0.27	0.61	1.00	0.82	-0.11	-0.34	0.65	0.47	0.10	0.92
FTSE	-0.25	0.61	0.82	1.00	-0.19	-0.33	0.63	0.48	0.07	0.83
SALWG	0.41	-0.06	-0.11	-0.19	1.00	0.58	-0.09	-0.18	0.15	-0.06
SLHTB	0.33	-0.17	-0.34	-0.33	0.58	1.00	-0.22	-0.16	0.01	-0.28
NASDQ	-0.20	0.80	0.65	0.63	-0.09	-0.22	1.00	0.53	0.19	0.81
NIKEI	-0.11	0.61	0.47	0.48	-0.18	-0.16	0.53	1.00	0.30	0.50
RICI	0.23	0.30	0.10	0.07	0.15	0.01	0.19	0.30	1.00	0.13
SPTR	-0.26	0.71	0.92	0.83	-0.06	-0.28	0.81	0.50	0.13	1.00

Source: Barclay Trading Group Ltd.

A REFERENCE GUIDE

As arcane as many of the details of futures trading might be, commodities exchanges are in the business of encouraging trading. Their liquidity depends on it. To help potential investors learn more about the ins and outs of trading, exchanges offer tours and brochures as well as education programs and seminars, for free and for a fee. Some even have special programs for children. All maintain Web sites packed with historical information about the markets, including charts and reports on trends. I have learned a lot from surfing the exchange Web sites, but I have also detected the occasional mistake. So be careful, and always double-check your information. The commodity exchanges in the U.S. and major ones abroad are:

U.S. Exchanges

Chicago Board of Trade (CBOT) www.cbot.com (corn, soybeans, meal and oil, wheat, oats, rough rice, and oilseeds)

Chicago Mercantile Exchange (CME) www.cme.com (livestock, corn, oats, soybeans, wheat)

Kansas City (Missouri) Board of Trade (KC) www.kcbot.com (wheat)

MidAmerica Commodity Exchange (MidAm) www.midam.com (wheat, corn, soybeans)

Minneapolis Grain Exchange (MPLS) www.mgex.com (corn, soybeans, wheat)

New York Board of Trade (NYBOT) www.nybot.com (cocoa, coffee, sugar, cotton, orange juice)

Divisions of NYBOT: New York Cotton Exchange (NYCE) www.nyce.com

Coffee, Sugar and Cocoa Exchange (CSCE) www.csce.com

New York Mercantile Exchange (NYMEX) www.nymex.com (oil, natural gas, and other energy products, along with precious and industrial metals)

Metals Division of NYMEX is COMEX www.comex.com

International Exchanges

Brazil's Bolsa de Mercadorias & Futuros (BM&F) www.bmf.com.br (sugar, ethanol, coffee, soy, and other agricultural products)

China's Dalian Commodity Exchange (DCE) www.dce.com.cn/english (soybeans, soy meal, and corn)

Shanghai Futures Exchange (SHFE) www.shfe.com.cn (aluminum, copper, rubber, and oil)

Zhengzhoa's Commodity Exchange (ZCE) www.english.czce.com.cn (wheat and cotton)

London's International Petroleum Exchange (IPE) www.theipe.com (oil and other energy products)

London International Financial Futures Exchange (LIFFE) www.liffe.com (cocoa, coffee, sugar, and wheat)

London Metal Exchange (LME) www.lme.co.uk (industrial metals)

Paris's Marche à Terme Internationale de France (MATIF) www.matif.fr (corn and wheat)

Sidney Futures Exchange (SFE) www.sfe.com.au (wool, cattle)

Tokyo Commodity Exchange (TOCOM) www.tocom.or.jp (precious and industrial metals, rubber, crude oil, and other energy products)

Tokyo Grain Exchange (TGE) www.tge.or.jp (corn, U.S. soybeans, soybean meal, azuki beans, coffee, and sugar)

Yokohama Commodity Exchange (YCE) www.y-com.or.jp/english (raw silk, dried cocoon, potato)

Winnipeg Commodity Exchange (WCE) www.wce.ca (canola, feed wheat, western barley, flaxseed)

Contract Guide

Futures contracts were invented as a way to standardize deals. But while the standards are the same for a given commodity, they vary from commodity to commodity. In addition, exchanges may change certain specifics of a given commodity from time to time, such as price limits or final trading days. As the New York Board of Trade puts it in its own postings of sample contracts, "specifications . . . may be subject to change. Verify information with your broker." Amen.

The following is a *guide* to the typical specifications of the futures contracts in the 36 most actively traded commodities in the world that make up the Rogers International Commodities Index, arranged according to category and based on the information that the exchanges publish on their products. I emphasize "guide." Treat this simply as a learning and research tool. It is not a substitute for an actual contract. Before you trade, check the details of each contract with your broker. (And when you do, you will note that every exchange has its own order for listing specifications. I have taken the liberty of creating my own uniform format.)

I have not included margin requirements, because they, too, change periodically, sometimes in the middle of a particularly volatile market in an effort to slow things down and protect speculators from themselves. The exchanges do post their current margin requirements on their Web sites. To underline what I said in my discussion of margins in the book, check the exchange minimums and double-check them with your broker and then make a decision on how much (or little) margin you want to use.

GRAIN AND OILSEED FUTURES

C   Corn (CBOT)

Contract Size	5,000 bushels
Price Quote	cents and ¼ cent/bu
Contract Months	Dec, Mar, May, Jul, Sep
Last Trading Day	The business day prior to the 15th calendar day of contract month.
Trading Hours	9:30 A.M.–1:15 P.M. Central Time, Mon.–Fri.
Tick Size*	¼ cent/bu ($12.50/contract)
Daily Price Limit	20 cents/bu ($1,000/contract) above or below the previous day's settlement price. No limit in the spot month (limits are lifted two business days before the spot month begins).
Delivery Period	The last delivery day is the second business day following the last trading day of the delivery month.

O   Oats (CBT)

Contract Size	5,000 bu
Price Quote	¼ cent/bu
Contract Months	Jul, Sep, Dec, Mar, May
Last Trading Day	The business day prior to the 15th calendar day of the contract month.
Trading Hours	9:30 A.M.–1:15 P.M. Central Time, Mon.–Fri.
Tick Size	¼ cent/bu ($12.50/contract)
Daily Price Limit	20 cents/bu ($1,000/contract) above or below the previous day's settlement price. No limit in the spot month.
Delivery Period	The last delivery day is the business day prior to the last trading day of the delivery month.

*Or Minimum Price Fluctuation.

S   Soybeans (CBOT)

Contract Size	5,000 bu
Price Quote	cents and ¼ cent/bu
Contract Months	Sep, Nov, Jan, Mar, May, Jul, Aug
Last Trading Day	The business day prior to the 15th calendar day of the contract month.
Trading Hours	9:30 A.M.–1:15 P.M. Central Time, Mon.–Fri.
Tick Size	¼ cent/bu ($12.50/contract)
Daily Price Limit	50 cents/bu ($2,500/contract) above or below the previous day's settlement price. No limit in the spot month (limits are lifted two business days before the spot month begins).
Delivery Period	The last delivery day is the second business day following the last trading day of the delivery month.

SM   Soybean Meal (CBOT)

Contract Size	100 tons (2,000 lbs/ton)
Price Quote	Dollars and cents/ton
Contract Months	Oct, Dec, Jan, Mar, May, Jul, Aug, Sep
Last Trading Day	The business day prior to the 15th calendar day of the contract month.
Trading Hours	9:30 A.M.–1:15 P.M. Central Time, Mon.–Fri.
Tick Size	10 cents/ton ($10/contract)
Daily Price Limit	$20/ton ($2,000/contract) above or below the previous day's settlement price. No limit in the spot month (limits are lifted two business days before the spot month begins).
Delivery Period	The last delivery day is the second business day following the last trading day of the delivery month.

BO   Soybean Oil (CBOT)

Contract Size	60,000 lbs
Price Quote	cents/lb
Contract Months	Oct, Dec, Jan, Mar, May, Jul, Aug, Sep
Last Trading Day	The business day prior to the 15th calendar day of the contract month.
Trading Hours	9:30 A.M.–1:15 P.M. Central Time, Mon.–Fri.
Tick Size	$\frac{1}{100}$ cent ($0.0001)/lb ($6/contract)
Daily Price Limit	2 cents per pound ($1,200/contract) above or below the previous day's settlement price. No limit in the spot month (limits are lifted two business days before the spot month begins).
Delivery Period	The last delivery day is the last business day of the delivery month.

RR   Rough Rice (CBOT)

Contract Size	2,000 cwt (hundredweight)
Price Quote	cents/cwt
Contract Months	Sep, Nov, Jan, Mar, May, Jul
Last Trading Day	Seventh business day preceding the last business day of the delivery month.
Trading Hours	9:15 A.M.–1:30 P.M. Central Time, Mon.–Fri.
Tick Size	$\frac{1}{2}$ cent/cwt ($10/contract)
Daily Price Limit	50 cents/cwt ($1,000/contract) above or below the previous day's settlement price. No limit in the spot month (limits are lifted two business days before the spot month begins).
Delivery Period	The last delivery day is the last business day of the delivery month.

W Wheat (CBOT)

Contract Size	5,000 bu
Price Quote	cents and ¼ cent/bu
Contract Months	Jul, Sep, Dec, Mar, May
Last Trading Day	Seventh business day preceding the last business day of the delivery month.
Trading Hours	9:30 A.M.–1:15 P.M. Central Time, Mon.–Fri.
Tick Size	¼ cent/bu ($12.50/contract)
Daily Price Limit	30 cents/bu ($1,500/contract) above or below the previous day's settlement price. No limit in the spot month (limits are lifted two business days before the spot month begins).
Delivery Period	The last delivery day is the seventh business day following the last trading day of the delivery month.

AB Barley (WCE)

Contract Size	20 tons
Price Quote	Canadian dollars/ton
Contract Months	Mar, May, Jul, Oct, Dec
Last Trading Day	Business day preceding the fifteenth calendar day of the delivery month.
Trading Hours	9:30 A.M.–1:15 P.M. (Central Time)
Tick Size	Canadian $0.10/ton ($2.00/contract)
Daily Price Limit	Canadian $7.50/ton above or below previous settlement.
Delivery Period	From first business day of delivery month until last business day.

RS Canola (WCE)

Contract Size	20 tons

Price Quote	Canadian dollars/ton
Contract Months	Jan, Mar, May, Jul, Sep, Nov
Last Trading Day	Business day preceding the fifteenth calendar day of the delivery month.
Trading Hours	9:30 A.M.–1:15 P.M. (Central Time)
Tick Size	Canadian $0.10/ton ($200/contract)
Daily Price Limit	Canadian $30.00/ton above or below previous settlement.
Delivery Period	From first business day of delivery month.

LIVESTOCK FUTURES

LC   Cattle—Live (CME)

Contract Size	40,000 pounds of steers averaging 1,100–1,300 pounds
Price Quote	cents/pound
Contract Months	Feb, Apr, Jun, Aug, Oct, Dec (only the three nearby contracts are listed).
Last Trading Day	The last business day of the contract month.
Trading Hours	9:05 A.M.–1:00 P.M. Central Time (Last Trading Day 12:00 P.M.)
Tick Size	0.025 cents/pound ($10.00/contract)
Daily Price Limit	$1.50 cents/pound ($600/contract)
Delivery Period	Any business day of the contract month (stockyard) and any slaughter day of the contract month (approved by packing-plant delivery) plus the first seven business days (and intervening slaughter days) of the next calendar month, except that deliveries may not be made prior to the seventh business day (stockyard delivery) and the fourth business day (approved packing-plant delivery) following the first Friday of the contract month.

LH   *Lean Hogs (CME)*

Contract Size	40,000 pounds
Price Quote	cents/pound
Contract Months	Feb, Apr, May, Jun, Jul, Aug, Oct, Dec (only the three nearby contracts listed).
Last Trading Day	The tenth business day of the contract month.
Trading Hours	9:10 A.M.–1:00 P.M. (LTD 12:00 P.M.) Central Time, Mon.–Fri.
Tick Size	.025 cents/pound ($10.00/contract)
Daily Price Limit	2.00 cents/pound ($10.00/contract)
Delivery Period	Same as for live cattle.

FOOD AND FIBER FUTURES

LB   *Lumber (CME)*

Contract Size	110,000 board feet of random lengths 2×4s (8 ft to 20 ft)
Price Quote	dollar/1,000 bd ft
Contract Months	Six months of Jan, Mar, May, Jul, Sep, Nov
Last Trading Day	Business day immediately preceding the 16th calendar day of the contract month.
Trading Hours	9:00 A.M.–1:05 P.M. (LTD 12:05 P.M.) Central Time, Mon.–Fri.
Tick Size	0.10 cents/1,000 bd ft ($11.00/contract)
Daily Price Limit	$10.00/thousand bd ft above or below the previous day's settlement price (expanded limits)
Delivery Period	Any business day of the delivery month.

CC   Cocoa (CSCE)

Contract Size	10 metric tons (22,406 pounds)
Price Quote	dollars/metric ton
Contract Months	Mar, May, Jul, Sep, Dec
Last Trading Day	One business day prior to last notice day.
Trading Hours	8:00 A.M.–11:50 A.M., Mon.–Fri.
Tick Size	$1.00/metric ton ($10.00/contract)
Daily Price Limit	None
Delivery Period	Any business day of the contract month.

KC   Coffee (CSCE)

Contract Size	37,500 pounds (approximately 250 bags)
Price Quote	cents/pound
Contract Months	Mar, May, Jul, Sep, Dec
Last Trading Day	One business day prior to last notice day.
Trading Hours	9:15 A.M.–12:30 P.M., Mon.–Fri.
Tick Size	$\frac{5}{100}$ cent/pound ($18.75/contract)
Daily Price Limit	None
Delivery Period	Any business day of the contract month.

SB   Sugar (CSCE)

Contract Size	112,000 pounds (50 long tons)
Price Quote	cents/pound
Contract Months	Mar, May, Jul, Oct
Last Trading Day	Last business day of the month preceding delivery month.

Trading Hours	9:00 A.M.–12:00 P.M., Mon.–Fri.
Tick Size	1/100 cent/pound ($11.20/contract)
Daily Price Limit	None
Delivery Period	Any business day of delivery month.

CT   Cotton (NYCE)

Contract Size	50,000 pounds net weight (approximately 100 bales)
Price Quote	cents and hundredths of a cent/pound
Contract Months	Current month plus one or more of the next 23 succeeding months (active trading months: Mar, May, Jul, Oct, Dec).
Last Trading Day	Seventeen business days from the end of spot month.
Trading Hours	10:30 A.M.–2:15 P.M., Mon.–Fri.
Tick Size	1/100 of a cent (one "point")/pound below 95 cents/pound; 5/100 of a cent (five "points")/pound at prices of 95 cents/pound and higher.
Daily Price Limit	Three cents above or below the previous day's settlement price. But if any contract month settles at or above $1.10/pound, all contract months will trade with 4 cent price limits. Should no month settle at or above $1.10/pound, price limits stay at (or revert to) 3 cents/pound. No limit for spot month or after first notice day, which is five business days from the end of the preceding month.
Delivery Period	Any business day of delivery month.

OJ   Orange Juice (NYCE)

Contract Size	15,000 pounds of orange solids (3% more or less)
Price Quote	cents and hundredths of a cent/pound
Contract Months	Jan, Mar, May, Jul, Sep, Nov (with at least two Jan months listed at all times)
Last Trading Day	14th business day prior to the last business day of the month.

Trading Hours	10:00 A.M.–1:30 P.M., Mon.–Fri.
Tick Size	$\frac{5}{100}$ of a cent/pound ($7.50/contract)
Daily Price Limit	5 cents ($750/contract)
Delivery Period	Any business day of the delivery month.

YZ   Azuki Beans (TGE)

Contract Size	2,400 kilograms (80 bags)
Price Quote	Japanese yen (JPY)/bag
Contract Months	6 consecutive months
Last Trading Day	2 business days prior to the delivery day.
Trading Hours	9:00 A.M., 11:00 A.M., 1:00 P.M. and 3:00 P.M. (9:00 A.M. and 11:00 A.M. on the last trading day) (Japanese time)
Tick Size	10 JPY/bag (800 JPY/contact)
Daily Price Limit	If the "standard price" (i.e. monthly average of closing prices for contract months) is under JPY 8,000, the price limit is JPY 300; if the standard price is JPY 8,000 or more under JPY 16,000 yen, the limit is JPY 350; if the standard price is JPY 16,000 or more, the limit is JPY 400. No price limits in the spot month from the fifteenth of delivery month.
Delivery Period	The business day prior to the last business day of the delivery month. If Dec 24 is not a business day, the delivery day is moved up to the nearest business day.

GW   Wool (SFE)

Contract Size	The greasy (i.e. unwashed) wool equivalent of 2,5000 kilograms clean weight of merino combing fleece (approximately 20 farm bales)
Price Quote	Australian cents/kilogram clean weight
Contract Months	Feb, Apr, Jun, Aug, Oct, Dec
Last Trading Day	Third Thursday of the contract month (trading ceases at 12:00 noon (Sidney time).

Trading Hours	5:10 P.M.–7:00 A.M. and 10:30 A.M.–4:00 P.M. (during U.S. daylight savings time); 5:10 P.M.–7:30 A.M. and 10:30 A.M.–4:00 P.M. (during U.S. non-daylight savings time)
Tick Size	Australian $0.01/kilogram (A$25/contract)
Daily Price Limit	Not listed
Delivery Period	Commences on the Friday prior to the third Thursday of the delivery month, unless that Friday is not a business day, in which case the delivery period commences on the business day immediately preceding, and in any event ends at the close of trade on the final day of trading.

JSK   Silk (YCE)

Contract Size	300 kilograms
Price Quote	U.S. dollars/kilogram
Contract Months	Feb, Apr, Jun, Aug, Oct, Dec within 12 month period
Last Trading Day	Fifteenth calendar day of the delivery month.
Trading Hours	"Morning 1st Session, Morning 2nd Session; Afternoon 1st Session; Afternoon Second Session"
Tick Size	$0.01/kilogram ($3.00/contract)
Daily Price Limit	If the standard price is less than $20, the price limit is US $0.65; if the price $20 to less than $30, the limit is $0.80; if the price is $30 and over, the limit is $0.95.
Delivery Period	From last trading day until end of delivery month.

JRU   Rubber (TOCOM)

Contract Size	10,000 kilograms (Ribbed Smoked Sheet No. 3)
Price Quote	Japanese yen (JPY)/kilogram
Contract Months	6 consecutive months from the current month
Last Trading Day	The fourth business day prior to the delivery day.
Trading Hours	9:45 A.M., 10:45 A.M., 1:45 P.M., 2:45 P.M., 3:30 P.M.

Tick Size	Japanese yen 0.1/kilogram

Daily Price Limit	If the "standard price" (i.e. a monthly average of closing prices for all contract months except the last three business days in the previous month) is less than JPY 70.0, the price limit is JPY 3.0/kilogram; if the standard prices is JPY 70.0–JPY 119.9, the price limit is JPY 4.0/kilogram; if the standard price is JPY 120.0–JPY 169.9, the price limit is JPY 5.0/kilogram; if the standard price is JPY 170.0 and over, the limit is JPY 6.0/kilogram.

Delivery Period	The last business day of each month except December, when it is the day preceding the last business day.

METALS FUTURES

HG   Copper—High Grade (CMX)

Contract Size	25,000 pounds
Price Quote	cents/pound
Contract Months	The current calendar month and the next 23 consecutive months.
Last Trading Day	Close of business on the third to last business day of the maturing delivery month.
Trading Hours	8:10 A.M.–1:00 P.M., Mon.–Fri.
Tick Size	$5/100$ of a cent/pound ($12.50/contract). Fluctuation of one cent is equivalent to $250/contract.
Daily Price Limit	Initial price limit, based upon the preceding day's settlement price, is $0.20/pound. Two minutes after either of the two most active months trades at the limit, trading in all months of futures and options will cease for a 15-minute period. Trading will also cease if either of the two active months is bid at the upper limit or offered at the lower limit for two minutes without trading. Trading will not cease if the limit is reached during the final 20 minutes of the day's trading. If the limit is reached during the final half hour of trading, trading will resume no later than 10 minutes before the normal closing time. When trading resumes after a cessation of trading,

the price limits will be expanded by increments of 100%.

Delivery Period	The first delivery day is the first business day of the delivery month; the last delivery day is the last business day of the delivery month.

GC   Gold (CMX)

Contract Size	100 troy ounces
Price Quote	dollars/troy ounce
Contract Months	Current calendar month, the next two calendar months, any Feb, Apr, Aug, or Oct thereafter falling within a 23-month period, and any Jun and Dec falling within a 60-month period beginning with the current month.
Last Trading Day	The close of business on the third to last business day of the maturing delivery month.
Trading Hours	8:20 A.M.–1:30 P.M., Mon.–Fri.
Tick Size	$0.10/troy ounce ($10/contract).
Daily Price Limit	Initial price limit, based upon the preceding day's settlement price is $75 per ounce. Two minutes after either of the two most active months trades at the limit, trades in all months of futures and options will cease for a 15-minute period. Trading will also cease if either of the two active months is bid at the upper limit or offered at the lower limit for two minutes without trading. Trading will not cease if the limit is reached during the final 20 minutes of a day's trading. If the limit is reached during the final half hour of trading, trading will resume no later than 10 minutes before the normal closing time. When trading resumes after a cessation of trading, the price limits will be expanded by increments of 100%.
Delivery Period	The first delivery day is the first business day of the delivery month; the last delivery day is the last business day of the delivery month.

PL   Platinum (NYMEX)

Contract Size	50 troy ounces

Price Quote	dollars/troy ounce
Contract Months	Trading is conducted over 15 months, beginning with the current month and the next two consecutive months before moving into the quarterly cycle of Jan, Apr, Jul, and Oct.
Last Trading Day	The close of business of the fourth business day prior to the end of the delivery month.
Trading Hours	8:20 A.M.–1:05 P.M., Mon.–Fri.
Tick Size	$0.10/troy ounce ($5.00/contract)
Daily Price Limit	No maximum daily limit during the current delivery month, the closest cycle month, and any months preceding it. In other months, the daily limit is $50 per ounce ($2,500 per contract). If the price in any of the back months settles at the limit for two consecutive days, limits will be expanded to $75 per ounce ($3,750 per contract) and, if the market settles at that limit for two consecutive days, prices will be expanded to the maximum daily limit of $100 per ounce ($5,000 per contract) on the following day.
Delivery Period	Delivery notice may be given by the seller to the exchange on the last business day prior to the end of the delivery month. The basis of delivery is the settlement price on the day the delivery notice is issued.

SI   Silver (CMX)

Contract Size	5,000 troy ounces
Price Quote	cents/troy ounce
Contract Months	Trading is conducted during the current calendar month, the next two calendar months, any Jan, Mar, May, or Sep thereafter falling within a 23-month period, and any Jul or Dec falling within a 60-month period beginning with the current months.
Last Trading Day	Close of business on the third to last business day of the maturing delivery month.
Trading Hours	8:25 A.M.–1:25 P.M., Mon.–Fri.
Tick Size	Multiples of ½ cent/troy ounce ($25.00/contract)

Daily Price Limit	Initial price limit, based upon the preceding day's settlement price, is $1.50. Two minutes after either of the two most active months trades at the limit, trades in all months of futures and options will cease for a 15-minute period. Trading will also cease if either of the two active months is bid at the upper limit or offered at the lower limit for two minutes without trading. Trading will not cease if the limit is reached during the final 20 minutes of a day's trading. If the limit is reached during the final half hour of trading, trading will resume no later than 10 minutes before the normal closing time. When trading resumes after a cessation of trading, the price limits will be expanded by increments of 100%.
Delivery Period	The first delivery day is the first business day of the delivery month; the last delivery day is the last business day of the delivery month.

PB   Lead (LME)

Contract Size	25 metric tons (in the form of ingots)
Price Quote	dollars/ton
Contract Months	Monthly out to 15 months forward
Trading Hours	Trading can be done 24 hours a day by phone. On the floor: First session: 12:05 P.M.–12:10 P.M.; 12:45 A.M.–12:50 A.M.; 1:15 P.M.–3:10 P.M.; Second session: 3:20–3:25 P.M., 4:00–4:05 P.M.; 4:35–4:50 P.M.
Tick Size	50 cents/metric ton ($12.50/contract)
Daily Price Limit	none
Delivery Period	Daily for three months forward and then every Wednesday for the next three months and then every third Wednesday of the month for the next nine months out to 15 months forward.

AL   Aluminum (LME)

Contract Size	44,000 pounds
Price Quote	cents/pound
Contract Months	25 consecutive months

Last Trading Day	Close of business on the third to last business day of the delivery month
Trading Hours	7:50 A.M.–1:15 P.M.
Tick Size	$0.0005/pound ($22.00/contract)
Daily Price Limit	$0.20/pound above or below the previous day's settlement price, unless one of the two closest delivery month's trades at or is offered or bid for two minutes at the limit. In that case, after a 15-minute halt, the market will reopen with limits expanded by $0.20 on either side of the previous limit. This can happen no more than twice in a session for a maximum $0.60 limit.
Delivery Period	From the first business day of the delivery month until the end of business hours of the last business day of that month.

N   Nickel (LME)

Contract Size	6 tons
Price Quote	dollars/ton
Contract Months	First month out to 27 months forward.
Last Trading Day	Not listed
Trading Hours	First Session: 12:15 P.M.–12:20 P.M., 1:00 P.M.–1:05 P.M.; 1:15 P.M.–3:10 P.M. Second session: 3:45 P.M.–3:50 P.M.; 4:25 P.M.–4:30 P.M.; 4:35 P.M.–4:55 P.M.
Tick Size	$5.00/ton ($30/contract)
Daily Price Limit	No price limits listed
Delivery Period	Daily for 3 months forward and then every Wednesday for the next three months and every third Wednesday of the month for the next 21 months out to 27 months forward.

PA   *Palladium (NYMEX)*

Contract Size	100 troy ounces
Price Quote	dollars/troy ounce
Contract Months	Trading is conducted over 15 months, beginning with the current month and the next two consecutive months before moving into the quarterly cycle of Mar, Jun, Sep, and Dec.
Last Trading Day	Close of business on the fourth business day prior to the end of the delivery month.
Trading Hours	8:30 A.M.–1:00 P.M.
Tick Size	$0.05/troy ounce ($5/contract)
Daily Price Limit	No price limits
Delivery Period	Notice may be given by the seller to the Exchange on the last business day preceding the delivery month or any subsequent business day up to the third business day prior to the end of the delivery month.

SN   *Tin (LME)*

Contract Size	5 tons
Price Quote	dollars/ton
Contract Months	Monthly from the first month out to 15 months forward.
Last Trading Day	Not listed
Trading Hours	First Session: 11:50 A.M.–11:55 A.M., 12:40 P.M.–12:45 P.M.; 1:15 P.M.–3:10 P.M. Second session: 3:40 P.M.–3:45 P.M.; 4:20 P.M.–4:25 P.M.; 4:35 P.M.–4:50 P.M.
Tick Size	$5/ton ($25/contract)
Daily Price Limit	No price limits listed
Delivery Period	Daily for three months forward and then every Wednesday for the next three months and then every third Wednesday of the month for the next 9 months out to 15 months.

ZN   *Zinc (LME)*

Contract Size	25 tons
Price Quote	dollars/ton
Contract Months	First month out to 27 months forward
Last Trading Day	Not listed
Trading Hours	First session: 12:10 P.M.–12:15 P.M., 12:50 P.M.–12:55 P.M.; 1:15 P.M.–3:10 P.M. Second session: 3:25 P.M.–3:30 P.M.; 4:05 P.M.–4:10 P.M.; 4:35 P.M.–4:55 P.M.
Tick Size	$0.50/ton ($12.50/contract)
Daily Price Limit	No price limits listed
Delivery Period	Daily for 3 months forward and then every Wednesday for the next three months and every third Wednesday of the month for the next 21 months out to 27 months forward.

PETROLEUM FUTURES

CL   *Crude Oil, Light Sweet (NYMEX)*

Contract Size	1,000 barrels
Price Quote	dollars/barrel
Contract Months	Thirty consecutive months plus long-dated futures initially listed 36, 48, 60, 72, and 84 months prior to delivery. "Additionally, trading can be executed at an average differential to the previous day's settlement prices for periods of two to 30 consecutive months in a single transaction."
Last Trading Day	The close of business on the third business day prior to the 25th calendar day of the month preceding the delivery month. If the 25th calendar day is a non-business day, trading shall cease on the third business day prior to the business day preceding the 25th calendar day.

Trading Hours	10 A.M.–2:30 P.M., Mon.–Fri.
Tick Size	$0.01/barrel ($10.00/contract)
Daily Price Limit	$10/barrel ($10,000/contract) for all months. If any contract is traded, bid, or offered at the limit for five minutes, trading is halted for five minutes. When trading resumes, the limit is expanded by $10 per barrel in either direction after each successive five-minute trading halt. There will be no maximum price fluctuation limits during any one trading session.
Delivery Period	All deliveries are ratable over the course of the month and must be initiated on or after the first calendar day and completed by the last calendar day of the delivery month.

HO   Heating Oil No. 2 (NYMEX)

Contract Size	42,000 gallons
Price Quote	dollars/gallon
Contract Months	Eighteen consecutive months commencing with the next calendar month (e.g., on January 6, 2004, trading occurs in all months from February 2004 through July 2005).
Last Trading Day	The close of business on the last business day of the month preceding the delivery month.
Trading Hours	10:00 A.M.–2:30 P.M., Mon.–Fri.
Tick Size	$0.0001 (0.01 cent)/gallon ($4.20/contract)
Daily Price Limit	For all months $0.25/gallon ($10,500/contract). If any contract is traded, bid, or offered at the limit for five minutes, trading is halted for five minutes. When trading resumes, the limit is expanded by $0.25 per gallon in either direction. If another halt were triggered, the market would continue to be expanded by $0.25 per gallon in either direction after each successive five-minute trading halt. There will be no maximum price-fluctuation limits during any one trading session.
Delivery Period	Deliveries may be initiated only the day after the fifth business day and must be completed before the last business day of the delivery month.

HU   *Gasoline—NY Unleaded (NYMEX)*

Contract Size	42,000 gallons
Price Quote	dollars/gallon
Contract Months	Twelve consecutive months
Last Trading Day	Close of business on the last business day of the month preceding the delivery month.
Trading Hours	10:05 A.M.–2:30 P.M., Mon.–Fri.
Tick Size	$0.0001 (0.01 cent)/gallon ($4.20/contract)
Daily Price Limit	For all months $0.25/gallon ($10,500/contract). If any contract is traded, bid, or offered at the limit for five minutes, trading is halted for five minutes. When trading resumes, the limit is expanded by $0.25 per gallon in either direction. If another halt were triggered, the market would continue to be expanded by $0.25 per gallon in either direction after each successive five-minute trading halt. There will be no maximum price-fluctuation limits during any one trading session.
Delivery Period	Deliveries may be initiated only the day after the fifth business day and must be completed before the last business day of the delivery month.

NG   *Natural Gas (NYM)*

Contract Size	10,000 million British thermal units (mmBtu)
Price Quote	dollars/mmBtu
Contract Months	Seventy-two consecutive months commencing with the next calendar month (e.g., on January 6, 2004, trading occurs in all months from February 2004 through January 2010).
Last Trading Day	Three business days prior to the first calendar day of the delivery month.
Trading Hours	10:00 A.M.–2:30 P.M., Mon.–Fri.
Tick Size	$0.001 (0.1 cent)/mmBtu ($10/contract)

Daily Price Limit   For all months $3.00/mmBtu ($30,000/contract). If
                         any contract is traded, bid, or offered at the limit for
                         five minutes, trading is halted for five minutes. When
                         trading resumes, the limit is expanded by $3 per
                         mmBtu in either direction. If another halt were trig-
                         gered, the market would continue to be expanded by
                         $3 per mmBtu in either direction after each succes-
                         sive five-minute trading halt. There will be no maxi-
                         mum price-fluctuation limits during any one trading
                         session.

Delivery Period   No earlier than the first calendar day of the delivery
                         month and shall be completed no later than the last
                         calendar day of the delivery month.

Born on October 19, 1942, JIM ROGERS had his first job at age five, picking up bottles at baseball games. After growing up in Demopolis, Alabama, he won a scholarship to Yale. Upon graduation, he attended Balliol College at Oxford where he earned his first Guinness record as coxswain of the crew. After a stint in the army, he began work on Wall Street. He co-founded the Quantum Fund, a global investment partnership. During the 1970s, the portfolio gained 4,200 percent, while the S&P rose less than 47 percent. Rogers then decided to retire—at age 37—but he did not remain idle.

Continuing to manage his own portfolio, Rogers served as a professor of finance at the Columbia University Graduate School of Business and as moderator of *The Dreyfus Roundtable* on WCBS and *The Profit Motive* on FNN. At the same time, he laid the groundwork for his lifelong dream, an around-the-world motorcycle trip: more than 100,000 miles across six continents, his second Guinness record. That journey became the subject of Rogers's first book, *Investment Biker* (1994).

Rogers's Millennium Adventure 1999–2001, his third Guinness record, took him and his wife through 116 countries, through half of the world's 30 civil wars, and over 152,000 miles. His second book, *Adventure Capitalist,* chronicled that incredible journey.

Now a contributor to Fox News and other news and print outlets, he lives with his wife and daughter in New York City.

He can be reached at www.jimrogers.com.